HILLSIDE HOMES

Design 9554

214 Sloping-Lot & Multi-Level Designs
1,040 to 6,628 square feet

 HOME PLANNERS, INC.

Published by Home Planners, Inc.
Editorial and Corporate Offices:
3275 West Ina Road, Suite 110
Tucson, Arizona 85741

Distribution Center:
29333 Lorie Lane
Wixom, Michigan 48393

Rickard D. Bailey, President and Publisher
Cindy J.C. Lewis, Publications Manager
Paulette Mulvin, Senior Editor
Amanda Kaufmann, Project Editor
Paul D. Fitzgerald, Book Designer

Photo Credits

Front Cover: Bob Greenspan

Back Cover: Bob Greenspan

First Printing, January 1996

10 9 8 7 6 5 4 3 2

Printed in the United States of America.
Library of Congress Catalog Card Number: 95-080233
ISBN: 1-881955-28-1

On the front cover: An elegant facade introduces fine livability in this
front-slope design, 9554. See page 34 for floor plans and more information. Cover photo shown in reverse of plans.

On the back cover: Traditionally styled, this home, Design 9573, meets the
modern family's demands. Page 19 has floor plans and descriptions.

Design 3645

Table Of Contents

About The Designers 4

Editor's Note 5

Homes For Front- Or Side-Sloping Lots 6

Traditional Homes With Walk-Out Basements 41

Contemporary Homes With Walk-Out Basements..................87

Plans With Livable Basements...131

Homes With Open Staircases...137

Bi-Level, Split-Level & Split-Foyer Designs 153

Homes With Raised Foundations 205

Ordering Blueprints..212

Additional Plans Books 222

About The Designers

The Blue Ribbon Designer Series™ is a collection of books featuring home plans of a diverse group of outstanding home designers and architects known as the Blue Ribbon Network of Designers. This group of companies is dedicated to creating and marketing the finest possible plans for home construction on a regional and national basis. Each of the companies exhibits superior work and integrity in all phases of the stock-plan business including modern, trendsetting floor planning, a professionally executed blueprint package and a strong sense of service and commitment to the consumer.

Design Basics, Inc.

For nearly a decade, Design Basics, a nationally recognized home design service located in Omaha, has been developing plans for custom home builders. Since 1987, the firm has consistently appeared in *Builder* magazine, the official magazine of the National Association of Home Builders, as the top-selling designer. The company's plans also regularly appear in numerous other shelter magazines such as *Better Homes and Gardens, House Beautiful* and *Home Planner.*

Design Traditions

Design Traditions was established by Stephen S. Fuller with the tenets of innovation, quality, originality and uncompromising architectural techniques in traditional and European homes. Especially popular throughout the Southeast, Design Traditions' plans are known for their extensive detail and thoughtful design. They are widely published in such shelter magazines as *Southern Living* magazine and *Better Homes and Gardens.*

Alan Mascord Design Associates, Inc.

Founded in 1983 as a local supplier to the building community, Mascord Design Associates of Portland, Oregon began to successfully publish plans nationally in 1985. With plans now drawn exclusively on computer, Mascord Design Associates quickly received a reputation for homes that are easy to build yet meet the rigorous demands of the buyers' market, winning local and national awards. The company's trademark is creating floor plans that work well and exhibit excellent traffic patterns. Their motto is: "Drawn to build, designed to sell."

Larry E. Belk Designs

Through the years, Larry E. Belk has worked with individuals and builders alike to provide a quality product. After listening to over 4,000 dreams and watching them become reality all across America, Larry's design philosophy today combines traditional exteriors with upscale interiors designed for contemporary lifestyles. Flowing, open spaces and interesting angles define his interiors. Great emphasis is placed on providing views that showcase the natural environment. Dynamic exteriors reflect Larry's extensive home construction experience, painstaking research and talent as a fine artist.

Home Planners, Inc.

Headquartered in Tucson, Arizona, with additional offices in Detroit, Home Planners is one of the longest-running and most successful home design firms in the United States. With over 2,500 designs in its portfolio, the company provides a wide range of styles, sizes and types of homes for the residential builder. All of Home Planners' designs are created with the care and professional expertise that fifty years of experience in the home-planning business affords. Their homes are designed to be built, lived in and enjoyed for years to come.

The Sater Design Collection

The Sater Design Collection has a long established tradition of providing South Florida's most diverse and extraordinary custom designed homes. Their goal is to fulfill each client's particular need for an exciting approach to design by merging creative vision with elements that satisfy a desire for a distinctive lifestyle. This philosophy is proven, as exemplifies by over 50 national design awards, numerous magazine features and, most important, satisfied clients. The result is an elegant statement of lasting beauty and value.

Home Design Services, Inc.

For the past fifteen years, Home Design Services of Longwood, Florida has been formulating plans for the sun-country lifestyle. At the forefront of design innovation and imagination, the company has developed award winning designs that are consistently praised for their highly detailed, free-flowing floor plans, imaginative and exciting interior architecture and elevations which have gained international appeal.

Design 3360, Rear

Editor's Note

Whether you just purchased that perfect view lot or are about to, this collection of *Hillside Homes* is sure to provide you with the home of your dreams. Over 200 of today's most tempting housing styles enclose floor plans for split-level, walkout-basement and even raised-foundation living.

Homes for front- or side-sloping lots are featured in the first section, pages 6-40. You'll find homes that incorporate split-foyer design, often in the form of two-story designs with partially "in-ground" first stories and no basements. Design 2788 on page 24 is a fine example of this. Its first story consists of a cozy family room and a study that may also serve as a bedroom with a full bath nearby. Several other homes incorporate lower-level garages, optional finished basements and fully livable second and third levels. There is a variety of slopes considered in this section, assuring ample opportunity to find the design that meets your demands.

Walk-out basements are the most popular way to handle lots that drop off to the rear. Two sections, pages 41-130, are devoted to this building strategy, covering both traditional and contemporary styles. There are many strategies to expanding living space with a walk-out basement plan. One is to take a one-story home, such as Design 9567 on page 43, and offer additional bedrooms and casual living areas on the lower level. Or build two-story like Design 8145 on page 84 and realize multiple levels with lots of livability.

A finished basement is an economical answer to furthering a one-story home's livability. A section on **homes with livable basements** presents plans with additional bedrooms and casual living spaces, all without extending building dimensions (and spending many more dollars!). A prime example is Design 7277 on page 132. As a one-story with a width of 32' and a depth of 46', it presents an economical answer as is. However, with two additional bedrooms and a family room downstairs, it will serve the growing family for years to come.

Homes with open staircases give living areas a spacious and roomy quality. The open staircase may ascend to an upper-level lounge or descend to family living areas. See pages 137-152 for your favorite.

Many homeowners opt for a **bi-level, split-level or split-foyer design** to accommodate their hillside. Bi-levels offer flexibility in design because the site determines which level becomes the entrance level. Full-story stairs then lead to living or sleeping areas. Split-level homes have two or three living levels and an optional third- or fourth-level basement. These homes provide clearly defined multiple living patterns. A selection of the most popular styles and floor plans appears in this book on pages 153-204.

Homes with raised foundations are popular in coastal areas, but also provide flexibility in construction for other regions. With the first floor above a garage or bonus space, lots may slope steeply or mildly underneath living levels. Design 6618 on page 207 offers an exclusive peek at this home-building style. An entry porch is actually situated over extra space. A carport may be incorporated underneath the first floor, site providing. Expansive views from both first and second living levels are a given.

Whatever your style, size or slope considerations, *Hillside Homes* shows that your sloping lot can become the perfect site for a practical, livable home. And, with the many home-design options offered by the Blue Ribbon Network of Designers, it's never been easier to realize your dream home. Our exclusive Quote One™ service allows you to estimate the costs of building select designs in this collection–see page 214 for more information. Complete ordering instructions, along with a host of helpful additional products, can be found at the back of the book. All are designed to make your homebuilding dreams come true!

Homes For Front- Or Side-Sloping Lots

Design 9571

First Floor: 1,574 square feet
Second Floor: 1,112 square feet
Total: 2,686 square feet

● This home fits sloping lots well. From the elegant terraced entry, a great interior unfolds. Formal living and dining rooms dominate the right side of the plan. To the left of the foyer is the private den with double doors. A family room is found to the rear, as are the breakfast room and attached island kitchen. Amenities include abundant counter space and a large island cooktop. The second floor holds two family bedrooms and an outstanding master suite with a compartmented toilet, a whirlpool tub and a large walk-in closet.

Design by
Alan Mascord
Design Associates, Inc.

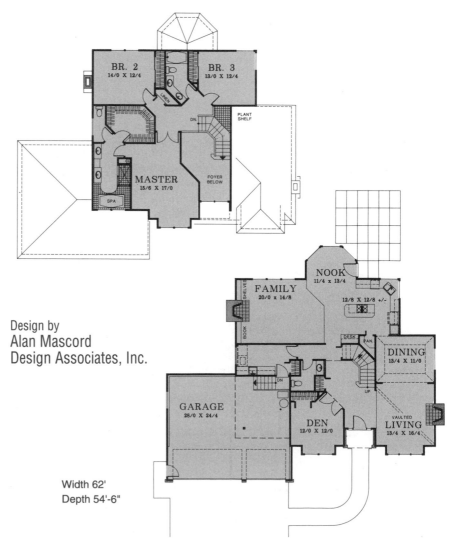

Width 62'
Depth 54'-6"

Design 9407

First Floor: 1,670 square feet

Second Floor: 1,257 square feet

Total: 2,927 square feet

● A great traditional-looking home for those lots that drop off from the street and slightly to the side. The rear part of the house is five feet lower than the entry level. The tall foyer overlooks the sunken living room and dining room beyond. The family room, nook and kitchen stretch across the back opening up to the out-door living area. A den is conveniently located on the main floor working well as guest bedroom or office. Four large bedrooms including a grand master suite round out the upper floor.

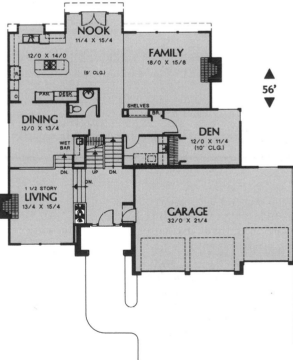

Design by
Alan Mascord
Design Associates, Inc.

7

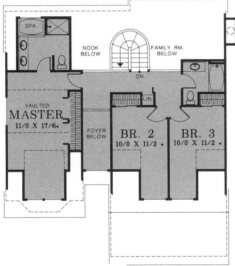

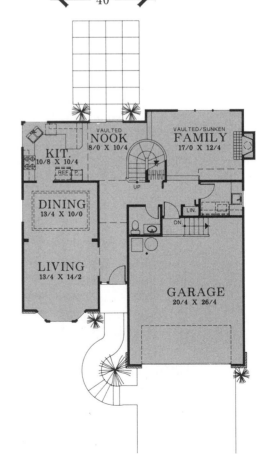

40'

46'

Design 9491

First Floor: 1,059 square feet
Second Floor: 872 square feet
Total: 1,931 square feet

● This home for the hillsides was designed to suit lots that slope up from the street 4 to 8 feet. Its first floor is dominated by formal and informal living areas. The living room has a bay window and attached dining area. The family room is sunken and features a vaulted ceiling and fireplace. The kitchen serves both areas nicely, as well as the casual nook eating area. Upstairs are three bedrooms. The master bedroom has a vaulted ceiling and luxurious bath. Two family bedrooms share a full bath. The upper floor balcony overlooks the nook and family room below.

Design by
Alan Mascord
Design Associates, Inc.

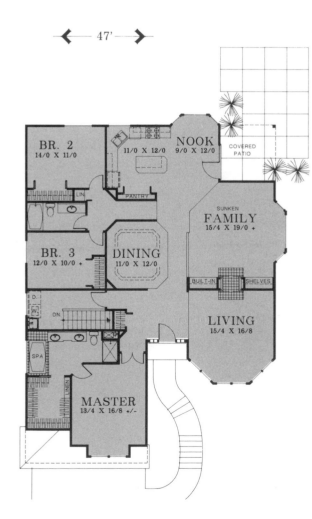

← 47' →

63'

BR. 2
14/0 X 11/0

NOOK
9/0 X 12/0

11/0 X 12/0

COVERED
PATIO

LIN

PANTRY

SUNKEN

FAMILY
15/4 X 19/0 +

BR. 3
12/0 X 10/0 +

DINING
11/0 X 12/0 +

DN.

BUILT-IN   SHELVES

SPA

LIVING
15/4 X 16/8

MASTER
13/4 X 16/8 +/-

CRAWLSPACE (OR FULL BASEMENT)

UP

WINE
CELLAR

GARAGE
20/8 X 23/8

Design 9492
Square Footage: 2,198

● This home is perfect for a sloping lot with the garage at the lower level and the remainder of the house above. Special features of the home include a see-through fireplace between the living and family rooms, a bay-windowed nook, a large walk-in closet and spa in the master bedroom and a wine cellar just off the garage. The family room is sunken and also has a bay window. A covered patio is found just off the nook.

Design by
Alan Mascord
Design Associates, Inc.

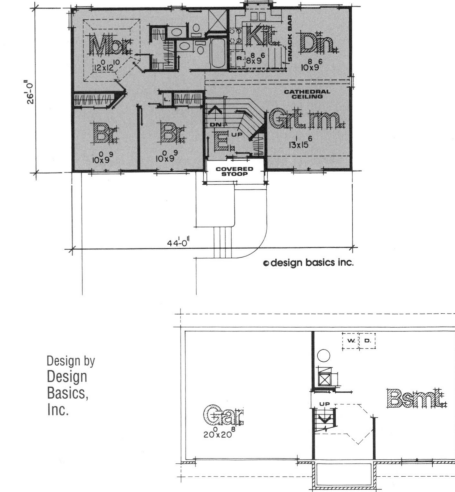

Design 7278
Square Footage: 1,125

● This convenient, split-entry ranch design features a two-car garage. The large entry, with its coat closet, is dramatic with an angled staircase that leads to the great room. A volume ceiling further expands the lofty feeling in the home. The efficient kitchen functions with a snack bar, a lazy Susan and a window over the sink. A hallway leads to the bedrooms. Double doors open to a large master bedroom with a vaulted ceiling. It contains a walk-in closet and a private bath. The secondary bedrooms share a convenient hall bath.

Design by
Design Basics, Inc.

Design 7279

Square Footage: 1,201

● Hilly sites are easily accommodated by this efficient home. The entry opens to a volume great room with a fireplace and a large boxed window. The conveniently located laundry room is only a half-flight down on the garage level. The well-planned kitchen features a wrapping counter, a corner sink with windows, a pantry, a lazy Susan and a snack bar serving the sunny dining area. The master bedroom, with walk-in closet space and a compartmented toilet and shower, provides comfort and convenience. Two secondary bedrooms share a full hall bath and enjoy lots of privacy.

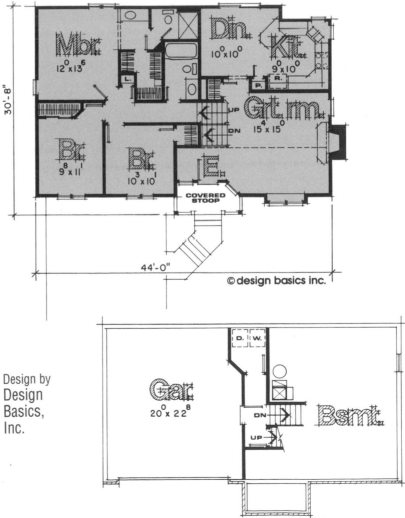

Design by
Design
Basics,
Inc.

© design basics inc.

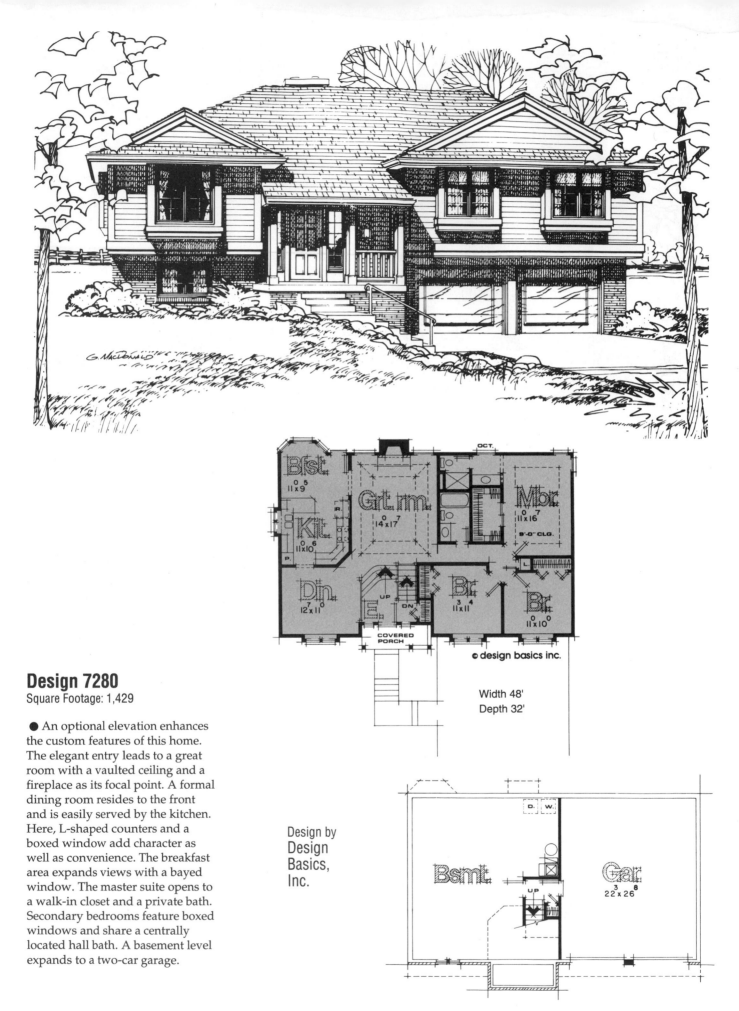

Design 7280

Square Footage: 1,429

● An optional elevation enhances the custom features of this home. The elegant entry leads to a great room with a vaulted ceiling and a fireplace as its focal point. A formal dining room resides to the front and is easily served by the kitchen. Here, L-shaped counters and a boxed window add character as well as convenience. The breakfast area expands views with a bayed window. The master suite opens to a walk-in closet and a private bath. Secondary bedrooms feature boxed windows and share a centrally located hall bath. A basement level expands to a two-car garage.

Width 48'
Depth 32'

Design by
Design Basics, Inc.

© design basics inc.

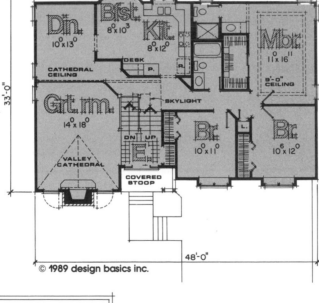

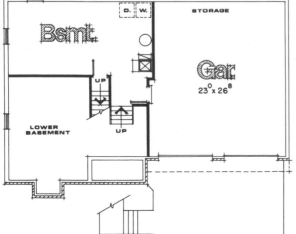

Design by
Design
Basics,
Inc.

Design 9291
Square Footage: 1,458

● From the volume entry, expansive views of the great room and dining room captivate homeowners and guests. The great room with a fireplace centered under the valley cathedral ceiling beckons. An efficient kitchen, which serves the bright dinette, has a pantry and planning desk. The cathedral ceiling in the dining room adds to the atmosphere of meals and entertaining. Two secondary bedrooms with boxed windows are accessed by the corridor hallway. Comfort abounds in the master suite with a nine-foot tiered ceiling plus mirrored bi-pass doors for the walk-in closet and private bath. The convenient garage accommodates a sloping site.

Design 9572

First Floor: 1,180 square feet
Second Floor: 1,025 square feet
Total: 2,205 square feet

● For lots that slope up from the street, this plan has much to offer. A three-car garage opens to a laundry room. Through here, family living areas gain attention with a family room, breakfast nook and ample kitchen setting the stage. Double doors lead to outdoor livability. Formal areas include a front-facing living room and a tier-ceilinged dining room. Upstairs, a spacious master bedroom enjoys a private luxury bath and a walk-in closet. Three family bedrooms include two with window seats.

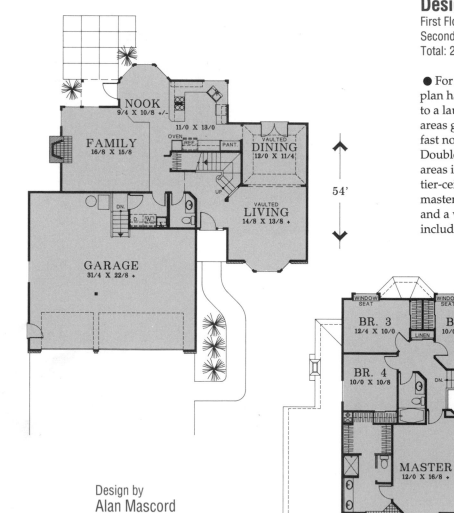

53'

54'

NOOK
9/4 X 10/8 +/-

11/0 X 13/0

FAMILY
16/8 X 15/8

OVEN
REF.   PANT.

VAULTED
DINING
12/0 X 11/4

DN.

UP

VAULTED
LIVING
14/8 X 13/8 +

GARAGE
31/4 X 22/8 +

Design by
Alan Mascord
Design Associates, Inc.

WINDOW SEAT

WINDOW SEAT

BR. 3
12/4 X 10/0

LINEN

BR. 2
10/0 X 13/2

BR. 4
10/0 X 10/8

DN.

FOYER BELOW

LIVING BELOW

MASTER
12/0 X 16/8 +

SPA

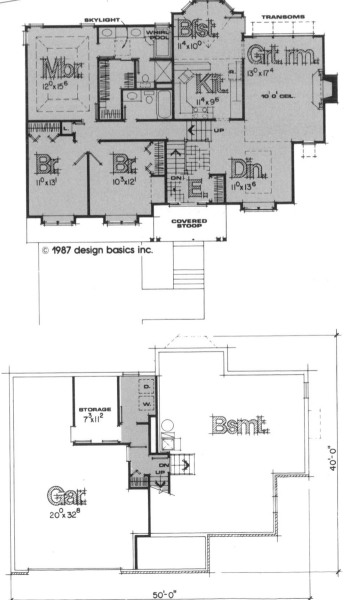

© 1987 design basics inc.

Design 9345

Main Level: 1,499 square feet
Lower Level: 57 square feet
Total: 1,556 square feet

● A high-impact entry defines the exterior of this special multi-level home design. A formal dining room with interesting ceiling detail and a boxed window is open to the entry. In the volume great room, homeowners will enjoy a handsome brick fireplace and large windows to the back. Wrapping counters, a corner sink, Lazy Susan and pantry add convenience to the thoughtful kitchen. The adjoining bayed breakfast area has a sloped ceiling and arched transom window. The three bedrooms in this home provide privacy from the main living areas. Two secondary bedrooms share the hall bath. Last, but not least, the master suite offers a vaulted ceiling, skylit dressing/bath area with double vanity, walk-in closet and whirlpool tub.

Design by
Design
Basics,
Inc.

15

Design 9570

First Floor: 1,766 square feet
Second Floor: 1,124 square feet
Total: 2,890 square feet

● Live like a king on a hill in this beautifully styled home. A three-car garage accommodates family vehicles as well as recreational equipment. The first floor of livability includes a two-story living room, a double-doored family room, an elegant dining room and an octagonal den. The kitchen serves a breakfast nook. Upstairs, the master suite draws attention with its vaulted ceiling, deck and pampering bath. Two secondary bedrooms will meet the needs of growing children or guests.

Design by
Alan Mascord
Design Associates, Inc.

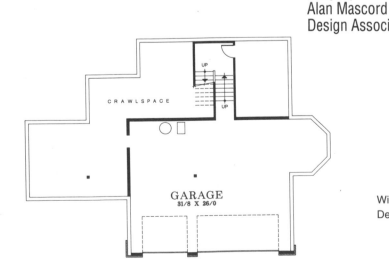

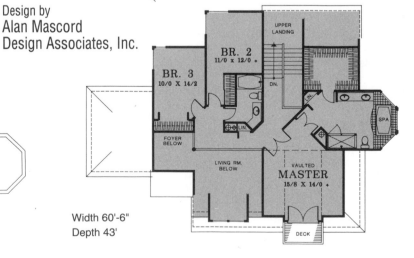

Width 60'-6"
Depth 43'

Width 73'
Depth 51'

Design 9448

First Floor: 1,820 square feet
Second Floor: 1,384 square feet
Total: 3,204 square feet

● For slightly sloping lots, this design puts its best foot forward. From the elegant terraced entry, a great interior unfolds. Formal living and dining rooms dominate the left side of the plan. To the right of the foyer is the private den with front-terrace access. A family room is found to the rear, as are the breakfast room and attached island kitchen. The second floor holds two family bedrooms and an outstanding master suite with its own hearth-warmed study, luxurious bath and immense walk-in closet.

Design by
Alan Mascord
Design Associates, Inc.

17

Design 9577

First Floor: 2,306 square feet
Second Floor: 1,941 square feet
Total: 4,247 square feet

● Luxurious describes this plan's many attributes. Designed to fit a hilly site, it begins with a three-car garage level. A striking entry opens to a lofty living room with a fireplace. A planter separates the living room from the dining room. The elaborate kitchen includes a cooktop island that extends far enough to double as a breakfast bar. The bright nook accommodates casual meals. A bookcase-lined family room also holds a fireplace. The master suite pampers with large proportions and a huge bath and walk-in closet. The upper level has three bedrooms, a den and a games room with an exercise area. Don't miss the laundry room and its counter space.

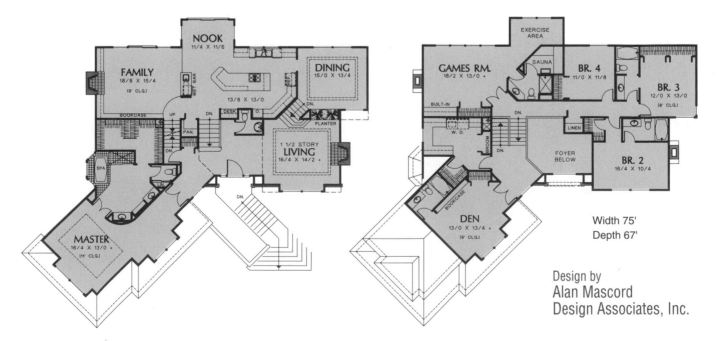

Width 75'
Depth 67'

Design by
Alan Mascord
Design Associates, Inc.

Width 50'
Depth 35'

Design 9573

First Floor: 1,502 square feet
Second Floor: 954 square feet
Total: 2,456 square feet

● Come home to the spectacular views and
livability supplied by this lovely hillside
home. It tucks a garage into the lower level;
two full stories accommodate family living
patterns. A two-story living room shares a
see-through fireplace with the formal dining
room. Quiet time may be spent in the den,
which opens through double doors to a
deck. The sunken family room also enjoys a
fireplace and isn't too far from the kitchen
and breakfast nook. The kitchen features a
cooktop island. On the top floor, a vaulted
master suite enjoys privacy from the two
secondary bedrooms. Both of these access a
full bath between.

Design by
Alan Mascord
Design Associates, Inc.

Design 9410

First Floor: 1,484 square feet
Second Floor: 1,402 square feet
Bonus Room: 430 square feet
Total: 3,316 square feet

● This impressive Tudor is designed for lots that slope up slightly from the street — the garage is five feet below the main floor. Just to the right of the entry, the den is arranged to work well as an office. Formal living areas include a living room with fireplace and an elegant dining room. The family room also has a fireplace and is close to the bumped-out nook — a great casual dining area. All the bedrooms are generously sized, especially the master which features all the amenities plus a huge walk-in closet. A large vaulted bonus room is provided with convenient access both from the family room and the upper hallway.

Design by
**Alan Mascord
Design Associates, Inc.**

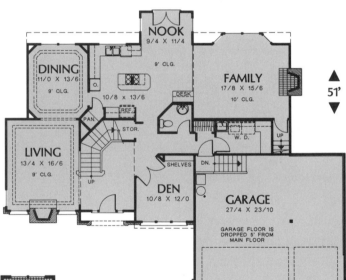

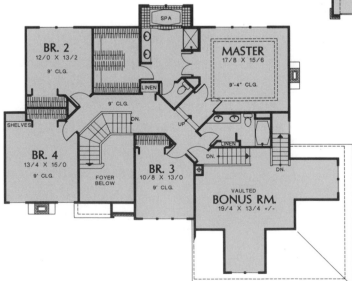

Design 9406

First Floor: 2,152 square feet
Second Floor: 1,248 square feet
Total: 3,400 square feet

● This spectacular plan is designed for a lot that slopes up from the street approximately sixteen feet—perfect for uphill view lots. The foyer opens up to the 1½-story living room on one side and the huge master suite with luxury bath on the other. The rear section of the home features a dramatic two-story family room and a breakfast nook overlooked by an upstairs bridge leading to the bedroom area. Three family bedrooms and a den are provided, plus 2 full bathrooms.

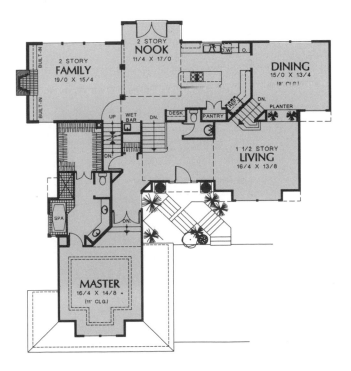

Width 60'
Depth 65'

Design by
Alan Mascord
Design Associates, Inc.

Design 6600

Square Footage: 1,795

● This engaging three-bedroom split plan is great for casual living both inside and out, offering contemporary amenities for convenient living. Built on a crawlspace designed for a sloping lot, this design assures flexible construction. The foyer opens to the formal dining room on the right, and straight ahead, the great room complete with a fireplace and a built-in entertainment center. Double French doors unfold onto a large veranda. The kitchen includes a large walk-in pantry, an eating bar and a bayed breakfast nook. The relaxing master suite enjoys access to a screened porch, His and Hers walk-in closets and a private bath with a glass-enclosed shower. Two secondary bedrooms offer privacy and plenty of storage.

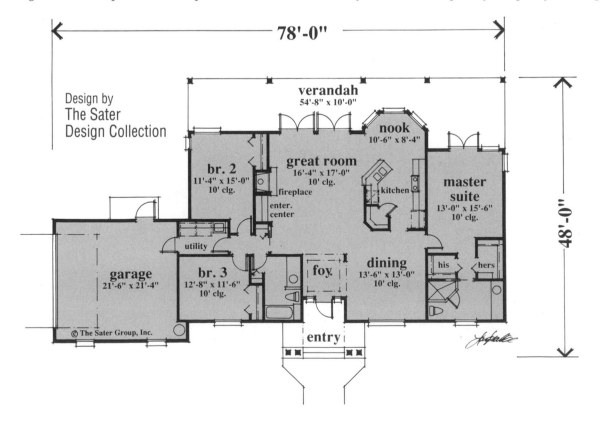

Design by
The Sater
Design Collection

78'-0"

48'-0"

verandah
54'-8" x 10'-0"

nook
10'-6" x 8'-4"

br. 2
11'-4" x 15'-0"
10' clg.

great room
16'-4" x 17'-0"
10' clg.

fireplace

enter.
center

kitchen

master
suite
13'-0" x 15'-6"
10' clg.

garage
21'-6" x 21'-4"

utility

br. 3
12'-8" x 11'-6"
10' clg.

foy.

dining
13'-6" x 13'-0"
10' clg.

his   hers

entry

22

Width 108'-2"
Depth 61'-6"

Design by
**Larry E. Belk
Designs**

OFFICE
14-0 X 21-6

BEDROOM 5
15-4 X 17-6

BATH
4

GAME ROOM
27-0 X 16-0

LIGHT WELL
ABOVE

ATTIC STORAGE

ATTIC STORAGE

Design 8084

First Floor: 3,328 square feet
Second Floor: 868 square feet
Total: 4,196 square feet

● The combination of stucco, stacked stone and brick adds texture and character to this Country French home. The foyer, with a twelve-foot ceiling, offers views to the study, the dining room and the living room. Columns with connecting arches define the entrances to the dining room and the living room. Notice the progression of step-ups throughout the floor plan, which make this home more adaptable to a sloping lot. Double French doors open to the study with built-in bookcases and a window seat overlooking the rear deck. A see-through fireplace serves both the living room and the study. The breakfast room features a built-in hutch for storage and the family room includes built-in bookcases perfect for stereo equipment and a television. The master suite is enhanced by a raised, corner fireplace and a bath with an exercise room.

WIDTH 108-2

GARAGE

SCREENED PORCH
14-6 X 10-6

PATIO WITH TRELLIS

DECK

EXERCISE RM
8-4 X 11-6
10 FT CEILING

MASTER
BATH
10 FT CEILING

PORCH

COVERED PORCH

HOT
TUB

LIN

BATH
3

WORK BENCH

FAMILY ROOM
15-6 X 16-0
10 FT CEILING

BREAKFAST
11-8 X 12-0
11 FT CEILING

LIVING ROOM
15-0 X 17-6
12 FT CEILING

WINDOW SEAT

STUDY/BEDROOM 3
14-6 X 13-6
10 FT CEILING

FP

MASTER BEDROOM
15-4 X 16-6
10 FT CEILING

ARCH

DEPTH 61-6

BEDROOM 4
11-6 X 13-0

PAN

10 FT CEILING

STEP

FOYER
12 FT CEILING

BATH
2

UTIL

KITCHEN
21-0 X 13-6

DINING ROOM
15-4 X 15-4
12 FT CEILING

BEDROOM 2
12-0 X 14-0
10 FT CEILING

PORCH

Design 2788
Upper Level: 1,795 square feet
Lower Level: 866 square feet
Total: 2,661 square feet

● This pleasing Tudor design accommodates the sloping site well. On the upper level, a large living room with a fireplace will make gatherings a real pleasure. The formal dining room is easily served by the efficient kitchen. Three bedrooms include a master bedroom suite with two closets, a private bath and a dressing room. On the lower level, a family room and a study further livability. The two-car garage opens to the side.

Design by
Home Planners, Inc.

Width 56'-4"
Depth 38'

Design by
Home Planners,
Inc.

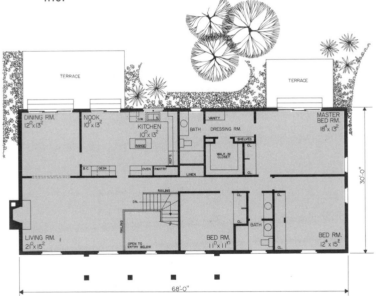

Design 2547
Upper Level: 1,946 square feet
Lower Level: 1,340 square feet
Total: 3,286 square feet

● This home offers the growing family plenty of space. On the lower level you'll find a huge activities room, perfect for parties. A versatile study or bedroom is also on this level. Upstairs, formal living includes the living room, which has a fireplace. The dining room is next to the kitchen and breakfast nook. In the kitchen, an island range adds to the modern efficiency of this area. Three bedrooms include a master suite with a dressing room, a walk-in closet and a full bath. The secondary bedrooms share a naturally lit hall bath.

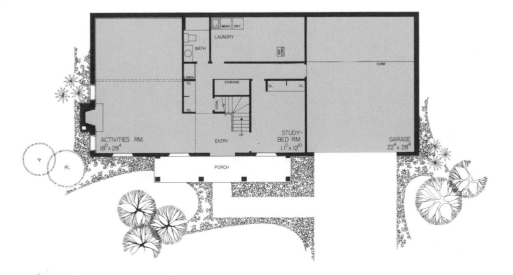

Design 4209

Entry Level: 800 square feet
Upper Level: 896 square feet
Total: 1,696 square feet

L

● Though small in size, this home's
leveled-living arrangement allows a
floor plan that easily accommodates
family lifestyles. Besides a sunken
living room with corner fireplace, a
handy L-shaped kitchen, powder
room, and dining room are found on
the entry level. Side patios extend the
possible eating areas, both formal and
informal. An indulgent master suite
on the second floor has its own fireplace and sitting room. Just a few
steps up are two family bedrooms.

Design by
**Home Planners,
Inc.**

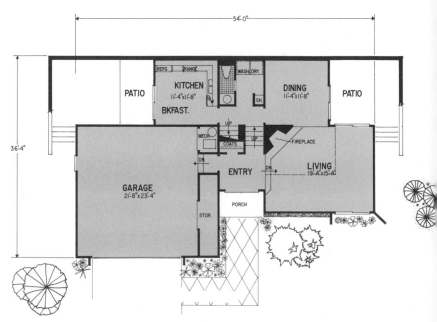

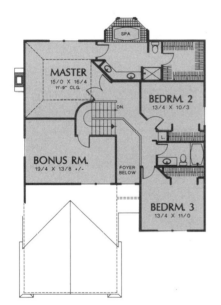

Design by
**Alan Mascord
Design Associates**

Design 9409

First Floor: 1,453 square feet
Second Floor: 1,016 square feet
Bonus Room: 251 square feet
Total: 2,720 square feet

● Designed for lots sloping up approximately eight feet, this compact home is just 39 feet wide. Its special features include a dramatic 1½-story living room, a dining room that is raised and allows views of the living room, and a den off the entry on the main floor. The large family room has a curved stairwell wall. Upstairs are three large bedrooms including a spacious master suite with spa tub and double vanity. Note the extra space available in the bonus room.

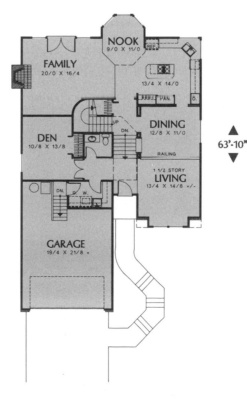

Design 9538

First Floor: 1,538 square feet
Second Floor: 1,089 square feet
Total: 2,627 square feet

● Accentuate your sloping lot with this attractive two-story home. The foyer opens to columned views. A volume great room with a deck, a fireplace and built-ins commands attention. The gourmet kitchen features an island cooktop, a sunny corner sink and a nook with a pass-through to the great room. A dining room, a double-doored den and a spacious laundry room with a nearby powder room complete the first floor. Upstairs, the master bedroom suite utilizes a scissor vault ceiling design. An attached, private luxury bath and a walk-in closet will surely satisfy. Two secondary bedrooms share a compartmented hall bath.

Design by
Alan Mascord
Design Associates, Inc.

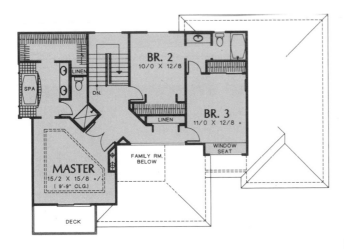

Design 9488

Main Level: 1,713 square feet
Upper Level: 998 square feet
Lower Level: 102 square feet
Total: 2,813 square feet

Design by
**Alan Mascord
Design Associates, Inc.**

Width 54'-6"
Depth 37'

● Designed for sloping lots, this home has much to offer in addition to its visual appeal. It is especially suited to homes that orient with a view to the front (note the decks in the master bedroom and den). The two-story family room, with through fireplace to the den, is complemented by the more formal parlor with 10'-1" ceiling. The parlor is separated from the dining room by a step with columned accents. The kitchen/nook area has an island range and is enhanced by a 9' ceiling. Three bedrooms upstairs include a master with lavish bath and 9'-9" tray ceiling. Two family bedrooms share a full bath.

Design 9569

First Floor: 1,108 square feet
Second Floor: 943 square feet
Total: 2,051 square feet

● This dapper home will grace a variety of sloping sites. The front door gives way to a two-story living room with a fireplace. A nearby formal dining room features double doors that lead to the outdoors. The family room enjoys a deck. In the kitchen, plenty of counter and cabinet space will make meal preparation a breeze. In the vaulted master suite, two closets and a superb bath add to the luxury. Two additional bedrooms each have private bath access.

Width 36'
Depth 34'

Design by
Alan Mascord
Design Associates, Inc.

Design 9509

Main Level: 1,022 square feet
Upper Level: 813 square feet
Total: 1,835 square feet

● This house not only accommodates a narrow lot, but it also fits a sloping site. Notice how the two-car garage is tucked away under the first level of the house. The angled corner entry gives way to a two-story living room with a tiled hearth. The dining room shares an interesting angled space with this area and enjoys easy service from the efficient kitchen. A large pantry and an angled corner sink add character to this area. The family room offers double doors to a refreshing balcony. A powder room and a laundry room complete the main level. Upstairs, three bedrooms include a vaulted master suite with a private bath. Bedrooms 2 and 3 each take advantage of direct access to a full bath.

Design by
Alan Mascord
Design Associates, Inc.

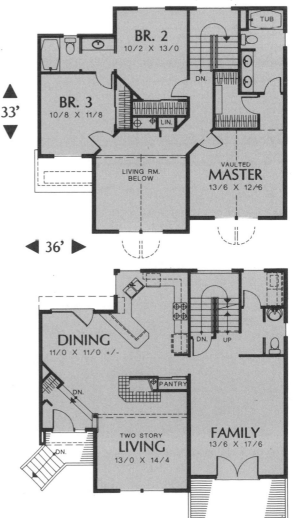

Design 2734

Main Level: 1,626 square feet; Upper Level: 1,033 square feet
Lower Level: 1,273 square feet; Total: 3,932 square feet

● If you have a desire for something delightfully different that offers unique, yet practical and enjoyable living patterns, then this house deserves careful study by all the members of your family. Having three bedrooms and a study on the upper level and a guest (or hobby) room on the lower level offers sleeping flexibility for the growing family. Notice how the living area looks down on the delightful planting area of the lower level. Also it shares a through-fireplace with the study. Other features of the study include a seven-foot-high book shelf, private balcony and separate stairs to the master bedroom. The outstanding U-shaped kitchen is flanked by the family and dining room. In addition to the living room, there is a huge, 32-foot activity room on the lower level. An abundance of storage space will be found in the three-car garage and the basement.

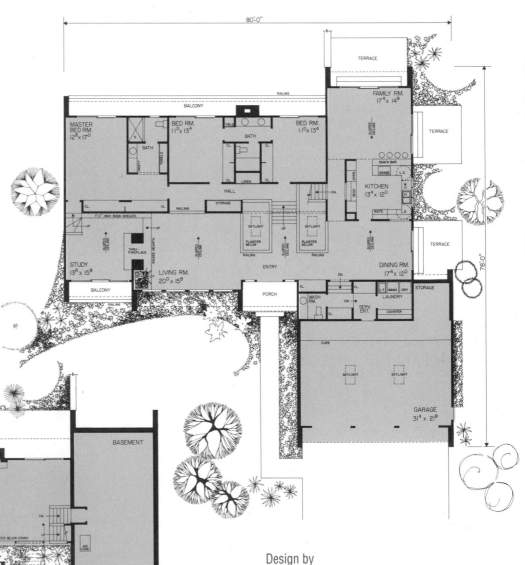

Design by
Home Planners,
Inc.

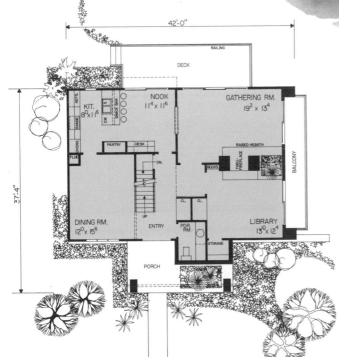

Design by
Home Planners,
Inc.

Design 2770

Main Level: 1,182 square feet
Upper Level: 998 square feet
Total: 2,180 square feet

● If you're looking for a home with loads of livability, then consider this contemporary version. It features main living areas made up of a formal dining room, a library and a gathering room with a raised hearth. The kitchen serves a nook. A full deck opens to the rear of the home. The sleeping level includes a master suite with a private bath, a dressing room and an outdoor balcony. The two secondary bedrooms share a full bath. The garage level has a laundry room and basement storage.

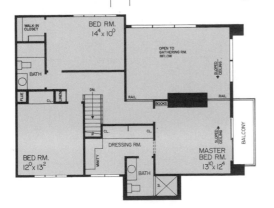

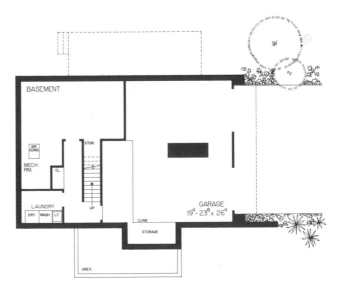

Design 9554

Main Level: 1,989 square feet
Upper Level: 1,349 square feet
Lower Level: 105 square feet
Total: 3,443 square feet
Bonus Room: 487 square feet

QUOTE ONE®

Cost to build? See page 214
to order complete cost estimate
to build this house in your area!

● Undeniable flair sets this design apart from the rest. On the lower level, a three-car garage, a shop and a bonus room are all very accommodating. Livability is the key on the main level where formal and informal spaces are located. A gallery outside the living room allows the display of fine art. A large den enjoys peace and quiet at the right side of the plan. Spacious kitchen planning includes a cooktop island and a nearby nook. Three bedrooms on the upper level all have walk-in closets. The master suite contains a fireplace and a private bath.

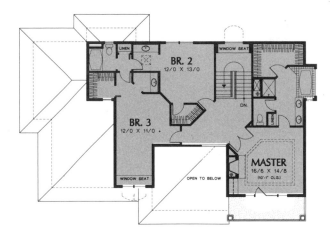

LINEN
BR. 2
12/0 X 13/0
WINDOW SEAT
BR. 3
12/0 X 11/0
DN.
LINEN
WINDOW SEAT
OPEN TO BELOW
MASTER
16/6 X 14/8
(10'-1" CLG.)

CRAWLSPACE
STORAGE
UP
SHOP
10/10 X 16/4
BONUS RM.
19/6 X 20/6
STORAGE/GAMES
GARAGE
32/10 X 25/10

Design by
Alan Mascord
Design Associates, Inc.

NOOK
10/0 X 17/0
WINDOW SEAT
FAMILY
18/0 X 16/0
12/0 X 16/0
GALLERY
DINING
13/6 X 14/8
VAULTED
LIVING
16/0 X 15/0
DEN
15/6 X 12/8 +/-
10' CLG.

Width 63'
Depth 48'

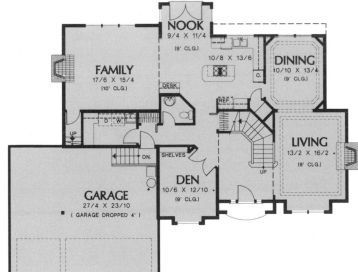

FAMILY
17/6 X 15/4
(10' CLG.)

NOOK
9/4 X 11/4
(9' CLG.)

DESK

10/8 X 13/6

DINING
10/10 X 13/4
(9' CLG.)

REF.

GARAGE
27/4 X 23/10
[GARAGE DROPPED 4']

SHELVES

DEN
10/6 X 12/10
(9' CLG.)

LIVING
13/2 X 16/2
(9' CLG.)

UP

DN.

UP

Width 63'
Depth 51'

SPA

MASTER
17/8 X 15/6

LINEN

BR. 2
12/0 X 13/2

UP

DN.

BONUS
19/4 X 13/4 +/-

DN.

BR. 3
10/8 X 13/0

FOYER
BELOW

BR. 4
13/4 X 15/0

Design by
Alan Mascord
Design Associates, Inc.

Design 9561

First Floor: 1,564 square feet
Second Floor: 1,422 square feet
Total: 3,416 square feet
Bonus Room: 430 square feet

● Stucco, a two-story entrance and thoughtful window treatment give this home a wonderful street presence. A gentle rise up from the street furthers its appeal. Inside, the whole family will find enough living area for every pursuit. A double-doored den opens off the foyer. A formal living and dining area includes a fireplace and boxed ceilings. In the rear of the plan, the kitchen opens to a sunny breakfast nook and a large family room. Upstairs, four bedrooms include a raised master bedroom suite with spacious closets and a spa tub. A bonus room over the garage will make an excellent play room for the kids. A three-car garage further enhances the plan.

Design 9576

First Floor: 1,894 square feet
Second Floor: 1,544 square feet
Total: 3,438 square feet

● Sleek, contemporary lines define the exterior of this home. Steps lead up a front-sloping lot to the bright entry. A front-facing den is brightly lit by a curving wall of windows. Built-ins enhance the utility of this room. A two-story living room offers a fireplace and lots of windows. The nearby dining room is capped by an elegant ceiling. The kitchen serves a sunny breakfast nook and an oversized family room. The family will find plenty of sleeping space with four bedrooms on the second level. The master bedroom suite is a real attention getter. Its roomy bath includes a spa tub and a separate shower.

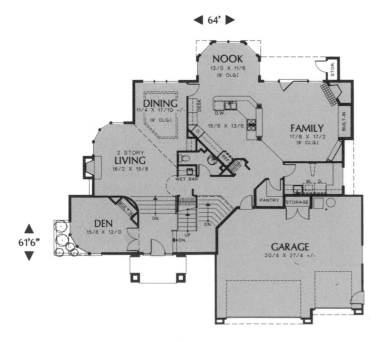

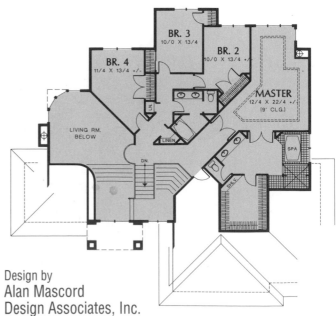

Design by
Alan Mascord
Design Associates, Inc.

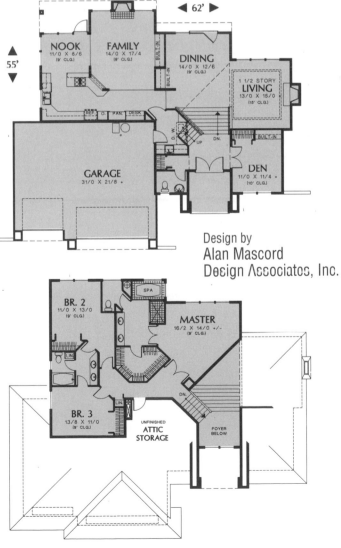

Design by
**Alan Mascord
Design Associates, Inc.**

Design 9574

First Floor: 1,532 square feet
Second Floor: 1,116 square feet
Total: 2,648 square feet

● For contemporary tastes, this sloping lot plan has few rivals. Double front doors lead to a private den with built-ins. To accommodate side-sloping lots, the plan steps down again to formal living areas. The 1½-story living room basks in details such as a tiered ceiling, a fireplace and bright windows. The dining room holds built-ins and also leads to outdoor livability. The family room is adjacent to the nook and the kitchen. Upstairs, an angled master bedroom suite contains a truly luxurious bath. The two secondary bedrooms access a full bath that connects them.

● If you like a contemporary plan with plenty of windows, this is the home for you. It offers a wealth of glass area throughout. Besides well-planned living areas on the first floor, there are four bedrooms and two full baths upstairs. The garage supplies a large storage area and is uniquely camouflaged as a wing of the house. Look also for abundant closet space, the screened porch and attached deck, and two-story foyer with open staircase to the second floor. All four bedrooms feature sloped ceilings.

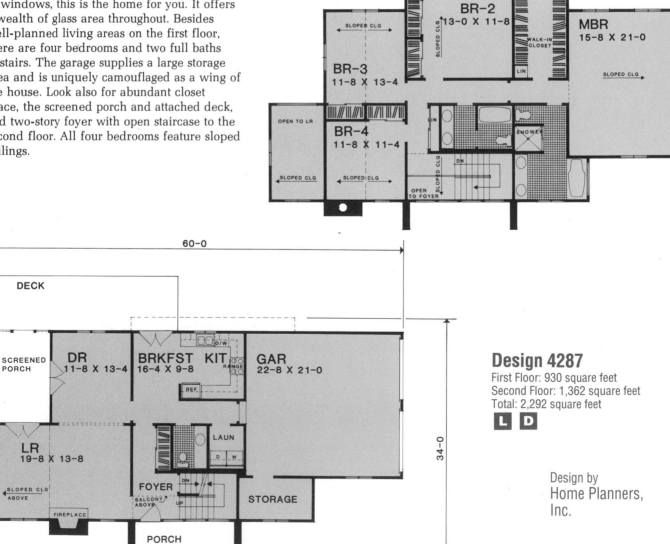

Design 4287

First Floor: 930 square feet
Second Floor: 1,362 square feet
Total: 2,292 square feet

L **D**

Design by
Home Planners,
Inc.

Design 9405

First Floor: 2,178 square feet
Second Floor: 1,297 square feet
Total: 3,475 square feet

● This impressive contemporary has a plan that works well for steep, sloping lots. A large, two-story covered entry has a curved balcony overlooking the front yard. The great master suite, with a private sun deck, is conveniently located on the same level as the entry and the living room. A stackable washer/dryer and a built-in ironing board are provided in the huge master bath. The 14-foot-high living room has a stair up to the overlooking dining room. Note the bridge on the upper level which has a view of the two-story nook on one side and the foyer on the other. Each of the four bedrooms and the den have direct access to a bathroom. This plan is designed with a flat roof.

◀ 66' ▶

▲ 48' ▼

Design by
Alan Mascord
Design Associates, Inc.

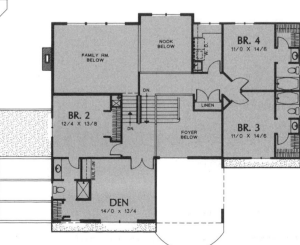

Design 3645

First Floor: 2,024 square feet
Second Floor: 800 square feet
Total: 2,824 square feet

L

Design by
Home Planners,
Inc.

● Tame the wild west with this handsome adobe-style home. Suitable for side-sloping lots, it contains a wealth of livability. A bee-hive fireplace graces the living room to enhance formal entertaining. The dining room is nearby. A den or sitting room is located near the master bedroom suite. All will enjoy the family room, which opens to outdoor spaces. Four bedrooms include a guest room. Split styling puts the master bedroom suite on the first floor of the plan. Here, a walk-in closet, curved shower and dual vanities bring a touch of luxury.

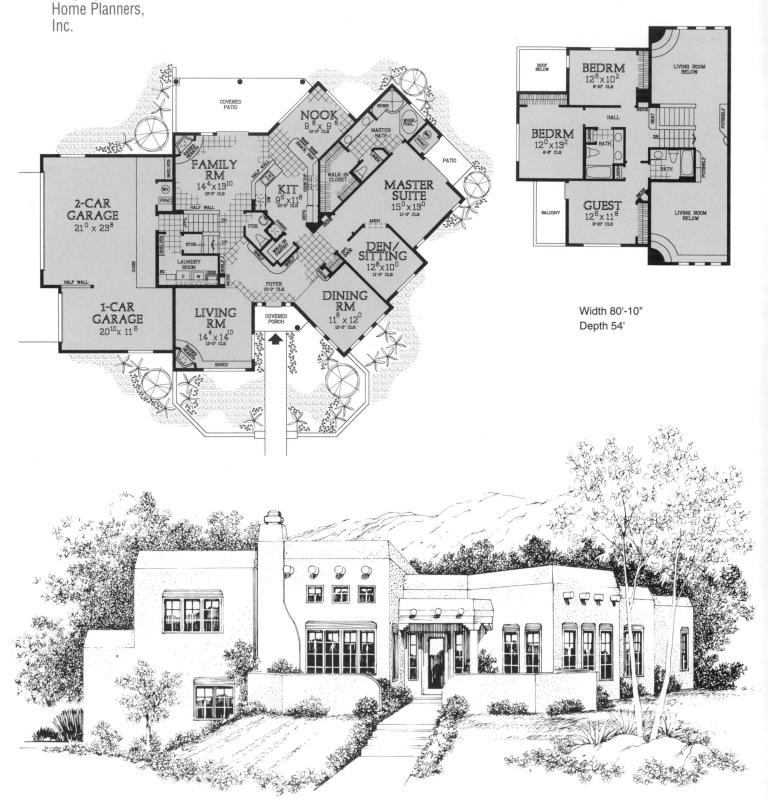

Width 80'-10"
Depth 54'

Traditional Homes With Walk-Out Basements

Design 9393

Main Level: 2,317 square feet
Finished Basement: 1,475 square feet
Total: 3,792 square feet

● A lower-level option turns this tidy one-story home into a much larger plan—and accommodates a hillside nicely. The main level contains the basic living areas: a great room with a through-fireplace to the hearth room, a formal dining room with a bay window and a kitchen with informal eating space.

The master bedroom, also on this level, has a wonderfully appointed bath and its own sitting room. An additional bedroom may serve as a den. The lower level, when finished, contains space for a family room with a wet bar and snack counter, plus two bedrooms and a bath.

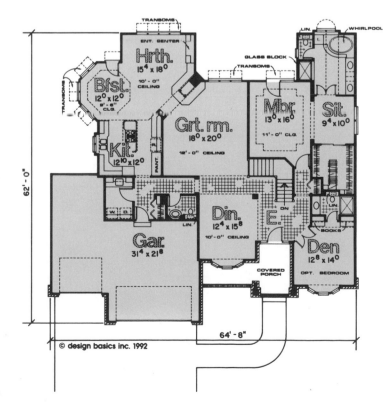

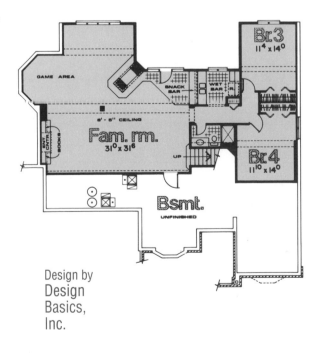

Design by
Design Basics, Inc.

Design 7281

Main Level: 1,595 square feet
Finished Basement: 790 square feet
Total: 2,385 square feet

● A columned entry and large windows mark this home's charming elevation. In the great room, a ten-foot ceiling and an angled, see-through fireplace create a cozy atmosphere. The dining room also features a ten-foot ceiling. The kitchen has room for a planning desk and an island counter. The breakfast area is served by the snack bar. An entertainment center is available in the bayed hearth room. The master bedroom overlooks a private, covered deck. The master bath includes a walk-in closet, a whirlpool tub and a dual-sink vanity. The optional finished basement has plans for additional bedrooms and a family room.

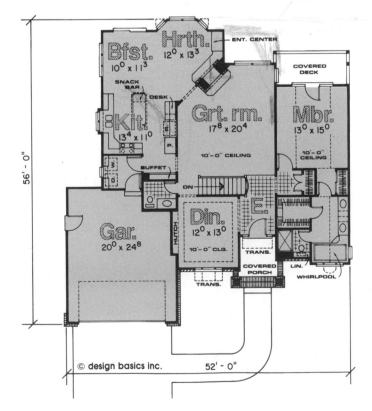

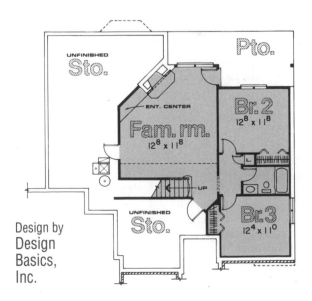

Design by
Design
Basics,
Inc.

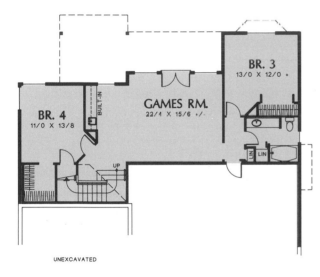

BR. 3
13/0 X 12/0 +

GAMES RM.
22/4 X 15/6 +/-

BR. 4
11/0 X 13/8

BUILT-IN

UP

UNEXCAVATED

Design by
Alan Mascord
Design Associates, Inc.

Design 9567

Main Level: 1,644 square feet
Lower Level: 1,012 square feet
Total: 2,656 square feet

● The character of this home is purely traditional. At the forefront is an elegant dining room open to the great room. The spacious kitchen is centered around a cooktop island. Double doors lead to a rear deck. The main-level master suite also opens to this area. A den or bedroom faces the front and is not far from a full bath, making it an ideal guest room. On the lower level, a games room and two more bedrooms reside. Built-ins and outdoor access make the games room versatile.

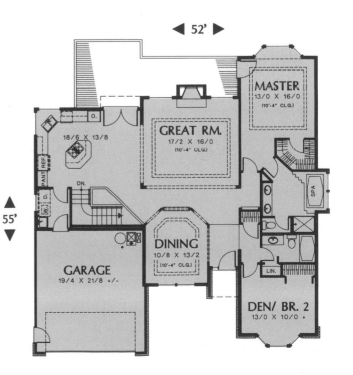

52'

55'

MASTER
13/0 X 16/0
(10'-4" CLG.)

GREAT RM.
17/2 X 16/0
(10'-4" CLG.)

18/6 X 13/8

SPA

DINING
10/8 X 13/2
(10'-4" CLG.)

GARAGE
19/4 X 21/8 +/-

DEN/ BR. 2
13/0 X 10/0

Design 9821

First Floor: 2,070 square feet
Second Floor: 790 square feet
Total: 2,860 square feet
Finished Basement: 914 square feet

QUOTE ONE®

Cost to build? See page 214
to order complete cost estimate
to build this house in your area!

● A striking combination of wood frame, shingles and glass creates the exterior of this classic cottage. The foyer opens to the main-level layout. To the left of the foyer is a study with a warming hearth and a vaulted ceiling. To the right is the formal dining room. A great room with an attached breakfast area is near the kitchen. A guest room is nestled in the rear of the plan for privacy. The master suite provides an expansive tray ceiling, a glass sitting area and easy passage to the outside deck. Upstairs, two bedrooms are accompanied by a loft for a quiet getaway. This home is designed with a walk-out basement.

Rear Elevation

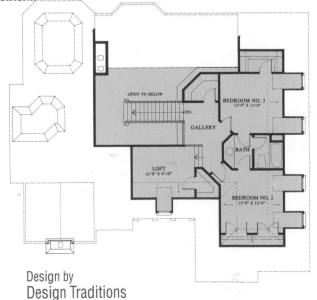

Design by
Design Traditions

WIDTH 58'-4"
DEPTH 54'-10"

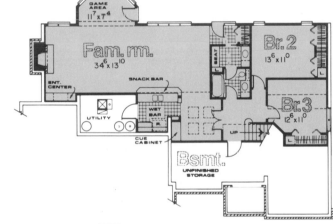

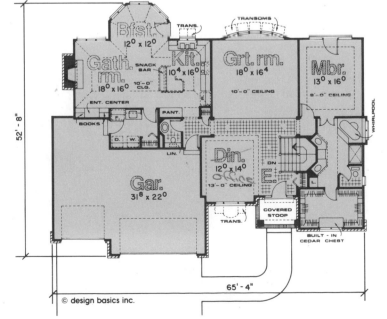

Design 7222

Main Level: 1,887 square feet
Lower Level: 1,338 square feet
Total: 3,225 square feet

● A majestic window and a brick exterior provide an extra measure of style to this handsome traditional home. Straight ahead, upon entering the foyer, is the spacious great room where bowed windows coupled with a high ceiling promote a light and airy feeling. The kitchen and breakfast area are integrated with the gathering room which features a fireplace and an entertainment center with built-in bookshelves, making this area a favorite for family gatherings. For more formal occasions, entertaining is easy in the adjacent dining room. The large, private master suite is highlighted by double doors opening into the master dressing area which features angled lavs and a huge walk-in closet complete with a cedar chest. The basement is designed for finishing as space is needed.

Design by
Design
Basics,
Inc.

Design 9484

Main Level: 1,573 square feet
Lower Level: 1,404 square feet
Total: 2,977 square feet

● There's something for every member of the family in this captivating hillside plan. The first floor holds a huge great room for family and formal gatherings, a dining room distinguished by columns, an island kitchen with an attached nook and outdoor deck area, and a master suite with a giant-sized bath. The game room downstairs is joined by three bedrooms or two bedrooms and a den. Look for another deck at this level.

Design by
**Alan Mascord
Design Associates, Inc.**

DECK

GAMES RM.
19/0 X 16/6

DEN/BR.4
12/10 X 11/2

BR. 3
11/10 X 12/10

BR. 2
11/0 X 16/6

LINEN

MECHANICAL

CRAWLSPACE

STOR.

UP

BUILT-IN

LINEN

D.W.

DECK

VAULTED
GREAT RM.
19/0 X 16/6

MASTER
14/0 X 15/8
(10' CLG.)

SPA

NOOK/KIT.
15/6 X 18/0
(11'-8" CLG.)

PANT.

DINING
11/0 X 12/0
(12'-8" CLG.)

DN.

GARAGE
32/2 X 21/4 +/-

Width 76'
Depth 43'

Design 9543 Main Level: 2,188 square feet
Lower Level: 1,049 square feet; Total: 3,237 square feet

● Carriage lamps and brick columns provide a dramatic element to the impressive entry to this one-story traditional. The well-designed floor plan flows nicely. The den is ideally located for use as an office if the need arises. To the left rests the formal living and dining area which provides nearby access to the step-saving kitchen. The family room is separated only by the breakfast nook, which provides access to the rear deck. The master suite, with its tray ceiling and luxurious bath, completes the first floor. The basement contains a recreation room, (with access to the rear grounds), two secondary bedrooms and a full bath.

Design by
Alan Mascord
Design Associates, Inc.

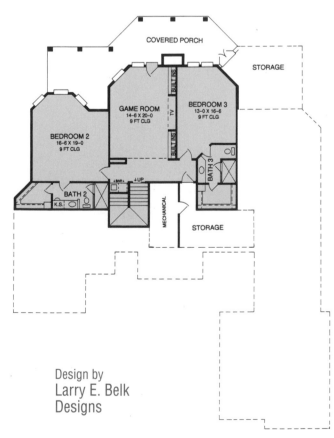

Design 8153

Main Level: 2,773 square feet
Lower Level: 1,214 square feet
Total: 3,987 square feet

● An understated stucco facade creates an elegant picture from the curb of this sloping-lot home. The grand foyer features a barrel-vaulted ceiling, which ties into the arched opening leading to the enormous great room and its fourteen-foot ceiling. Created for outdoor living, the ground floor provides views for the master suite, the great room, the kitchen and breakfast room. All of these areas provide access to the large deck that wraps the rear of the home. Downstairs, the basement includes two roomy bedrooms with private baths. The game room is a perfect location for a big-screen TV. Nine-foot ceilings in the basement give the rooms an open, spacious feeling. This home may also be built with a slab foundation.

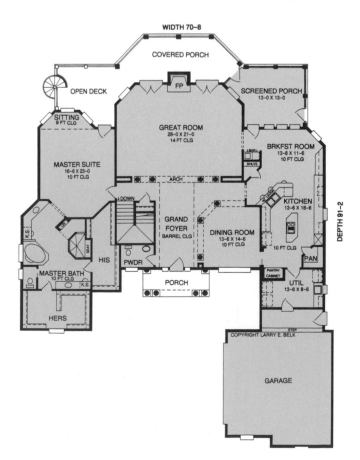

WIDTH 70–8
COVERED PORCH
OPEN DECK
SCREENED PORCH 13-0 X 13-0
SITTING 9 FT CLG
GREAT ROOM 28-0 X 21-0 14 FT CLG
BRKFST ROOM 13-6 X 11-6 10 FT CLG
MASTER SUITE 16-6 23-0 10 FT CLG
ARCH
KITCHEN 13-6 X 18-6
GRAND FOYER BARREL CLG
DINING ROOM 13-6 X 14-6 10 FT CLG
HIS
PWDR
PAN
MASTER BATH 10 FT CLG
PORCH
UTIL 13-6 X 8-6
HERS
DEPTH 91–2

GARAGE

COVERED PORCH
STORAGE
GAME ROOM 14-6 X 20-0 9 FT CLG
BEDROOM 3 13-0 X 16-6 9 FT CLG
BEDROOM 2 16-6 X 19-0 9 FT CLG
BATH 3
BATH 2
MECHANICAL
STORAGE

Design by
Larry E. Belk
Designs

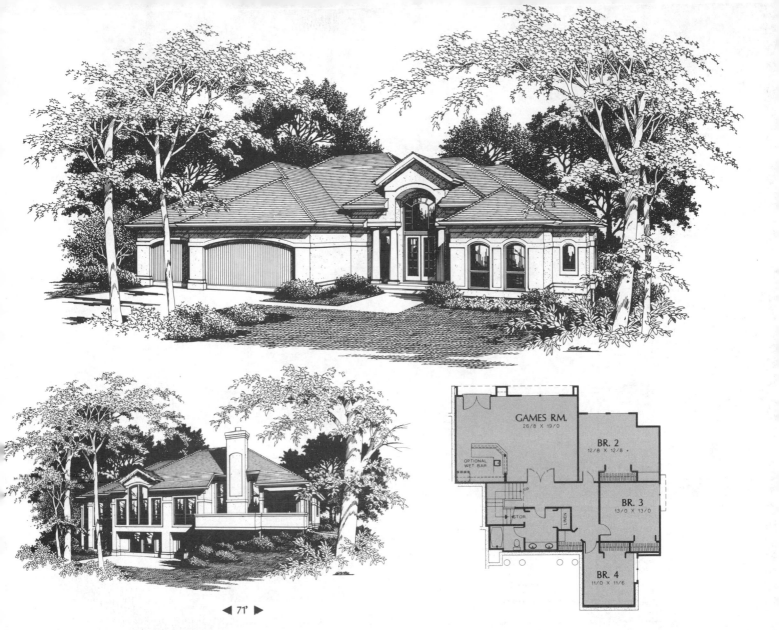

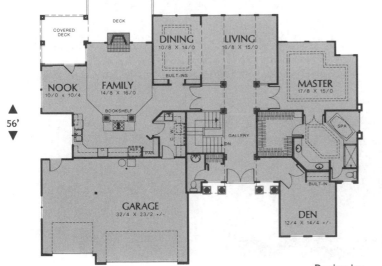

◀ 71' ▶

▲
56'
▼

COVERED DECK

DECK

DINING
10/8 X 14/0

BUILT-INS

LIVING
16/8 X 15/0

NOOK
10/0 X 10/4

FAMILY
14/8 X 16/0

BOOKSHELF

MASTER
17/8 X 15/0

SPA

GALLERY

DN

BUILT-IN

GARAGE
32/4 X 23/2 +/-

DEN
12/4 X 14/4 +/-

GAMES RM.
26/8 X 19/0

OPTIONAL
WET BAR

UP

STOR.

LINEN

BR. 2
12/8 X 12/8

BR. 3
13/0 X 13/0

BR. 4
11/0 X 11/6

Design by
**Alan Mascord
Design Associates, Inc.**

Design 9417

Main Level: 2,196 square feet
Lower Level: 1,542 square feet
Total: 3,738 square feet

● This refined home is designed for lots that fall off toward the rear and works especially well with a view out the back. The kitchen and eating nook wrap around the vaulted family room with its arched transom windows flanking the fireplace. Directly off the nook is a covered deck. Don't miss the huge game room on the lower level.

Design 2846
Main Level: 2,341 square feet; Lower Level: 1,380 square feet; Total: 3,721 square feet

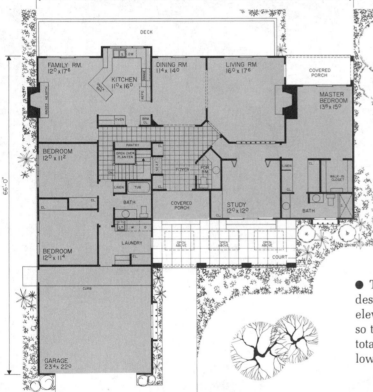

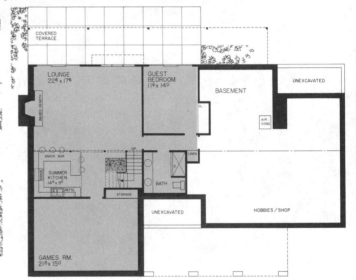

● The street view of this Spanish design shows a beautifully designed one-story home, but now take a look at the rear elevation. This home has been designed to be built into a hill so the lower level can be opened to the sun. By so doing, the total livability is almost doubled. A unique feature of the lower level is the summer kitchen.

Design by
Home Planners,
Inc.

PLAN IS DESIGNED FOR
DAYLIGHT BASEMENT LOTS.

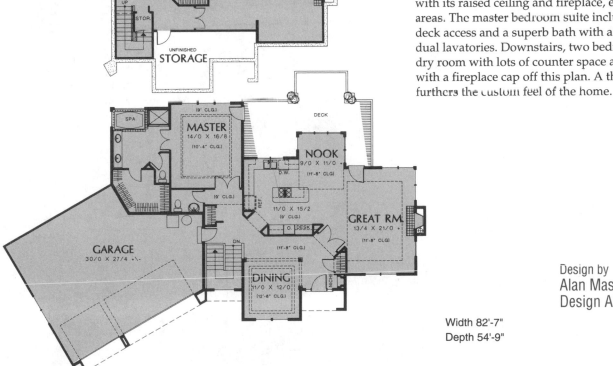

Design 9537

Main Floor: 1,687 square feet
Lower Floor: 1,251 square feet
Total: 2,938 square feet

● This striking home is perfect for daylight basement lots. An elegant dining room fronts the plan. It is near an expansive kitchen that features plenty of cabinet and counter space. A nook surrounded by a deck adds character and the comfortable great room, with its raised ceiling and fireplace, enhances these areas. The master bedroom suite includes private deck access and a superb bath with a spa tub and dual lavatories. Downstairs, two bedrooms, a laundry room with lots of counter space and a rec room with a fireplace cap off this plan. A three-car garage furthers the custom feel of the home.

Design by
Alan Mascord
Design Associates, Inc.

Width 82'-7"
Depth 54'-9"

Design 8160

Main Level: 1,709 square feet
Lower Level: 1,051 square feet
Total: 2,760 square feet

● Designed for a sloping lot, this home is complete with a roomy front porch and a Southern character. The ground floor features nine-foot ceilings to give the home a spacious feeling. A covered balcony is located off the breakfast room and makes a perfect place to sit and view the lake or woods beyond. His and Hers walk-in closets and vanities are among the luxuries found in the master suite. The basement features two bedrooms, each with a private bath. A large den completes the downstairs plan. This home may be built with a slab or basement foundation. Please specify when ordering.

Design by
**Larry E. Belk
Designs**

Width 60'-10"
Depth 69'-3"

Design 2847

Main Level: 1,874 square feet
Lower Level: 1,131 square feet
Total: 3,005 square feet

L

● This is a magnificent Tudor hillside plan, complete with a main-level fireplace, easy-to-reach rear deck (four different rooms lead to it) and plenty of storage space. The lower level is a delight. Note the fireplace, summer kitchen with snack bar, rear terrace, space for an extra bedroom (or two), built-ins galore and lots of bonus space that could easily be a workroom, exercise room or both.

Design by
**Home Planners,
Inc.**

Width 78'-10'
Depth 43'-5"

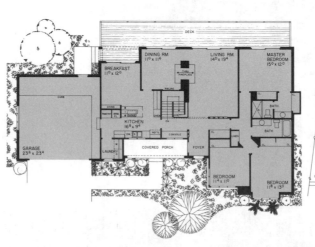

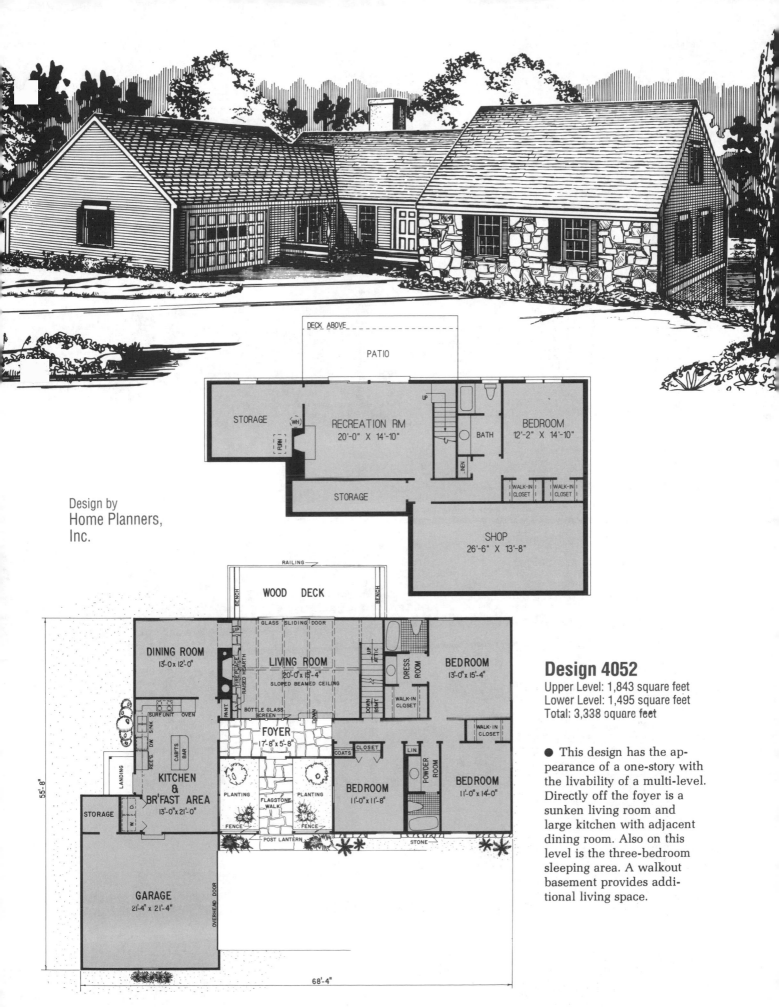

DECK ABOVE

PATIO

STORAGE

RECREATION RM
20'-0" X 14'-10"

WH

FURN

BATH

BEDROOM
12'-2" X 14'-10"

UP

LINEN

WALK-IN CLOSET   WALK-IN CLOSET

STORAGE

SHOP
26'-6" X 13'-8"

Design by
Home Planners,
Inc.

RAILING

WOOD   DECK

BENCH

BENCH

GLASS   SLIDING   DOOR

DINING ROOM
13'-0 x 12'-0"

UP

FIRE PLACE
RAISED HEARTH

LIVING ROOM
20'-0" x 15'-4"
SLOPED BEAMED CEILING

UP
ATTIC

DRESS. ROOM

BEDROOM
13'-0" x 15'-4"

DOWN
BSMT.

WALK-IN
CLOSET

PANTRY

SURF UNIT   OVEN

REF'G   DW   SINK

CAB'T'S
BAR

BOTTLE GLASS
SCREEN

FOYER
17'-8" x 5'-8"

DOWN

WALK-IN
CLOSET

KITCHEN
&
BR'FAST AREA
13'-0" x 21'-0"

LANDING

PLANTING

FLAGSTONE
WALK

PLANTING

COATS   CLOSET

LIN.

POWDER
ROOM

BEDROOM
11'-0" x 11'-8"

BEDROOM
11'-0" x 14'-0"

STORAGE

W. D.

FENCE

POST LANTERN

FENCE

STONE

55'-8"

GARAGE
21'-4" x 21'-4"

OVERHEAD DOOR

STORAGE

68'-4"

Design 4052

Upper Level: 1,843 square feet
Lower Level: 1,495 square feet
Total: 3,338 square feet

● This design has the appearance of a one-story with the livability of a multi-level. Directly off the foyer is a sunken living room and large kitchen with adjacent dining room. Also on this level is the three-bedroom sleeping area. A walkout basement provides additional living space.

Design 4300

Main Level: 1,824 square feet
Lower Level: 811 square feet
Total: 2,635 square feet

● This cozy ranch house makes a great starter home. Directly off the foyer is the spacious living room with a beamed ceiling and an enormous stone fireplace. Nearby is the kitchen with an island work center and a breakfast room. A walk-out basement provides room for future expansion. The three-bedroom sleeping area features a master bedroom with access to the rear deck. The secondary bedrooms each enjoy plenty of closet space and direct access to a bath with dual lavatories.

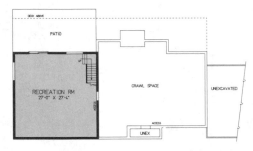

Design by
Home Planners,
Inc.

Width 88'
Depth 32'-8"

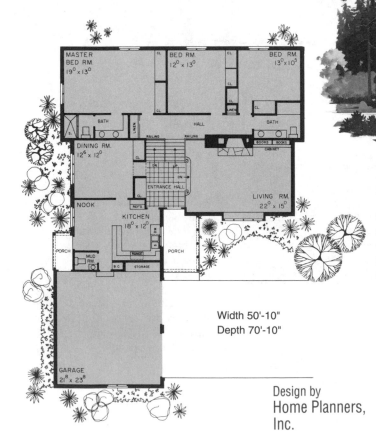

Width 50'-10"
Depth 70'-10"

Design by
Home Planners,
Inc.

Design 2354
Main Level: 936 square feet
Upper Level: 971 square feet; Lower Level: 971 square feet
Total: 2,878 square feet

● This English flavored tri-level design may be built on a flat site. Its configuration permits a flexible orientation on the site with either the garage doors or the front door facing the street. The interior offers a unique and practical floor plan layout.

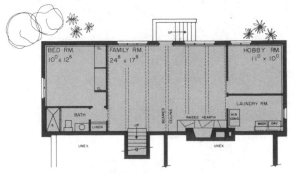

Design by
Home Planners,
Inc.

Design 3360

Main Level: 2,673 square feet
Lower Level: 1,389 square feet
Total: 4,062 square feet

L

● This plan has the best of both worlds — a traditional exterior and a modern, multi-level floor plan. The central foyer routes traffic effectively to all areas: the kitchen, gathering room, sleeping area, media room and the stairs leading to the lower level. Highlights include a master suite with luxurious bath and lower-level activities room with fireplace and kitchen. Also note the bedroom on this level.

Width 60'
Depth 72'

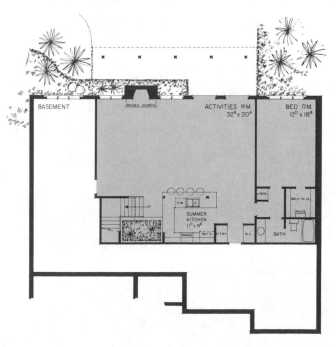

QUOTE ONE™
Cost to build? See page 214
to order complete cost estimate
to build this house in your area!

Design 1739 Main Level: 1,281 square feet; Sleeping Level: 857 square feet; Lower Level: 687 square feet; Total: 2,825 square feet

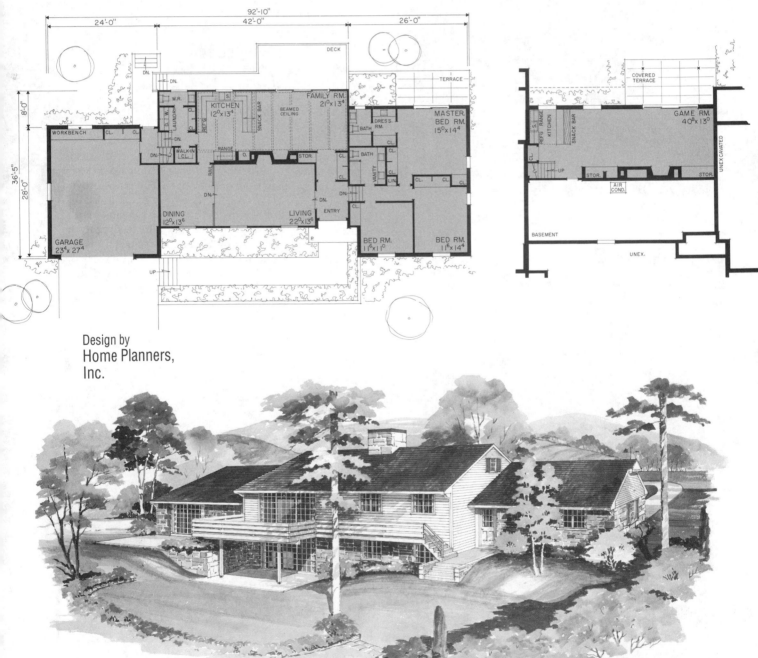

Design by
Home Planners,
Inc.

Design 1974 Main Level: 1,680 square feet; Lower Level: 1,344 square feet; Total: 3,024 square feet

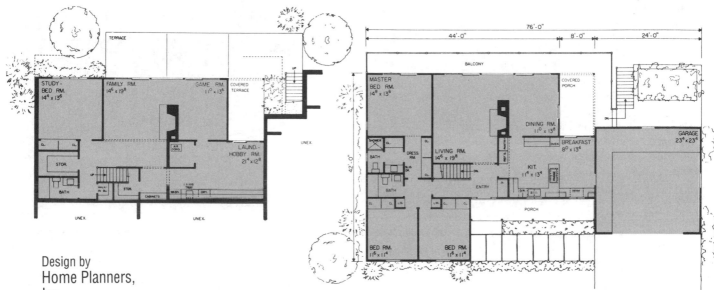

Design by
Home Planners,
Inc.

● You would never guess from looking at the front of this traditional design that it possessed such a strikingly different rear. From the front, you would guess that all of its livability is on one floor. Yet, just imagine the tremendous amount of livability that is added to the plan as a result of exposing the lower level - 1,344 square feet of it. Living in this hillside house will mean fun. Obviously, the most popular spot will be the balcony. Then again, maybe it could be the terrace adjacent to the family room. Both the terrace and the balcony have a covered area to provide protection against unfavorable weather. The interior of the plan also will serve the family with ease.

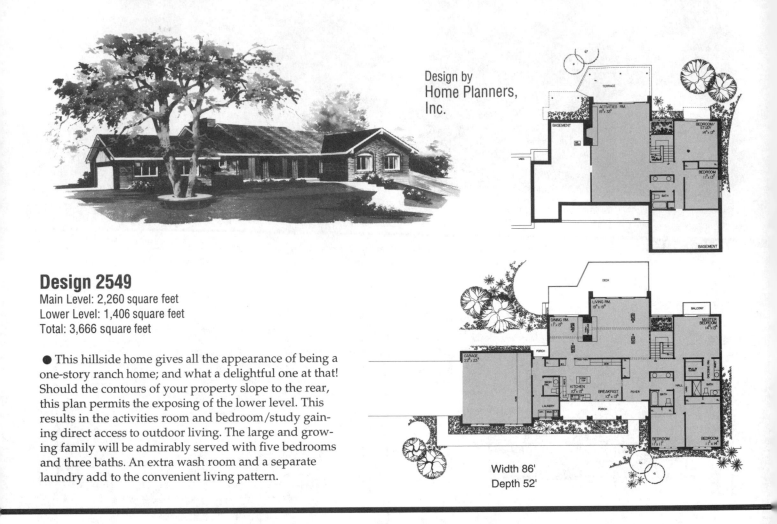

Design by
Home Planners,
Inc.

Design 2549

Main Level: 2,260 square feet
Lower Level: 1,406 square feet
Total: 3,666 square feet

● This hillside home gives all the appearance of being a one-story ranch home; and what a delightful one at that! Should the contours of your property slope to the rear, this plan permits the exposing of the lower level. This results in the activities room and bedroom/study gaining direct access to outdoor living. The large and growing family will be admirably served with five bedrooms and three baths. An extra wash room and a separate laundry add to the convenient living pattern.

Width 86'
Depth 52'

Design by
Home Planners,
Inc.

Design 2769

Main Level: 1,898 square feet
Lower Level: 1,134 square feet
Total: 3,032 square feet

Width 70'-8"
Depth 54'-4"

● This traditional hillside design has fine architectural styling. Its floor plan allows for split sleeping areas and a separation of formal and informal living areas.

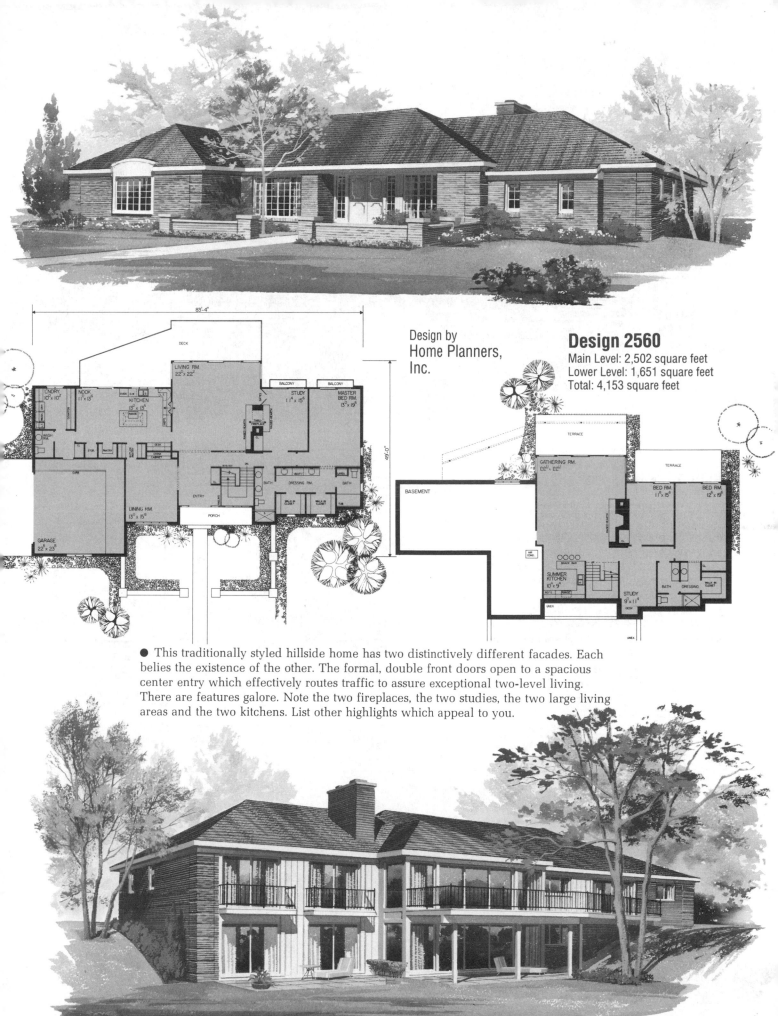

Design by Home Planners, Inc.

Design 2560

Main Level: 2,502 square feet
Lower Level: 1,651 square feet
Total: 4,153 square feet

● This traditionally styled hillside home has two distinctively different facades. Each belies the existence of the other. The formal, double front doors open to a spacious center entry which effectively routes traffic to assure exceptional two-level living. There are features galore. Note the two fireplaces, the two studies, the two large living areas and the two kitchens. List other highlights which appeal to you.

Design 8648

Square Footage: 2,500
Basement Level: 492 square feet

● This Florida "Cracker"-style home is warm and inviting. Space which is unpretentious is the hallmark of the Florida Cracker. This design shows the style at its best. Private baths for each of the bedrooms are a fine example of this. The huge great room, which sports a volume ceiling, opens to the expansive rear back porch for extended entertaining. Traditional Cracker homes had sparse master suites. Not this one! It has a lavish bed chamber and a luxurious bath with His and Hers closets and a corner soaking tub. Perfect for a sloping lot, this home can be expanded with a lower garage and bonus space in the basement.

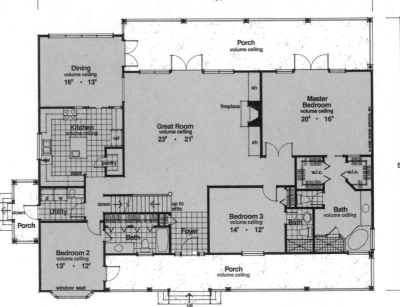

Design by
Home Design
Services, Inc.

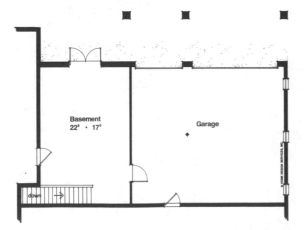

PORCH

BEDROOM 3
11-0 X 18-0
9 FT CLG

BEDROOM 4
13-6 X 14-0
9 FT CLG

GAME ROOM
15-0 X 20-0
9 FT CLG

FP

BEDROOM 2
13-6 X 15-8
9 FT CL

BUILT INS

LIN

BUILT INS

MECHANICAL

DRESSING

BATH 2

DRESSING

Design 8116

Main Level: 1,917 square feet
Lower Level: 1,579 square feet
Total: 3,496 square feet

● This country charmer starts with a large front porch. The rear of the home offers a huge deck, a portion of which is covered for outdoor protection. The ground floor features ten-foot ceilings throughout. The dining room is visible through a series of columns connected by arched openings. The kitchen, the breakfast room and the keeping room are open to one another. The master bedroom is located on the ground floor for privacy. The basement includes three bedrooms, a large bath with separate dressing areas and a game room with access to another outdoor covered porch.

OPEN DECK

COVERED DECK

OPEN DECK

Width 74'-2"
Depth 66'-1"

KEEPING ROOM
12-0 X 11-8
10 FT CLG

BRKFST AREA
13-6 X 14-6
10 FT CLG

LIVING ROOM
15-0 X 20-0
10 FT CLG

FP

MASTER BEDRM
13-6 X 14-6
10 FT CLG

KITCHEN
15-0 X 14-0
10 FT CLG

PAN

BUILT INS

HIS

CHEST

HERS

COPYRIGHT LARRY E. BELK

PWDR

DINING ROOM
13-0 X 12-6
10 FT CLG

ARCH

ARCH

FOYER
10 FT CLG

MASTER
BATH

10 FT CLG

GARAGE

UTIL
11-0 X 8-0

PORCH

STORAGE

Design by
Larry E. Belk
Designs

Design by
Design Traditions

Design 9839

Square Footage: 1,800
Lower Level: 981 square feet

● This European-inspired cottage contains one of the most efficient floor plans available. From the formal dining room at the front of the plan to the commodious great room at the rear, it accommodates various lifestyles in less than 2,000 square feet. An opulent master suite with deck access and grand bath dominates the right wing of the house. Two family bedrooms and a full bath are found to the left. There's even a powder room for guests. The gourmet-style kitchen has an attached breakfast area with glassed bay for sunny brunches. Bonus space in the basement allows for future development.

WIDTH 54'
DEPTH 52'

Design 9994

First Floor: 2,270 square feet
Second Floor: 1,128 square feet
Total: 3,398 square feet
Finished Basement: 1,271 square feet

● Designed for lovers of the outdoors, this 1½-story home crafts native creek stone and rugged lap siding into a design inspired by the rambling ski lodges of the high country. Massive stone fireplaces and soaring vaulted ceilings set the scene for casual living in the living room, great room, master bedroom and breakfast area. An island kitchen provides comfortable work space while the wide rear porch invites outside entertaining. A separate vestibule leads to the elegant downstairs master bedroom with a luxurious master bath and room-size walk-in closet. Upstairs are three more bedrooms and two full baths, one private. This home is designed with a walk-out basement.

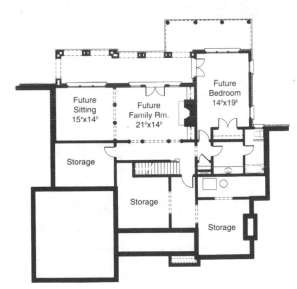

Width 62'-3"
Depth 59'-9"

Design by
Design Traditions

Design 9984

First Floor: 2,421 square feet
Second Floor: 1,322 square feet
Total: 3,743 square feet
Finished basement: 1,414 square feet

● This lovely farmhouse welcomes you home with a friendly front porch, perfect for outdoor relaxation. Inside, a warming hearth graces the living room. The dining room is across the foyer. A great room caters to more casual living with a porch and deck nearby. The kitchen serves a breakfast nook. An L-shaped counter and a walk-in pantry add to convenience. The first-floor master suite includes a pampering bath. Upstairs, three bedrooms each enjoy a walk-in closet. One even has its own bath. This home's walk-out basement provides found space.

Rear Elevation

Width 66'-9"
Depth 63'

Design by
Design Traditions

Design 9850

First Floor: 1,960 square feet
Second Floor: 905 square feet
Total: 2,865 square feet
Finished Basement: 1,243 square feet

QUOTE ONE®
Cost to build? See page 214
to order complete cost estimate
to build this house in your area!

Width 69'-8"
Depth 59'

Rear Elevation

Design by
Design Traditions

● This Georgian country-style home displays an impressive appearance. The front porch and columns frame the elegant, elliptical entrance. Textures of brick and wood are used to reflect this architectural period perfectly. Georgian symmetry balances the living room and dining room to the right and left of the foyer. Both are framed by columns, while the living room features its own fireplace. The main level continues into the two-story great room with built-in cabinetry, fireplace and a large bay window that overlooks the rear deck. A dramatic tray ceiling, a wall of glass and access to the rear deck complete the master bedroom. Left of the great room, the main level includes a large kitchen that opens to the breakfast area and staircase. Upstairs, from one of three bedrooms to another, you will pass the open railing overlooking the great room. Each bedroom features ample closet space and direct access to a bathroom. This home is designed with a walk-out basement.

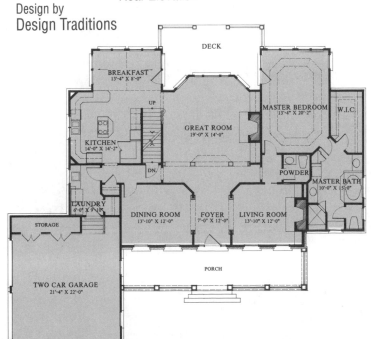

Design 9852

First Floor: 1,840 square feet
Second Floor: 950 square feet
Total: 2,790 square feet
Finished Basement: 1,840 square feet

● The appearance of this Early American home brings the past to mind with its wraparound porch, wood siding and flower-box detailing. The uniquely-shaped foyer leads to the dining room accented by columns, a vaulted ceiling and a bay window. Columns frame the great room as well, while a ribbon of windows creates a wall of glass at the back of the house from the great room to the breakfast area. The asymmetrical theme continues through the kitchen as it leads back to the hallway, accessing the laundry and two-car garage. Left of the foyer lies the living room with a warming fireplace. The master suite begins with double doors that open to a large bedroom with an octagonal tray ceiling and a bay window. The spacious master bath and walk-in closet complete the suite. Stairs to the second level lead from the breakfast area to an open landing overlooking the great room. Three family bedrooms are found on this level. This home is designed with a walk-out basement.

Rear Elevation

Width 58'-6"
Depth 62'

Design by
Design Traditions

Rear Elevation

Design 9910

First Floor: 2,565 square feet
Second Floor: 1,375 square feet
Total: 3,940 square feet
Finished Basement: 1,912 square feet

● A symmetrical facade with twin chimneys makes a grand statement. A covered porch welcomes visitors and provides a pleasant place to spend cool evenings. The entry foyer is flanked by formal living areas: a dining room and a living room, each with a fireplace. A third fireplace is the highlight of the expansive great room to the rear. The deck is accessible through the great room, the sun room or the master bedroom. The second floor offers three bedrooms, two full baths and plenty of storage space. This home is designed with a walkout basement.

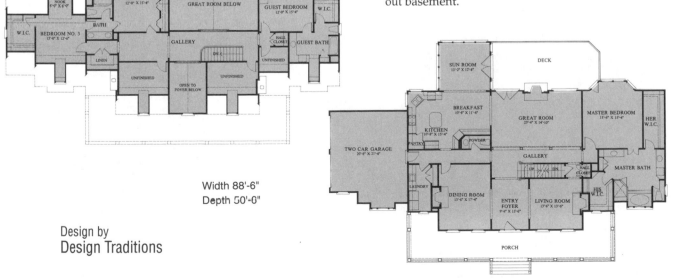

Width 88'-6"
Depth 50'-6"

Design by
Design Traditions

Design 9982

First Floor: 2,174 square feet
Second Floor: 1,113 square feet
Total: 3,287 square feet
Finished Basement: 2,174 square feet

● Front and back porches and old Southern charm give this home extra appeal. The foyer is flanked by a dining room and a living room (or a study). You'll also find a great room with a fireplace for family livability. The kitchen and breakfast room are not far away from here. The master suite is contained on the first floor. It contains porch access, a private bath and a large walk-in closet. Upstairs, secondary bedrooms accommodate the children or guests. This home's basement plan increases the overall square footage.

Rear Elevation

Design by
Design Traditions

Width 73'-6"
Depth 67'

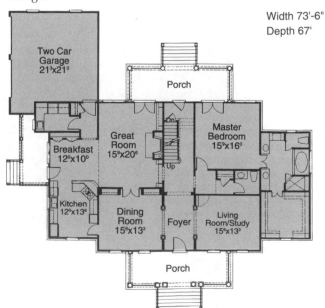

Two Car Garage 21³x21³

Porch

Great Room 15⁹x20⁶

Master Bedroom 15⁹x16⁰

Breakfast 12⁰x10⁰

Kitchen 12⁰x13⁶

Dining Room 15⁶x13³

Foyer

Living Room/Study 15⁶x13³

Porch

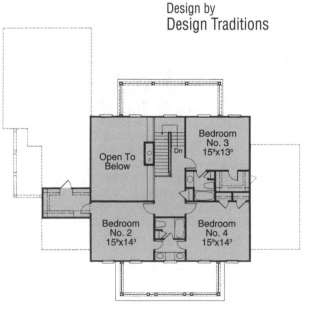

Open To Below

Bedroom No. 3 15⁹x13⁰

Bedroom No. 2 15⁹x14³

Bedroom No. 4 15⁹x14³

Design 9823

First Floor: 1,960 square feet
Second Floor: 905 square feet
Total: 2,865 square feet
Bonus Room: 297 square feet
Finished Basement: 1,243 square feet

● The classical styling of this Colonial home will be appreciated by traditionalists. The foyer opens to both a banquet-sized dining room and formal living room with fireplace. Just beyond is the two-story great room. The entire right side of the main level is taken up by the master suite. The other side of the main level includes a large kitchen and breakfast room just steps away from the detached garage. Upstairs, each bedroom features ample closet space and direct access to bathrooms. The detached garage features an unfinished office or studio on its second level. This home is designed with a walk-out basement.

Rear Elevation

Design by
Design Traditions

Width 69'-6"
Depth 74'-6"

QUOTE ONE®

Cost to build? See page 214
to order complete cost estimate
to build this house in your area!

Design 9822

First Floor: 1,944 square feet
Second Floor: 954 square feet
Total: 2,898 square feet
Finished Basement: 1,216 square feet

● This story-and-a-half home combines warm informal materials with a modern livable floor plan to create a true Southern classic. The dining room, study and great room work together to create one large, exciting space. Just beyond the open rail, the breakfast room is lined with windows. Plenty of counter space and storage make the kitchen truly usable. The master suite, with its tray ceiling and decorative wall niche, is a gracious and private owners' retreat. Upstairs, two additional bedrooms each have their own vanity within a shared bath while the third bedroom or guest room has its own bath and walk-in closet. This home is designed with a walk-out basement.

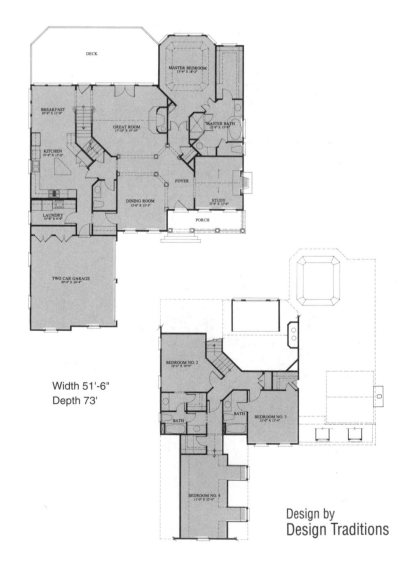

Width 51'-6"
Depth 73'

Design by
Design Traditions

Rear Elevation

Width 48'-6"
Depth 70'-11"

Design by
Design Traditions

Rear Elevation

Design 9812

First Floor: 1,580 square feet
Second Floor: 595 square feet
Total: 2,175 square feet
Bonus Room: 290 square feet
Finished Basement: 1,340 square feet

● This home features a front porch which warmly welcomes family and visitors, as well as protecting them from the weather—a true Southern Original. Inside, the spacious foyer leads directly to a large vaulted great room with massive fireplace. The dining room also receives the vaulted ceiling treatment. The grand kitchen offers both storage and large work areas opening up to the breakfast room. In the privacy and quiet of the rear of the home is the master suite with its garden bath, His and Hers vanities, and oversized closet. The second floor provides two additional bedrooms with a shared bath along with a balcony overlook to the foyer below. Ample amounts of storage space or an additional bedroom can be created in space over the garage. This home is designed with a walk-out basement.

QUOTE ONE®

Cost to build? See page 214
to order complete cost estimate
to build this house in your area!

Design 9967

First Floor: 1,567 square feet
Second Floor: 1,895 square feet
Total: 3,462 square feet
Finished Basement:1,567 square feet

● This home's fine proportions contain formal living areas, including a dining room and a living room. At the back of the first floor you'll find a fine kitchen that serves a breakfast nook. A great room with a fireplace and a bumped-out window makes everyday living very comfortable. A rear porch allows for outdoor dining and relaxation. Upstairs, four bedrooms include a master suite with lots of notable features. A boxed ceiling, a lavish bath, a large walk-in closet and a secluded sitting room (which will also make a nice study or exercise room) assure great livability. One of the secondary bedrooms contains a full bath. This home is designed with a walk-out basement.

Rear Elevation

Width 63'
Depth 53'-6"

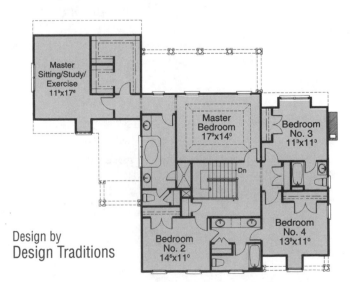

Design by
Design Traditions

Copyright 1992 Stephen S. Fuller, Inc.

Rear Elevation

Design 9869 First Floor: 1,475 square feet
Second Floor: 1,460 square feet; Total: 2,935 square feet
Finished Basement: 911 square feet

● Through this home's columned entry, the two-story foyer opens to the living room with wet bar. The media room features a fireplace and is accessed by double doors. The kitchen design is ideal with breakfast bar and preparation island. The dining room is ideal for formal entertaining. The upper level begins with the balcony landing overlooking the great room. The master bedroom features a bay-windowed sitting area and a tray ceiling. This home is designed with a basement foundation.

QUOTE ONE®
Cost to build? See page 214 to order complete cost estimate to build this house in your area!

Design by
Design Traditions

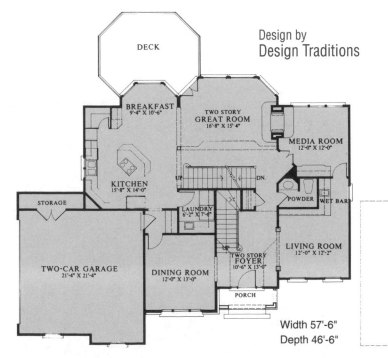

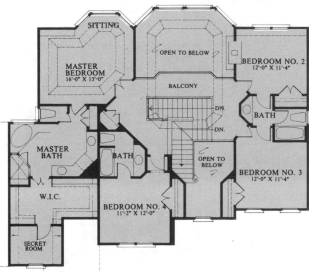

Width 57'-6"
Depth 46'-6"

Design 9993

First Floor: 1,634 square feet
Second Floor: 1,598 square feet
Total: 3,232 square feet
Bonus Room: 273 square feet
Finished Basement: 1,018

● Only a sloping pediment above double front windows adorns this simple, midwestern-style house, where a side-entry garage looks like a rambling addition. The wide porch signals a welcome that continues throughout the house. A front study doubles as a guest room with an adjacent full bath. A large dining room is ideal for entertaining and a sun-filled breakfast room off a spacious kitchen provides comfortable space for casual family meals. The open, contemporary interior plan flows from a stair hall at the heart of the house. On the private second level, the master bedroom includes a luxurious bath; two other bedrooms share a bath with dual vanities. An extra room over the kitchen makes a perfect children's play area. This home is designed with a walk-out basement.

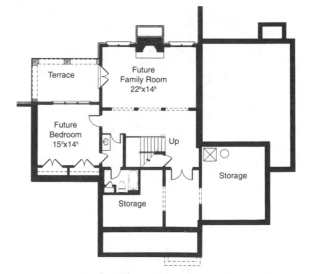

Width 62'
Depth 54'-9"

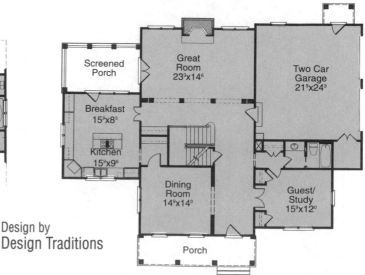

Design by
Design Traditions

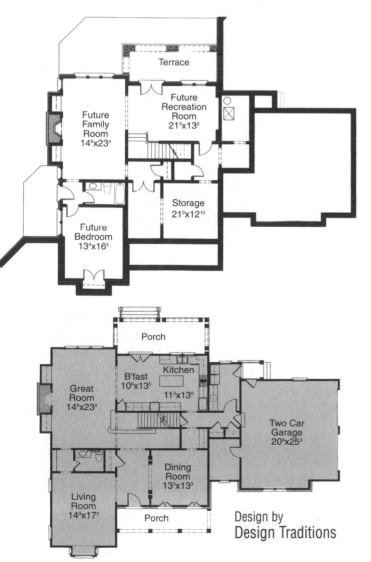

Terrace

Future Recreation Room
21⁰x13⁹

Future Family Room
14⁶x23⁴

Storage
21⁰x12¹⁰

Future Bedroom
13⁴x16⁴

Design 9992

First Floor: 1,704 square feet
Second Floor: 1,449 square feet
Total: 3,153 square feet
Bonus Room: 455 square feet
Finished Basement: 1,172 square feet

● The fieldstone exterior and cupola evoke rural Southern appeal. The distinctive railed balcony, bay windows and porch arches recall Colonial detail. Inside, formal and informal spaces are separated by a graceful central stair hall that opens off the front foyer. French doors lead from the front porch into a formal dining room that links both the stair hall and the foyer. The living room, which also opens off the entrance foyer, leads to a cheerful great room that features a fireplace and built-in bookcases. An adjoining breakfast area opens onto a columned rear porch. Upstairs, a spacious master suite overlooks the rear yard. Two additional bedrooms share a convenient hall bath. A generous bonus space above the garage is also available. This home is designed with a walk-out basement.

Porch

Great Room
14⁹x23⁹

B'fast
10⁹x13⁰

Kitchen
11³x13⁹

Two Car Garage
20⁸x25³

PWDR

Dining Room
13³x13³

Living Room
14⁹x17³

Porch

Design by
Design Traditions

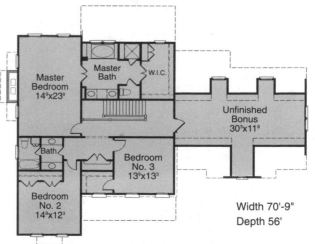

Master Bedroom
14⁹x23⁹

Master Bath

W.I.C.

Unfinished Bonus
30³x11⁹

Bath

Bedroom No. 3
13³x13³

Bedroom No. 2
14⁹x12³

Width 70'-9"
Depth 56'

Rear Elevation

Design by
Design Traditions

Design 9981

First Floor: 1,828 square feet
Second Floor: 1,552 square feet
Total: 3,380 square feet
Finished Basement: 1,828 square feet

● A stately appearance and lots of living space give this home appeal. The foyer introduces formal living and dining rooms. For more humble occasions, a great room opens to the back. The breakfast room has convenient proximity to these informal areas. The kitchen has plenty of work space. Four bedrooms on the second floor enjoy complete privacy. In the master bedroom suite, a short hallway flanked by closets leads to a lovely bath with a spa tub, a compartmented toilet, a separate shower and dual lavatories. This home is designed with a walk-out basement.

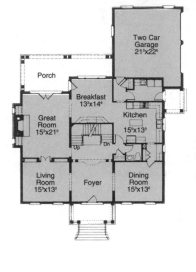

Width 54'-3"
Depth 70'-3"

Design 9991

First Floor: 2,496 square feet
Second Floor: 1,373 square feet
Total: 3,869 square feet
Finished Basement:1,620 square feet

● Classical symmetry prevails inside in same-size living and dining rooms that open off either side of the entrance foyer. The less formal living spaces beyond flow easily into one another from a central stair hall. Dormers bathe interior spaces in natural light. A dramatic vaulted great room with three dormers, a window-wrapped breakfast area and a master suite in the right wing all open onto a private rear porch. Five dormers on the front elevation distinguish a second story that includes three bedrooms, two baths and an optional linen closet or a cozy seating area. This home is designed with a walk-out basement.

Width 78'
Depth 53'-3"

Design by
Design Traditions

Rear Elevation

Design 9979

First Floor: 1,698 square feet
Second Floor: 1,542 square feet
Total: 3,240 square feet
Finished Basement: 1,207 square feet

● Make your mark with this brick traditional. With a walk-out basement, there's lots of room to grow. On the first floor, such attributes as informal/formal zones, a gourmet kitchen and a solarium, deck and screened porch are immediate attention getters. In the kitchen, meal preparation is a breeze with an island work station and plenty of counter space. Four bedrooms make up the second floor of this plan. One of the family bedrooms possesses a personal bath. The master bedroom has its own bath and a giant walk-in closet. This home is designed with a walk-out basement.

Design by
Design Traditions

Width 61'-6"
Depth 51'

Design 2841

Main Level: 1,044 square feet; Upper Level: 851 square feet
Lower Level: 753 square feet; Total: 2,648 square feet

L

● This spacious tri-level home provides optimal comfort and promotes outdoor living for today's active family. The rear opens to balconies and a deck that creates a covered patio below. An optional first-floor master suite is provided by the main-level study. Casual living is enhanced with a two-story gathering room found on the main level and an activities room, optional bunk room and full bath on the lower level. The master bedroom—located on the upper level—sports a private balcony, as does the large bunk room. A lounge and full bath complete this level.

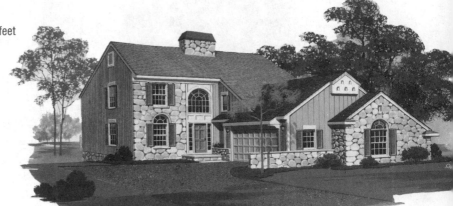

Design by
Home Planners, Inc.

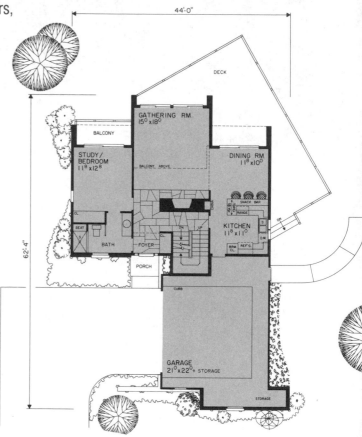

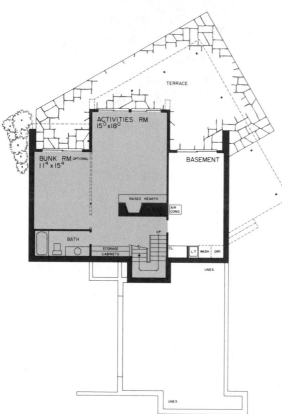

Design by
Home Planners,
Inc.

Design 3366

Main Level: 1,638 square feet
Upper Level: 650 square feet
Lower Level: 934 square feet
Total: 3,222 square feet

L

● There is much more to this design than
meets the eye. While it may look like a 1½-story
plan, bonus recreation and hobby space in the
walk-out basement adds almost 1,000 square
feet. The first floor holds living and dining
areas as well as the master bedroom suite. Two
family bedrooms on the second floor are connected by a balcony area that overlooks the
gathering room below. Notice the covered
porch beyond the breakfast and dining rooms.

QUOTE ONE™

Cost to build? See page 214
to order complete cost estimate
to build this house in your area!

Design 9575

Main Level: 1,887 square feet
Upper Level: 1,382 square feet
Lower Level: 906 square feet
Total: 4,175 square feet

● Graceful curves and ceiling treatments are showcased in this hillside home. Double front doors give passage to the airy foyer. An octagonal library impresses with its double-door entry and built-ins. The living and dining rooms remain open to each other, guaranteeing good flow for entertaining. The exceptional kitchen caters to family activities with a nook and a family room located nearby. The master suite provides a getaway with its elegant styling and planning. Three other bedrooms are on the second floor. The walk-out basement contains a games room and a guest bedroom next to a full bath.

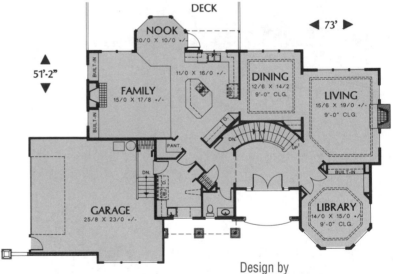

Design by
Alan Mascord
Design Associates, Inc.

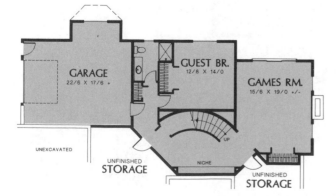

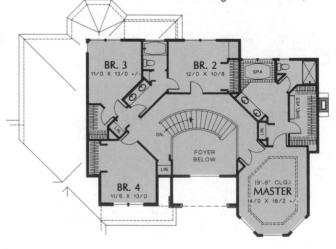

Design 2842

Entrance Level: 156 square feet; Upper Level: 1,038 square feet
Lower Level: 1,022 square feet; Total: 2,216 square feet

D

● This house can be built on a narrow lot to cut down overall costs. Yet its dramatic appeal surely is worth a million. The projecting front garage creates a pleasing curved drive. Enter through the covered porch to the entrance-level foyer. At this point, the stairs lead down to the walk-out living area consisting of a formal living room, family room, kitchen and dining area. Upstairs, four bedrooms and two full baths create the sleeping area. A balcony stretches across the rear.

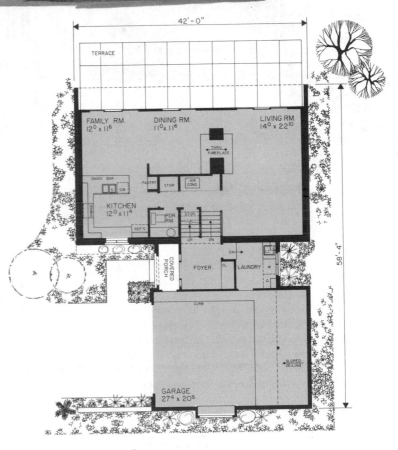

Design 4396

First Floor: 1,772 square feet
Second Floor: 674 square feet
Lower Level: 908 square feet
Total: 3,354 square feet

L

● Reminiscent of French country
houses, this delightful two-story
offers a wealth of extras. Two
wood decks flank the great room
on either side and are also accessed
through the breakfast room and the
master bedroom. Storage space
abounds with walk-in closets in
three bedrooms and extra store
rooms in the garage extension.
Downstairs, a walk-out basement
is fully livable with its family
room, bedroom and bath.

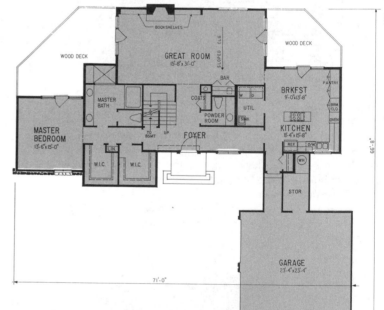

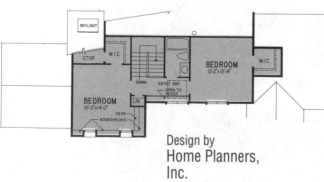

Design by
Home Planners,
Inc.

Floor Plans

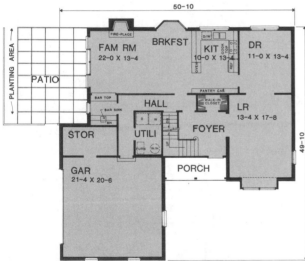

FAM RM 22-0 X 13-4
BRKFST
KIT 10-0 X 13-
DR 11-0 X 13-4
FIRE-PLACE
PATIO
PLANTING AREA
BAR TOP
BAR SINK
HALL
PANTRY CAB
WALK-IN CLOSET
LR 13-4 X 17-8
STOR
UTILI
FURN
FOYER
GAR 21-4 X 20-6
PORCH
50-10
49-10

HALL
STO
FOYER
PANTRY CAB
WALK-IN CLOSET
W

OPTIONAL FOR CRAWL FOUND.

Design 4278

First Floor: 1,269 square feet
Second Floor: 1,203 square feet
Lower Level: 1,232 square feet
Total: 3,704 square feet

D

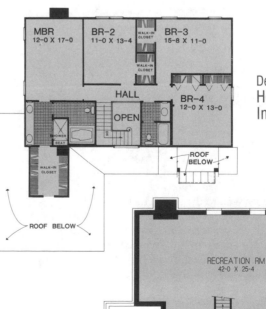

MBR 12-0 X 17-0
BR-2 11-0 X 13-4
BR-3 15-8 X 11-0
WALK-IN CLOSET
HALL
OPEN
BR-4 12-0 X 13-0
SHOWER
SEAT
WALK-IN CLOSET
ROOF BELOW
ROOF BELOW

Design by
Home Planners, Inc.

RECREATION RM 42-0 X 25-4
UNEX
UNEX
UP

● Beyond the welcoming front covered porch, this plan offers a lot to those looking for a two-story design, and then some. Besides the primary living areas found in the family room, living room, dining room, and breakfast room, there is lower-level space to really spread out. Notice that there are four bedrooms on the second floor. The master bedroom is a treat with an oversized walk-in closet and well-appointed bath.

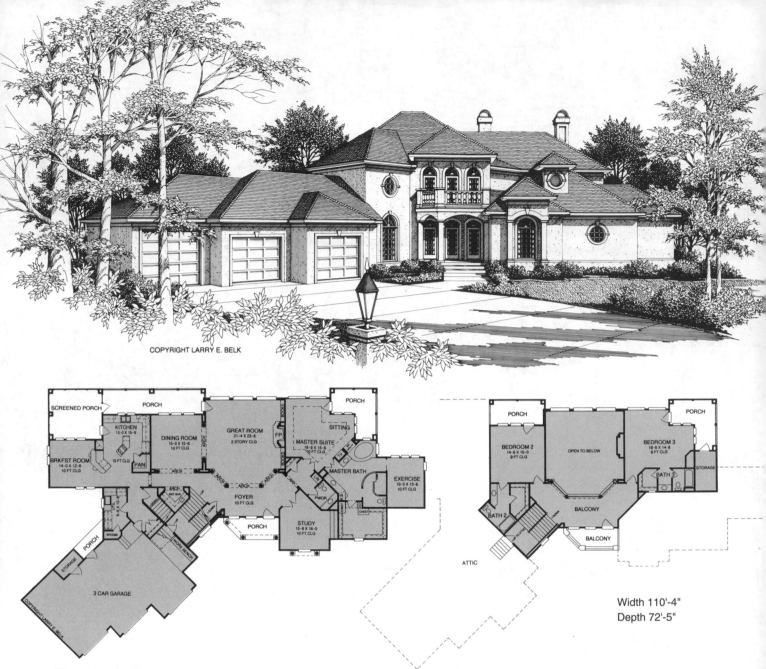

COPYRIGHT LARRY E. BELK

Width 110'-4"
Depth 72'-5"

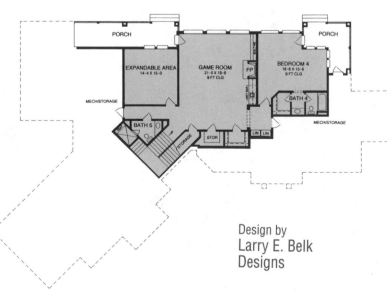

Design 8145

Main Level: 2,959 square feet
Upper Level: 1,055 square feet
Lower Level: 1,270 square feet
Total: 5,284 square feet

● Designed for a sloping lot, this fantastic Mediterranean features all the views to the rear making it the perfect home for an ocean, lake or golf-course view. Inside, the two-story great room features a full window wall to the rear. The breakfast room, kitchen, dining room and master suite all have rear views. A tri-level series of porches is located on the back for outdoor entertaining. Two bedroom suites are located upstairs. Each has a private bath and a porch. The basement of this home features another bedroom suite and a large game room. An expandable area can be used as an office or Bedroom 5. This home may also be built with a slab foundation. Please specify your preference when ordering.

Design by
Larry E. Belk
Designs

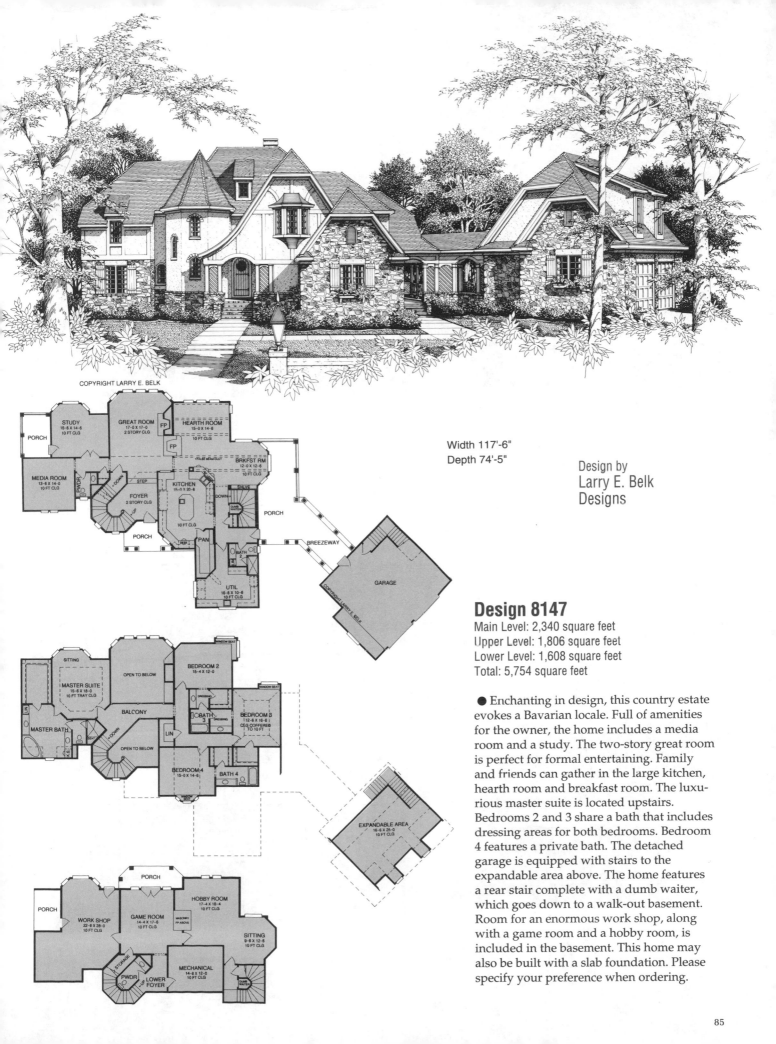

COPYRIGHT LARRY E. BELK

STUDY 15-6 X 14-6 10 FT CLG

GREAT ROOM 17-0 X 17-0 2 STORY CLG

HEARTH ROOM 15-0 X 14-6 10 FT CLG

FP

FP

PORCH

MEDIA ROOM 13-6 X 14-0 10 FT CLG

PWDR

BRKFST RM 12-0 X 12-6

STEP

KITCHEN 15-0 X 20-6

FOYER 2 STORY CLG

10 FT CLG

DOWN

DUMB WAITER

SHLVS

PORCH

PAN

BATH 2

PORCH

BREEZEWAY

UTIL 16-6 X 10-6 10 FT CLG

GARAGE

COPYRIGHT LARRY E. BELK

Width 117'-6"
Depth 74'-5"

Design by
**Larry E. Belk
Designs**

SITTING

MASTER SUITE 15-6 X 18-0 10 FT TRAY CLG

OPEN TO BELOW

BEDROOM 2 15-4 X 12-0

WINDOW SEAT

BALCONY

MASTER BATH

LIN

BATH 3

DRESSING

BEDROOM 3 12-6 X 15-6 CLG COFFERED TO 10 FT

WINDOW SEAT

LIN

OPEN TO BELOW

BEDROOM 4 15-0 X 14-6

BATH 4

WINDOW SEAT

EXPANDABLE AREA 16-6 X 25-0 10 FT CLG

Design 8147

Main Level: 2,340 square feet
Upper Level: 1,806 square feet
Lower Level: 1,608 square feet
Total: 5,754 square feet

● Enchanting in design, this country estate evokes a Bavarian locale. Full of amenities for the owner, the home includes a media room and a study. The two-story great room is perfect for formal entertaining. Family and friends can gather in the large kitchen, hearth room and breakfast room. The luxurious master suite is located upstairs. Bedrooms 2 and 3 share a bath that includes dressing areas for both bedrooms. Bedroom 4 features a private bath. The detached garage is equipped with stairs to the expandable area above. The home features a rear stair complete with a dumb waiter, which goes down to a walk-out basement. Room for an enormous work shop, along with a game room and a hobby room, is included in the basement. This home may also be built with a slab foundation. Please specify your preference when ordering.

PORCH

PORCH

WORK SHOP 22-6 X 28-0 10 FT CLG

GAME ROOM 14-4 X 17-6 10 FT CLG

HOBBY ROOM 17-4 X 18-4 10 FT CLG

MASONRY FP ABOVE

SITTING 9-6 X 12-6 10 FT CLG

STORAGE

PWDR

UP LOWER FOYER

MECHANICAL 14-6 X 12-0 10 FT CLG

DUMB WAITER

Design 4506

First Floor: 2,270 square feet
Second Floor: 865 square feet
Lower Level: 1,345 square feet
Total: 4,480 square feet

L **D**

● This multi-level home with its one-story antebellum Greek Revival exterior was designed for maximum flexibility for family requirements. On the first floor, Bedroom 2 easily converts into a sitting room to create a private suite for the master bedroom. Bedroom 3 could be a library or home office. The two upstairs bedrooms could be omitted or could be left unfinished for future development. The basement-level bedroom furnishes a private guest room.

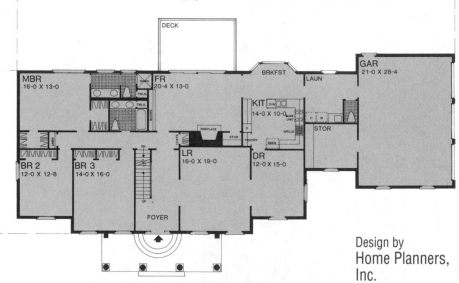

Design by
Home Planners, Inc.

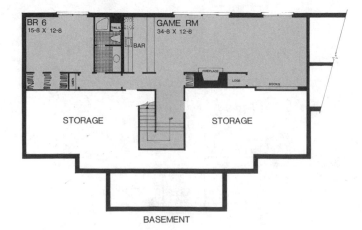

Contemporary Homes With Walk-Out Basements

Design 9539

Main Level: 2,219 square feet
Lower Level: 1,324 square feet
Total: 3,543 square feet

● Sleek lines define the contemporary feel of this home. Double entry doors lead to a columned gallery and an expressive great room. It showcases a fireplace, built-ins and a curving wall of windows. The nearby kitchen utilizes efficient zoning. A nook here opens to a wraparound deck. A dining room and a den finish the first-floor living areas. In the master bedroom suite, large proportions and an elegant bath with a see-through fireplace aim to please. The two bedrooms in the lower level have in-room vanities; one has direct access to the compartmented bath. A games room with a fireplace and built-ins leads to outdoor activities.

Design by
Alan Mascord
Design Associates, Inc.

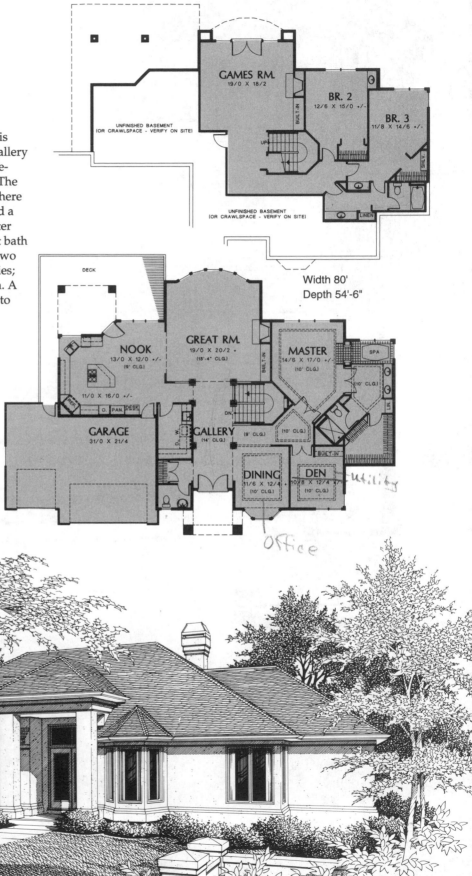

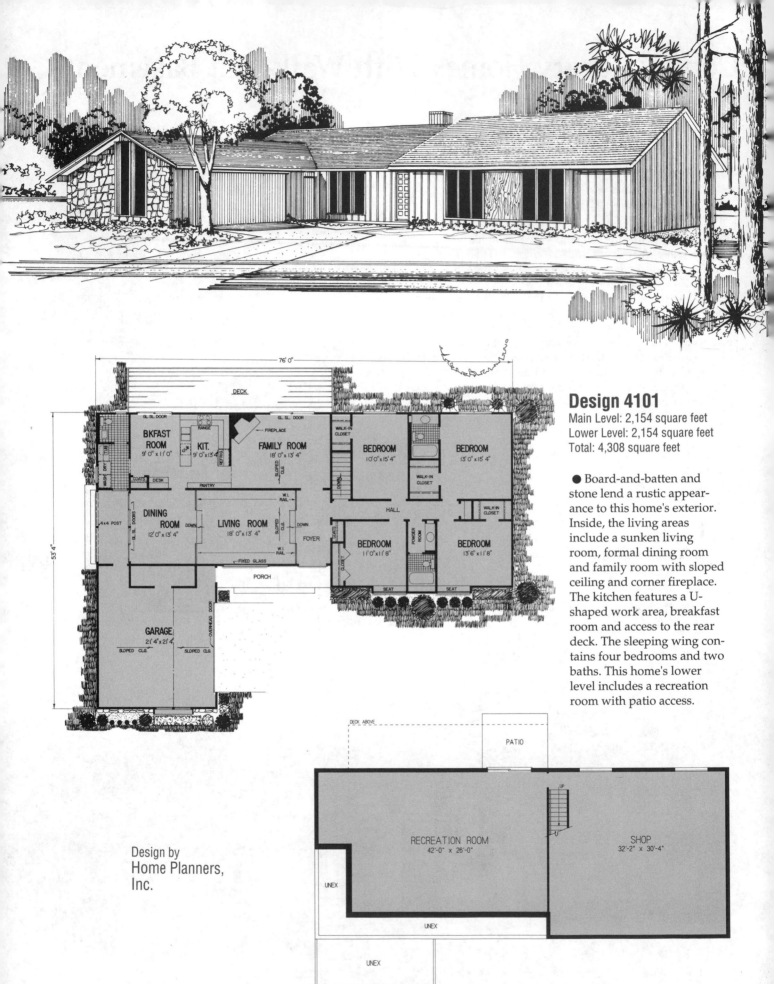

Design 4101

Main Level: 2,154 square feet
Lower Level: 2,154 square feet
Total: 4,308 square feet

● Board-and-batten and
stone lend a rustic appearance to this home's exterior.
Inside, the living areas
include a sunken living
room, formal dining room
and family room with sloped
ceiling and corner fireplace.
The kitchen features a U-
shaped work area, breakfast
room and access to the rear
deck. The sleeping wing contains four bedrooms and two
baths. This home's lower
level includes a recreation
room with patio access.

Design by
**Home Planners,
Inc.**

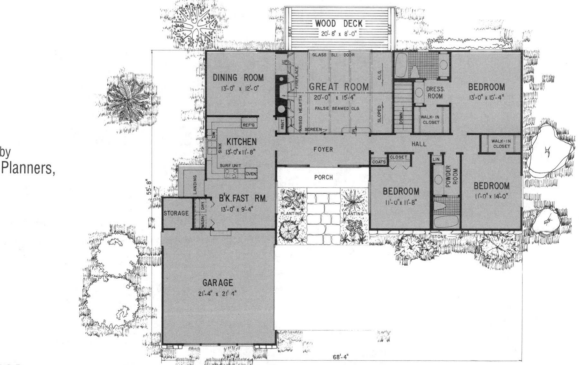

Design by
Home Planners,
Inc.

Design 4090

Main Level: 1,858 square feet
Lower Level: 1,538 square feet
Total: 3,396 square feet

● A wonderful combination of wood and stone accents the exterior of this clean-lined home while a gracious floor plan meets the needs of a busy family. Besides a great room with attached deck on the main level, there is a children's play room and plenty of storage area on the lower level. Three bedrooms on the main level are complemented by a fourth below. Note the convenient placement of baths and the many extras such as a raised-hearth fireplace and large walk-in closets.

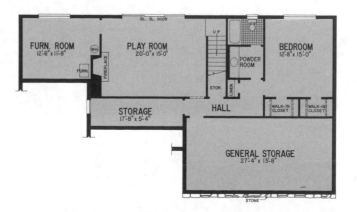

Design 3311

First Floor: 2,662 square feet
Lower Level: 1,548 square feet
Total: 4,210 square feet

L **D**

● Here's a hillside haven
for family living with plenty
of room to entertain in style.
Enter the main level from a
dramatic columned portico
that leads to a large entry
hall. The gathering room is
straight back and adjoins a
formal dining area. A true
gourmet kitchen with plenty
of room for casual eating
and conversation is nearby.
The abundantly appointed
master suite on this level is
complemented by a luxuri-
ous bath. Note the media
room to the front of the
house. On the lower level
are two more bedrooms, a
full bath, a large activity
area with fireplace and a
convenient summer kitchen.

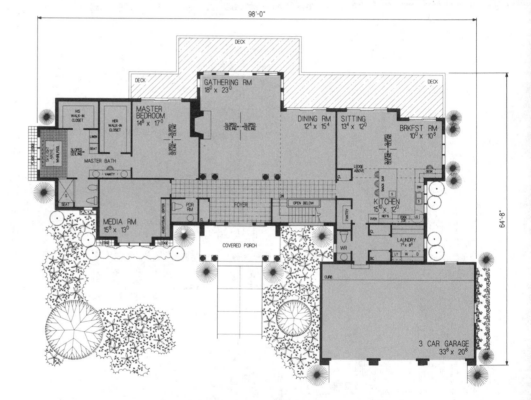

Design by
Home Planners,
Inc.

Design 3361

Main Level: 3,548 square feet
Lower Level: 1,036 square feet
Total: 4,584 square feet

L

QUOTE ONE®

Cost to build? See page 214
to order complete cost estimate
to build this house in your area!

Design by
**Home Planners,
Inc.**

● Here's a dandy hillside home that can easily accommodate the largest of families and is perfect for both formal and informal entertaining. Straight back from the entry foyer is a grand gathering room/dining room combination. It is complemented by the breakfast room and a front-facing media room. The sleeping wing contains three bedrooms and two full baths. On the lower level is an activities room with summer kitchen and a fourth bedroom that makes the perfect guest room.

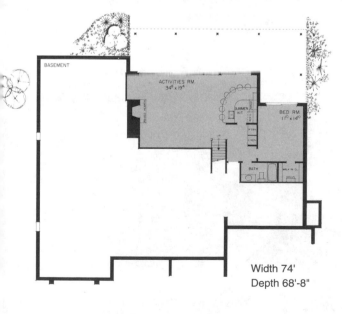

Width 74'
Depth 68'-8"

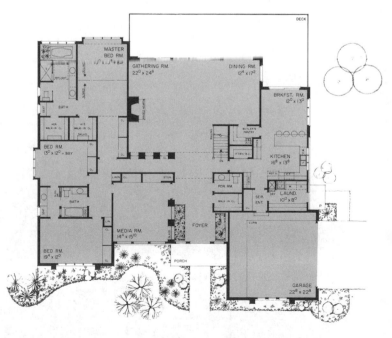

Design 2934

Main Level: 2,472 square feet
Lower Level: 2,136 square feet
Total: 4,608 square feet

D

Width 83'
Depth 50'-10"

Design by
**Home Planners,
Inc.**

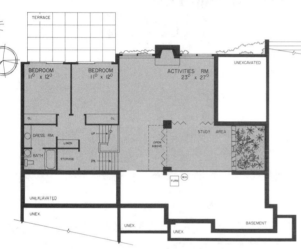

Design 2936

Main Level: 1,357 square feet; Master Bedroom Level: 623 square feet
Lower Level: 623 square feet; Activity Room 852 square feet
Total: 3,455 square feet

L

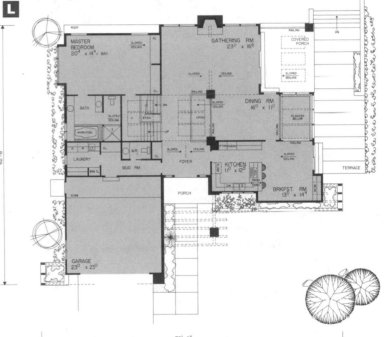

● This dramatic contemporary multi-level will offer the active family exciting new living patterns. The main level is spacious. Sloping ceilings and easy access to the outdoor living areas contribute to that feeling of openness. Imagine the enjoyment to be experienced when passing through the dining area and looking down upon the planting area of the activities level. Observe that the parents and the children each have a separate sleeping level. Don't miss the laundry, covered porch, and basement utility area.

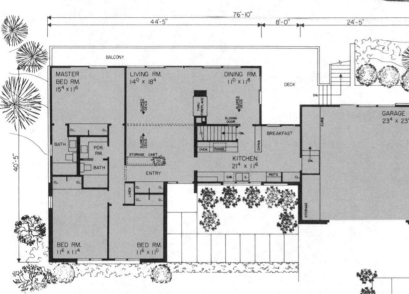

Design 1298

Main Level: 1,578 square feet
Lower Level: 1,184 square feet
Total: 2,762 square feet

Design by
Home Planners, Inc.

● Here, is a design which appears to be a one-story ranch in the front, yet, it has two full stories in the rear! Its basic main level floor plan is a completely livable unit which has three bedrooms, two baths, bright and cheerful living and dining rooms, an informal breakfast area and a most efficient kitchen. From this level, glass sliding doors open to the outdoor living areas. This amount of livability in 1,578 square feet is in itself outstanding. However, as a result of "exposing the basement," this basic one story home now assumes an entirely different character, for approximately 70 percent more livable floor area is gained.

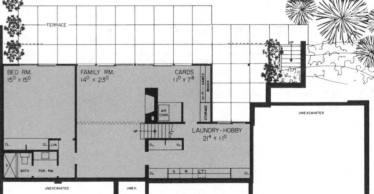

Design 2504

Main Level: 1,918 square feet
Lower Level: 1,910 square feet; Total: 3,828 square feet

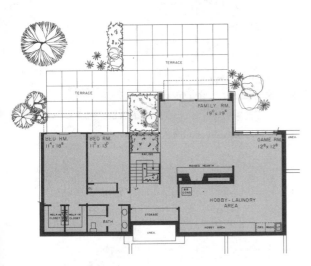

● Taking advantage of that sloping site can result in the opening up of a lower level which can double the available living area. Such has been the case in this hillside design. Study the interior carefully. This design offers tremendous living potential to the active family.

Design by
Home Planners,
Inc.

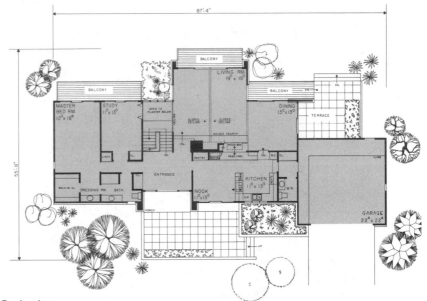

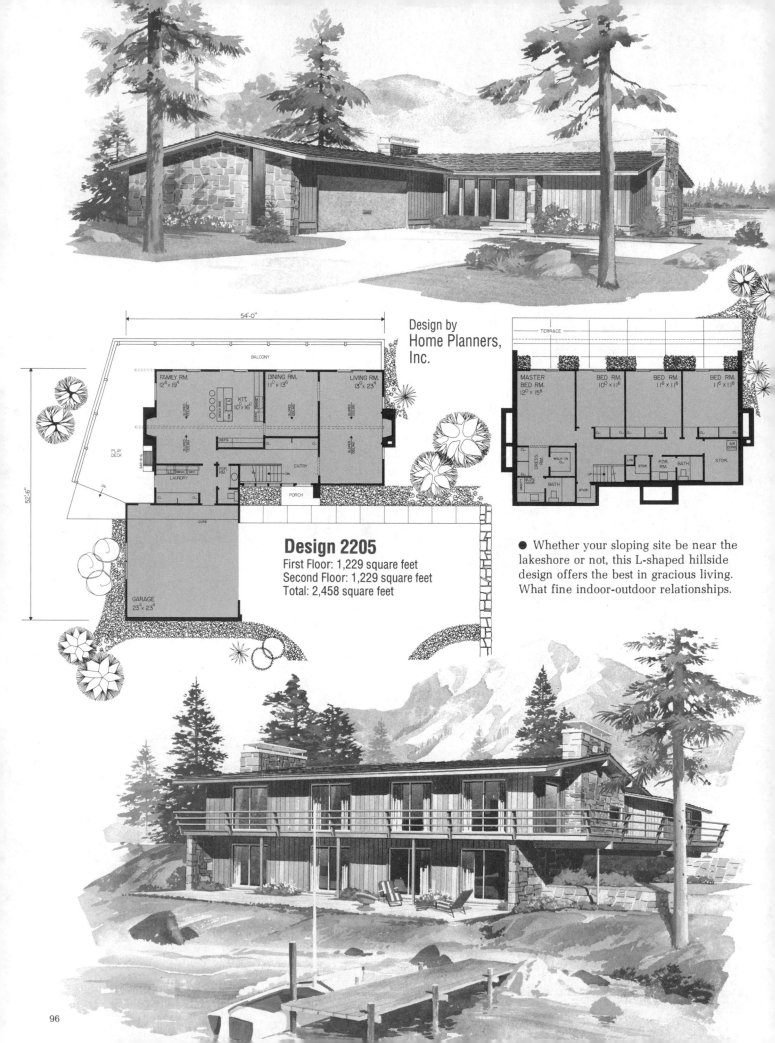

Design by
Home Planners, Inc.

54'-0"

52'-6"

BALCONY

FAMILY RM.
12⁸ x 19⁴

DINING RM.
11⁰ x 13⁶

LIVING RM.
13⁰ x 23⁴

KIT.
10⁰ x 16⁶

PLAY DECK

REF'G.

LAUNDRY

PDR. RM.

ENTRY

PORCH

GARAGE
23⁴ x 23⁴

CURB

TERRACE

MASTER BED RM.
12⁰ x 15⁸

BED RM.
10⁰ x 11⁶

BED RM.
11⁶ x 11⁶

BED RM.
11⁶ x 11⁶

DRESS. RM.

WALK-IN CL.

BATH

PDR. RM.

BATH

STOR.

AIR COND.

Design 2205

First Floor: 1,229 square feet
Second Floor: 1,229 square feet
Total: 2,458 square feet

● Whether your sloping site be near the lakeshore or not, this L-shaped hillside design offers the best in gracious living. What fine indoor-outdoor relationships.

Design 2502 Main Level: 2,606 square feet
Lower Level: 1,243 square feet; Total: 3,849 square feet

L

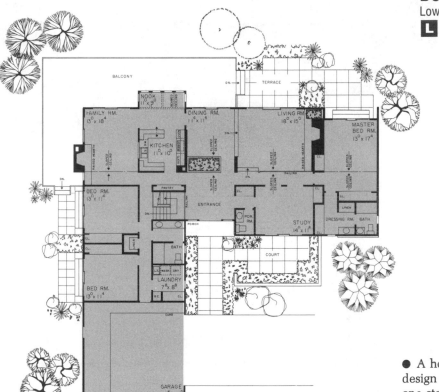

Width 71'-8"
Depth 71' 8"

Design by
Home Planners,
Inc.

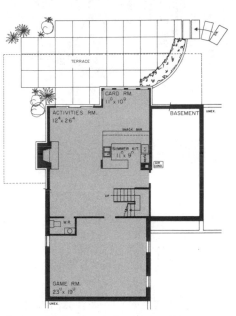

● A home with two faces. From the street this design gives all the appearances of being a one-story, L-shaped home. One can only guess at the character of the rear elevation as dictated by the sloping terrain. A study of the interior of this design reveals a tremendous convenient living potential.

● This attractive exterior comes with a floor plan in two different sizes to accommodate differently sized budgets. Each plan features a sunken great room with deck access and a fireplace, a dining room, a kitchen with an island cooktop and a breakfast area, and a three-bedroom sleeping area with two baths. An optional walk-out basement adds extra living and storage space.

Design by
**Home Planners,
Inc.**

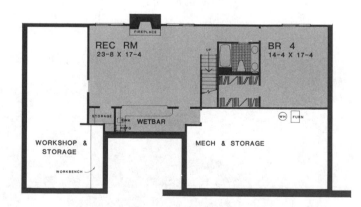

Lower Level: 1,130 square feet

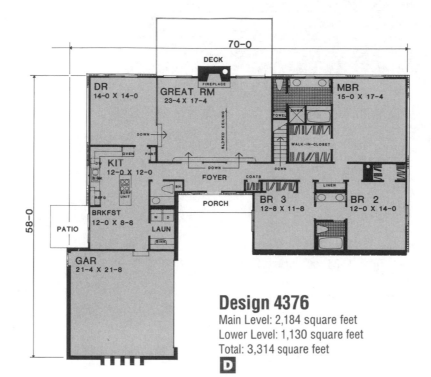

Design 4376

Main Level: 2,184 square feet
Lower Level: 1,130 square feet
Total: 3,314 square feet

D

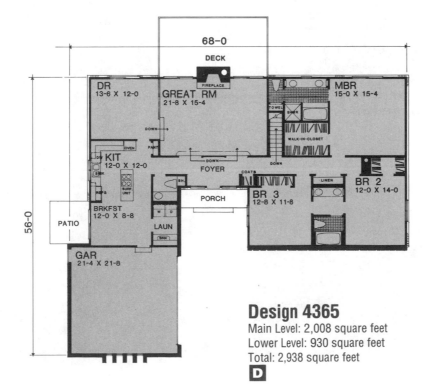

Design 4365

Main Level: 2,008 square feet
Lower Level: 930 square feet
Total: 2,938 square feet

D

Design 2761
Main Level: 1,242 square feet
Lower Level: 1,242 square feet; Total: 2,484 square feet

L

● Here is another one-story that doubles its livability by exposing the lowest level at the rear. Formal living on the main level and informal living, the activity room and study, on the lower level. Observe the wonderful outdoor living facilities. The deck acts as a cover for the terrace.

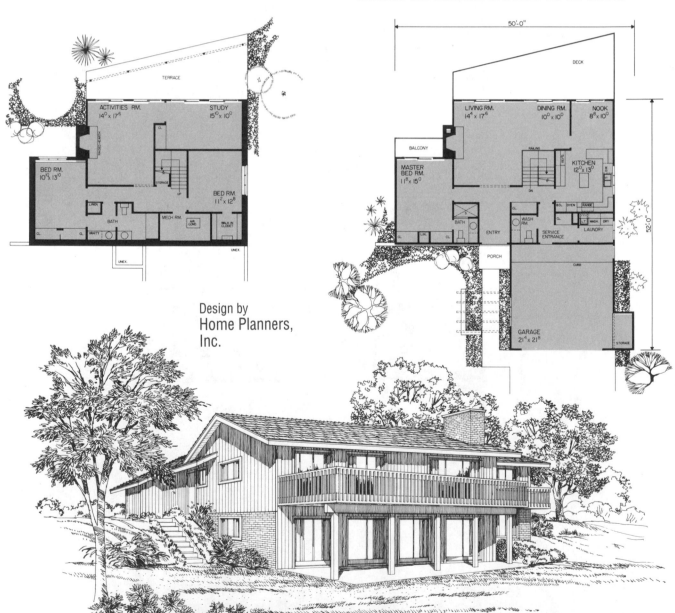

Design by
Home Planners,
Inc.

● Four bedrooms! Or three plus a study, it's your choice. A fireplace in the study/bedroom guarantees a cozy atmosphere. The warmth of a fireplace also will be enjoyed in the gathering room and activities room. Lots of living space, too. An exceptionally large gathering room with sliding glass doors that open onto the main terrace to enjoy the scenic outdoors. A formal dining room, too. And a kitchen that promises to turn a novice cook into a pro. Check out the counter space, the pantry and the island range. This house is designed to make living pleasant.

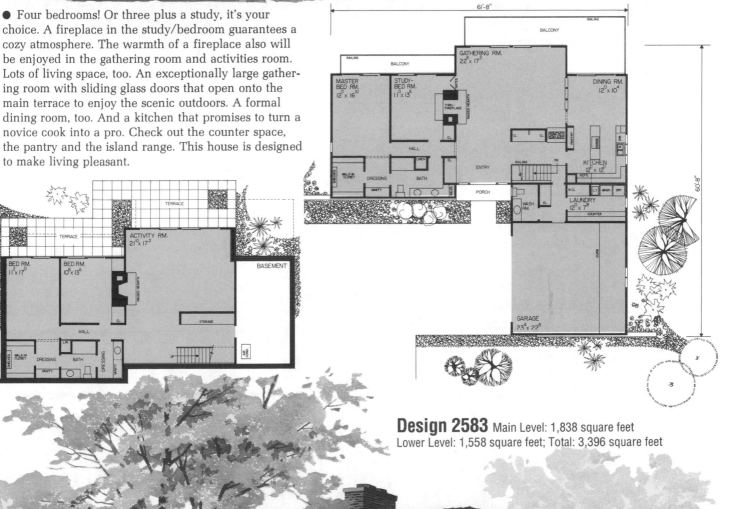

Design 2583 Main Level: 1,838 square feet
Lower Level: 1,558 square feet; Total: 3,396 square feet

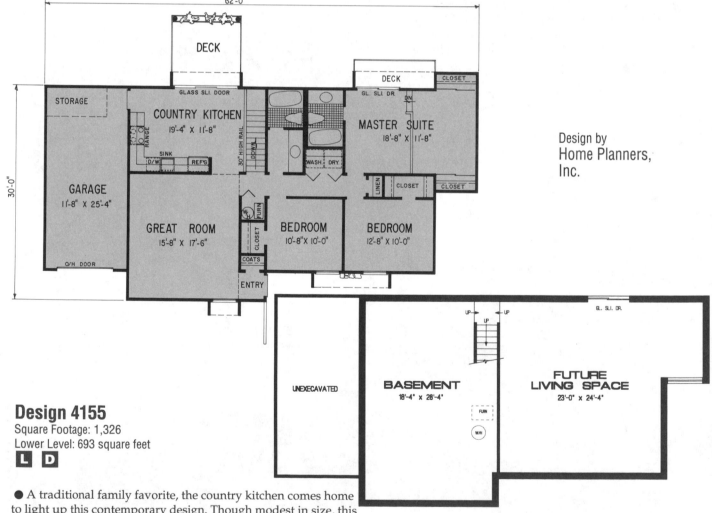

DECK

62'-0"

STORAGE

COUNTRY KITCHEN
19'-4" X 11'-8"

DECK

CLOSET

GLASS SLI. DOOR

GL. SLI. DR.

DN.

MASTER SUITE
18'-8" X 11'-8"

30'-0"

RANGE

SINK

D/W

REF'G

30" HIGH RAIL

WASH.

DRY.

LINEN

CLOSET

CLOSET

GARAGE
11'-8" X 25'-4"

GREAT ROOM
15'-8" X 17'-6"

W.H.

FURN

CLOSET

BEDROOM
10'-8" X 10'-0"

BEDROOM
12'-8" X 10'-0"

COATS

O/H DOOR

ENTRY

Design by
**Home Planners,
Inc.**

UP   UP

UP

GL. SLI. DR.

UNEXECAVATED

BASEMENT
18'-4" X 28'-4"

FURN

W/H

**FUTURE
LIVING SPACE**
23'-0" x 24'-4"

Design 4155
Square Footage: 1,326
Lower Level: 693 square feet

L **D**

● A traditional family favorite, the country kitchen comes home
to light up this contemporary design. Though modest in size, this
home provides a wealth of livability. Notice the abundance of
special amenities: entryway coat closet, two rear decks, open
staircase to the basement, laundry area near bedrooms, large storage area in the garage. The master suite has two levels; one will
serve nicely as a sitting room. A walk-out basement furthers living potential.

68'-0"

DECK

GLASS SLI. DOOR

GLASS SLI. DOOR | GLASS SLI. DR. | FIREPLACE | GLASS SLI. DR.

COUNTRY KITCHEN
23'-4" X 14'-0"

GREAT ROOM
20'-0" X 12'-4"

MASTER BEDROOM
17'-8" X 14'-0"

WALK-IN CLOSET

DRESSING

RANGE

46'-8"

LDRY

WASH

DOWN

SH. BOOKS SH.

ENTRY

LINEN DRESSING

OVERHEAD DOOR

COATS COATS

GARAGE
23'-4" X 20'-0"

BRIDGE

BEDROOM
11'-6" X 11'-8"

BEDROOM
11'-6" X 15'-4"

STORAGE

STORAGE

CLOSET

CLOSET

Design by
Home Planners,
Inc.

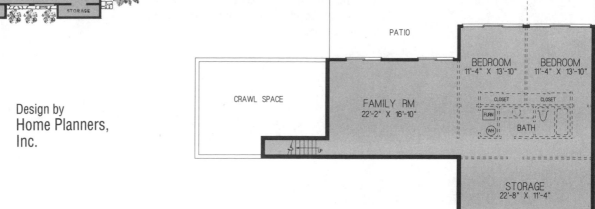

DECK ABOVE

PATIO

CRAWL SPACE

FAMILY RM
22'-2" X 16'-10"

BEDROOM
11'-4" X 13'-10"

BEDROOM
11'-4" X 13'-10"

CLOSET

CLOSET

FURN

WH

BATH

UP

STORAGE
22'-8" X 11'-4"

Design 4122

Main Level: 1,711 square feet
Lower Level: 1,322 square feet
Total: 3,033 square feet

D

● This distinctive design features diagonal and horizontal siding, projecting wings and a clerestory above the entry. For gathering and entertaining there's a spacious great room off the foyer. Notice the large fireplace. Next door is an enormous country kitchen with efficient work area and space for both dining and sitting areas. Three large bedrooms occupy their own wing. Note lower-level potential.

Design 4537

First Floor: 2,208 square feet
Second Floor: 773 square feet
Lower Level: 1,080 square feet
Total: 4,061 square feet

● This design features an especially well-planned interior. The entry foyer routes traffic effectively to the living and dining rooms and the kitchen. A U-shape and a pass-through to the breakfast room make the kitchen a pleasure to prepare meals in. The rear family room delights with a fireplace and passage to a patio. A guest room adjacent to a full bath and a master bedroom with a deck complete this level. Upstairs, two secondary bedrooms provide privacy and share a full hall bath with dual lavatories. The walk-out basement level features a large play room, a powder room and a laundry room.

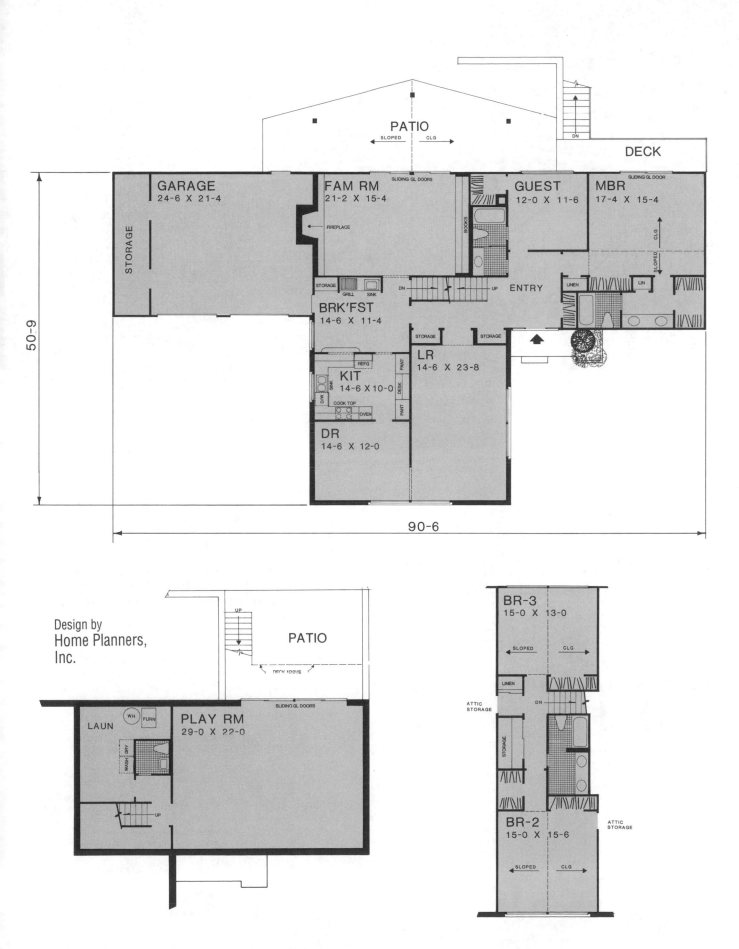

PATIO
← SLOPED | CLG →

DECK

GARAGE
24-6 X 21-4

STORAGE

FAM RM
21-2 X 15-4

SLIDING GL DOORS

FIREPLACE

STORAGE | GRILL | SINK

BRK'FST
14-6 X 11-4

BOOK'S

GUEST
12-0 X 11-6

MBR
17-4 X 15-4

SLIDING GL DOOR

CLG
SLOPED

DN ← | UP → ENTRY

LINEN | LIN

REFG

KIT
14-6 X 10-0

SINK
DFW
COOK TOP | OVEN

PANT | DESK | PANT

STORAGE | STORAGE

LR
14-6 X 23-8

DR
14-6 X 12-0

50-9

90-6

Design by
Home Planners,
Inc.

UP

PATIO

DECK ABOVE

SLIDING GL DOORS

LAUN
WH | FURN

WASH | DRY

PLAY RM
29-0 X 22-0

UP

BR-3
15-0 X 13-0

← SLOPED | CLG →

LINEN

ATTIC
STORAGE

STORAGE

DN

BR-2
15-0 X 15-6

ATTIC
STORAGE

← SLOPED | CLG →

Design 4408

First Floor: 2,016 square feet
Second Floor: 763 square feet
Lower Level: 1,028 square feet
Total: 3,807 square feet

● Be sure to investigate this 1½-story design for its outstanding features: outdoor spaces galore, a sunken great room with fireplace and built-in bookcases, expansion potential in the half story. The kitchen/breakfast room is a fitting complement to the formal dining room with built-in china cabinets. The lower-level features a garage, shop and recreation room.

Design by
Home Planners,
Inc.

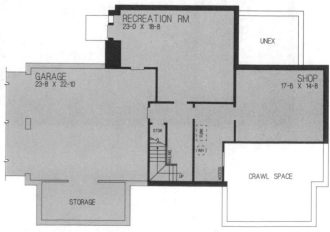

● Development of this home's hill-side possibilities adds to its already great floor plan. Besides the wrap-around deck that spans the dining room and kitchen/breakfast room, another private deck graces the master bedroom. Open floor planning is found in a sunken great room that is well-lighted and big enough for all types of get-togethers. Don't miss the abundance of storage.

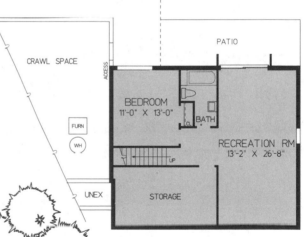

CRAWL SPACE

DECK ABOVE

ACCESS

FURN

WH

UNEX

PATIO

BEDROOM
11'-0" X 13'-0"

BATH

RECREATION RM
13'-2" X 26'-8"

STORAGE

RAILING

DECK

PLANTER

GL. SLD. DR.

DINING AREA

BOOTH

B'KFAST

DECK

STORAGE

WASH/DRY

LAUNDRY

FIXED GLASS ABOVE

RAILING

SINK

D/W

RANGE

KITCHEN
14'-6"x10'-0"

RAILING

DECK

GL. SLD. DR.

BEDROOM
13'-6"x13'-4"

SLOPE CLG.

GARAGE
22'-0" x 21'-0"

GREAT ROOM
15'-0"x 27'-4"

SLOPE CLG.

PANTRY

FLUE

REFG.

COATS

FURNACE & W/H
LOCATION W/OUT BASEM'T.

DOWN

WALK-IN
CLOSET

LINEN

CLOSET

CLOSET

DN

FOYER

GARAGE DOOR

PORCH

BEDROOM
13'-6"x10'-4"

WALK-IN
CLOSET

BEDROOM
13'-6"x11'-4"

STONE

36'-4"

76'-0"

Design 4197
Main Level: 1,502 square feet
Basement Level: 902 square feet
Total: 2,404 square feet

Design by
**Home Planners,
Inc.**

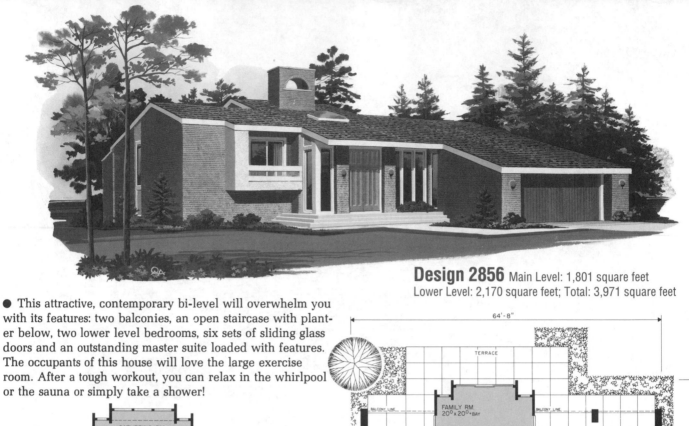

Design 2856 Main Level: 1,801 square feet
Lower Level: 2,170 square feet; Total: 3,971 square feet

● This attractive, contemporary bi-level will overwhelm you with its features: two balconies, an open staircase with planter below, two lower level bedrooms, six sets of sliding glass doors and an outstanding master suite loaded with features. The occupants of this house will love the large exercise room. After a tough workout, you can relax in the whirlpool or the sauna or simply take a shower!

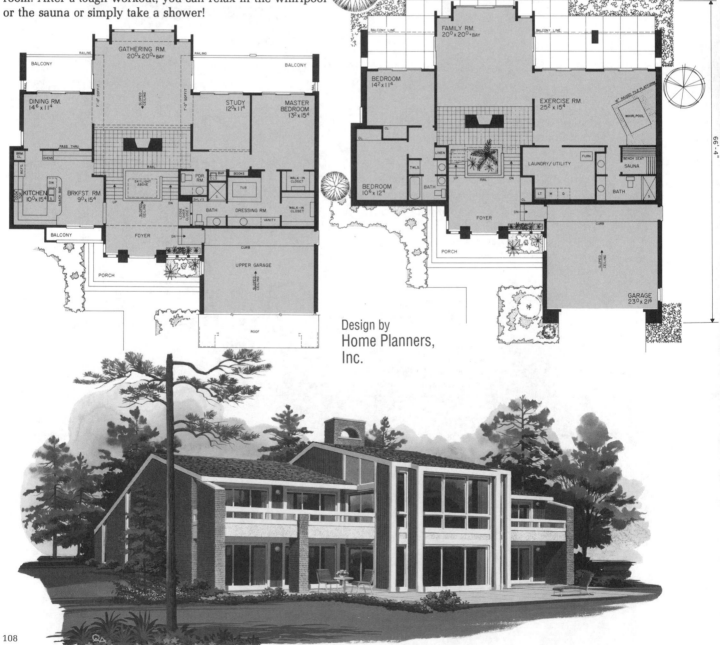

Design by
Home Planners,
Inc.

65'-0"

57'-3"

DECK
BREAKFAST RM. 12⁰x13⁴
DINING RM. 12⁸x13⁴
LIVING RM. 14⁰x21⁰
BALCONY
MASTER BEDROOM 13⁰x17⁰
BATH
WHIRL-POOL
RAISED HEARTH
RAILING
OPEN
DRESSING RM.
KITCHEN 12⁰x11⁶
LAUNDRY
LT. W. D.
PDR. RM.
FOYER
DN.
RAILING
STUDY/ SITTING RM. 15⁰x10⁴
COOK TOP
DW.
REF'S.
OVENS
BRM CL.
PLANTER
BALCONY
COVERED PORCH
CURB
ENTRANCE COURT
GARAGE 23⁴x21⁸

Design by
Home Planners,
Inc.

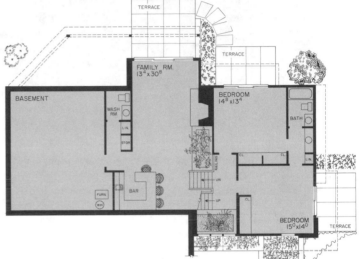

TERRACE
TERRACE
FAMILY RM. 13⁴x30⁸
BEDROOM 14⁸x13⁴
BASEMENT
WASH RM.
LIN.
STOR.
BATH
RAILING
UP
CL.
LIN.
FURN.
BAR
W.H.
UP
CL.
BEDROOM 15⁰x14⁰
TERRACE

Design 2679 Main Level: 1,179 square feet
Upper Level: 681 square feet; Family Room Level: 643 square feet
Lower Level: 680 square feet; Total: 3,183 square feet

● This spacious modern Contemporary home offers plenty of livability on many levels. Main level includes a breakfast room in addition to a dining room. Adjacent is a sloped-ceiling living room with raised hearth. The upper level features isolated master bedroom suite with adjoining study or sitting room and balcony. Family room level includes a long rectangular family room with adjoining terrace on one end and adjoining bar with washroom at the other end. A spacious basement is included. Two other bedrooms are positioned in the lower level with their own view of the terrace and quiet privacy. Note the rear deck.

Design 2848 Main Level: 2,028 square feet; Lower Level: 1,122 square feet; Total: 3,150 square feet

● This contemporary design is characterized by the contrast in diagonal and vertical wood siding. The private front court adjacent to the covered porch is a nice area for evening relaxation and creates an impressive entry. Once inside the house, the livability begins to unfold. Three bedrooms are arranged to one side of the entry with two baths sharing back-to-back plumbing. The master bedroom has a balcony. A view of the front court will be enjoyed from the kitchen and breakfast room. Along with the breakfast room, both the formal dining room and the screened porch will have easy access to the kitchen. A formal living room will be enjoyed on many occasions. It is detailed by a sloped ceiling and the warmth of a fireplace. A fourth bedroom is on the lower level. This level is opened to the outdoors by three sets of sliding glass doors. A second fireplace, this one with a raised hearth, is in the family room. A full bath and two work rooms also are located on the lower level.

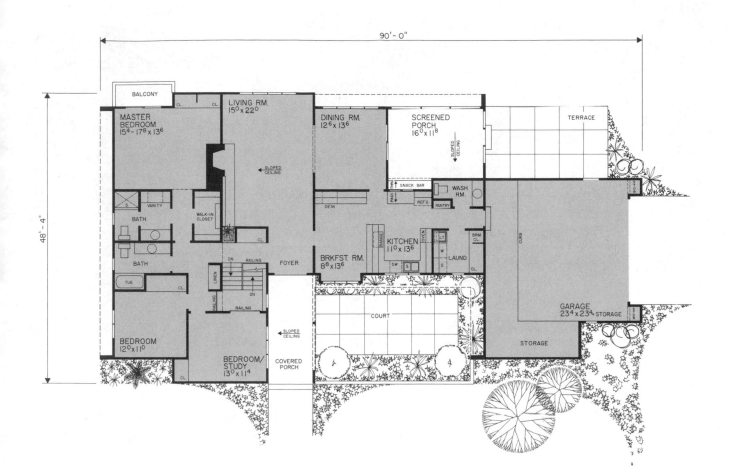

MASTER BEDROOM
15⁴ - 17⁸ x 13⁶

BALCONY

CL. CL.

LIVING RM.
15⁰ x 22⁰

DINING RM.
12⁶ x 13⁶

SCREENED PORCH
16⁰ x 11⁸

SLOPED CEILING

TERRACE

SLOPED CEILING

BATH

VANITY

WALK-IN CLOSET

CL.

SNACK BAR

WASH RM.

REF'G

PANTRY

BATH

FOYER

BRKFST. RM.
8⁸ x 13⁶

DESK

RANGE

KITCHEN
11⁰ x 13⁶

OVEN

LT

BRM. CL.

CURB

DN RAILING

LINEN

DN

RAILING

RAILING

DW S

W

LAUND.

D

CL.

TUB

CL.

BEDROOM
12⁰ x 11⁰

BEDROOM/STUDY
13⁰ x 11⁴

COVERED PORCH

SLOPED CEILING

COURT

STORAGE

GARAGE
23⁴ x 23⁴ STORAGE

CL.

90' - 0"

48' - 4"

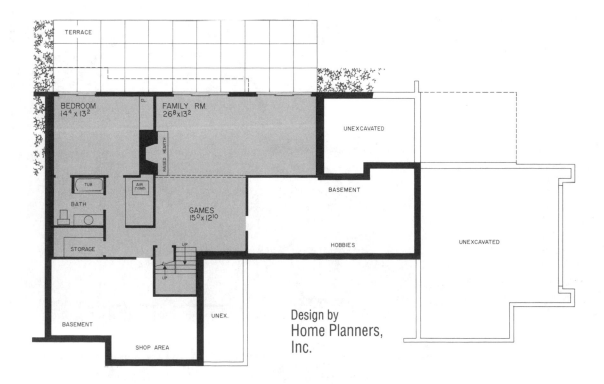

TERRACE

BEDROOM
14⁴ x 13²

CL.

FAMILY RM.
26⁸ x 13²

UNEXCAVATED

TUB

BATH

AIR COND.

RAISED HEARTH

BASEMENT

GAMES
15⁰ x 12¹⁰

STORAGE

UP

UP

HOBBIES

UNEXCAVATED

BASEMENT

UNEX.

SHOP AREA

Design by
Home Planners, Inc.

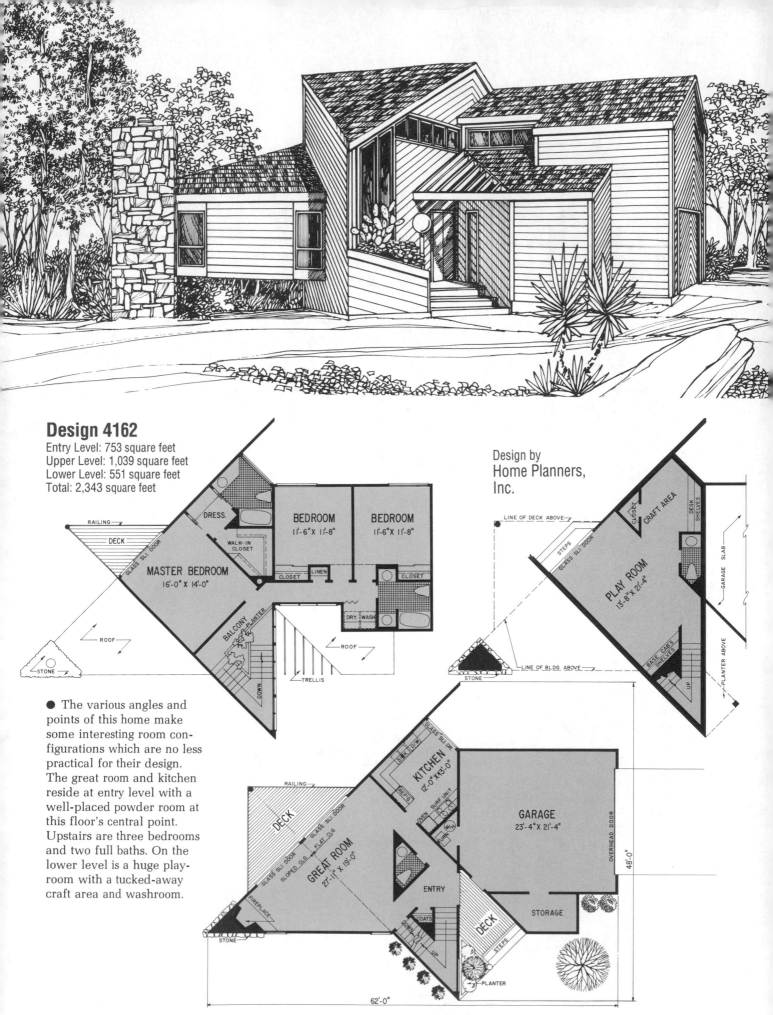

Design 4162

Entry Level: 753 square feet
Upper Level: 1,039 square feet
Lower Level: 551 square feet
Total: 2,343 square feet

Design by
Home Planners, Inc.

● The various angles and points of this home make some interesting room configurations which are no less practical for their design. The great room and kitchen reside at entry level with a well-placed powder room at this floor's central point. Upstairs are three bedrooms and two full baths. On the lower level is a huge playroom with a tucked-away craft area and washroom.

Design by
**Home Planners,
Inc.**

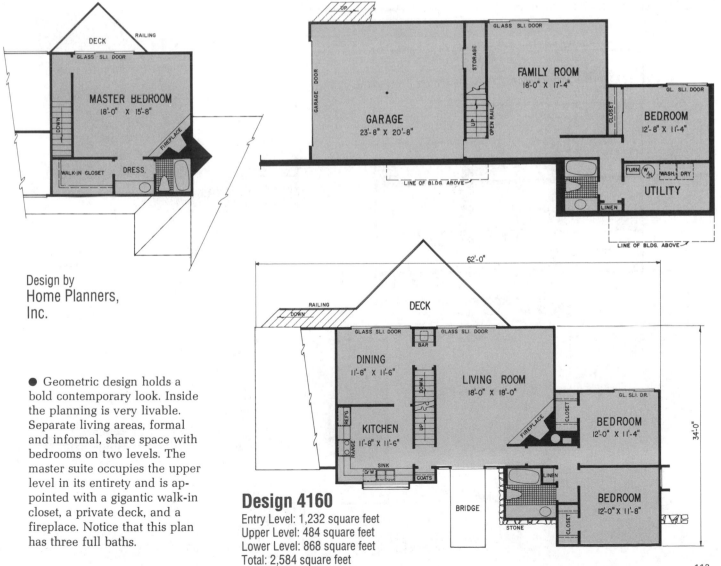

● Geometric design holds a
bold contemporary look. Inside
the planning is very livable.
Separate living areas, formal
and informal, share space with
bedrooms on two levels. The
master suite occupies the upper
level in its entirety and is appointed with a gigantic walk-in
closet, a private deck, and a
fireplace. Notice that this plan
has three full baths.

Design 4160

Entry Level: 1,232 square feet
Upper Level: 484 square feet
Lower Level: 868 square feet
Total: 2,584 square feet

● You can't help but feel spoiled by this design. Behind the handsome facade lies a spacious, amenity-filled plan. Downstairs from the entry is the large living room with sloped ceiling and fireplace. Nearby is the U-shaped kitchen with a pass-through to the dining room — a convenient step-saver. Also on this level, the master suite boasts a fireplace and a sliding glass door onto the deck. The living and dining rooms also feature deck access. Upstairs are two bedrooms and shared bath. A balcony sitting area overlooks the living room. The enormous lower-level playroom includes a fireplace, a large bar, and sliding glass doors to the patio. Also notice the storage room with built-in workbench.

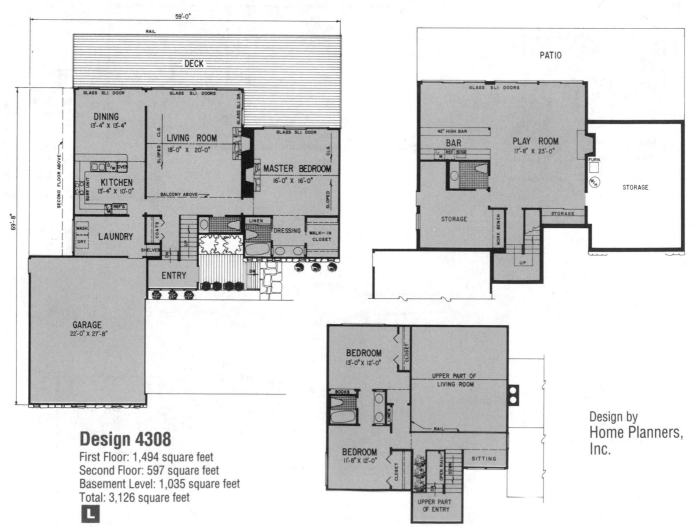

Design 4308

First Floor: 1,494 square feet
Second Floor: 597 square feet
Basement Level: 1,035 square feet
Total: 3,126 square feet

L

Design by
Home Planners,
Inc.

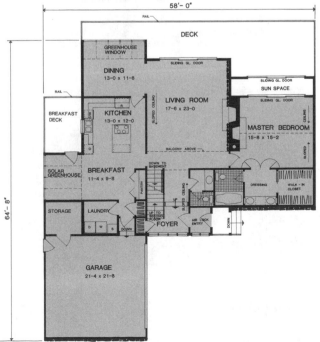

Design 4334

First Floor: 1,838 square feet
Second Floor: 640 square feet
Total: 2,478 square feet

● Grand sloping rooflines and a design created for southern orientation are the unique features of this contemporary home. Outdoor living is enhanced by a solar greenhouse off the breakfast room, a sun space off the master bedroom, a greenhouse window in the dining room, a casual breakfast deck, and full-width deck to the rear. The split-bedroom plan allows for the master suite (with fireplace, and huge walk-in closet) to be situated on the first floor and two family bedrooms and a full bath to find space on the second floor. Be sure to notice the balcony overlook to the sloped-ceiling living room below.

Design by
Home Planners,
Inc.

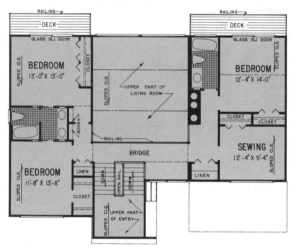

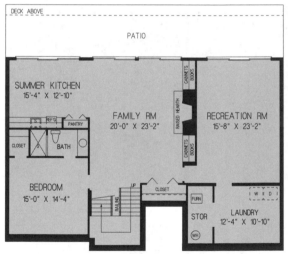

Design 4141

Main Level: 1,809 square feet
Upper Level: 1,293 square feet
Lower Level: 1,828 square feet
Total: 4,930 square feet

● A spacious two-story living room is the centerpiece of this plan with its large fireplace and access to the rear deck. Next door is the kitchen and breakfast room and adjacent formal dining room. Also on this level is an enormous master bedroom with fireplace. Upstairs are three bedrooms and a sewing room linked by a balcony overlooking the living room. The lower level pleases with a summer kitchen, a family room, a recreation room and a bedroom.

Design by
Home Planners,
Inc.

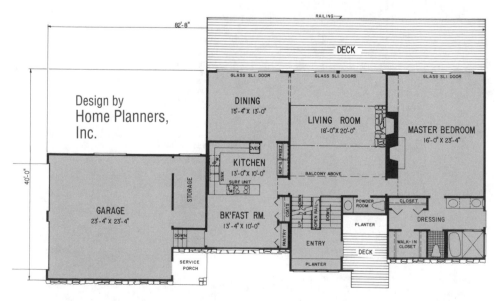

Design 4241

First Floor: 1,580 square feet
Second Floor: 702 square feet
Basement: 967 square feet
Total: 3,249 square feet

L

● Contemporary styling gives this home a sleek appearance. The floor plan caters to multiple living patterns. On the entry level, formal and informal dining revolve around the U-shaped kitchen. A large living room opens to a large deck. The master bedroom has a fireplace, deck access and a private bath. Upstairs, two bedrooms flank a full bath. The lower level offers an expansive play room with a bar and a powder room. A two-car garage is accessible from this level.

Design by
Home Planners,
Inc.

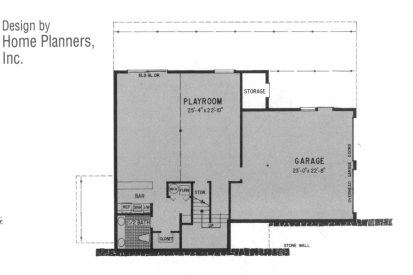

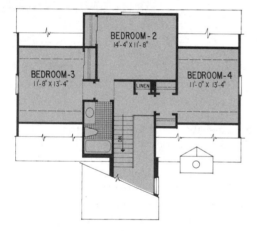

Design 4254

Main Level: 1,160 square feet
Upper Level: 715 square feet
Lower Level: 614 square feet
Total: 2,489 square feet

● Unique siding and masonry work make this hillside home a showplace. Inside there's plenty of living space in the lower-level family room and main-level great room. The kitchen with breakfast area is conveniently adjacent to the great room. The split sleeping area thoughtfully places the master bedroom on the main level and the remaining three bedrooms on the upper level for utmost peace and quiet.

Design by
Home Planners, Inc.

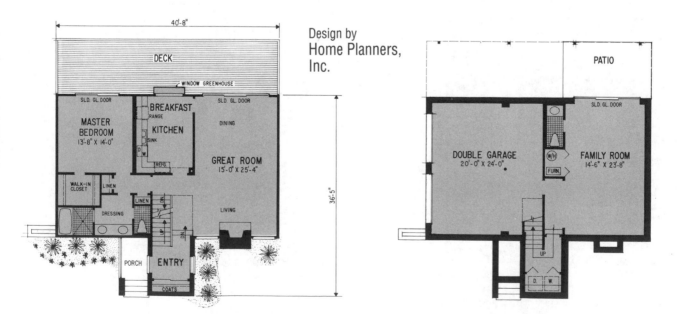

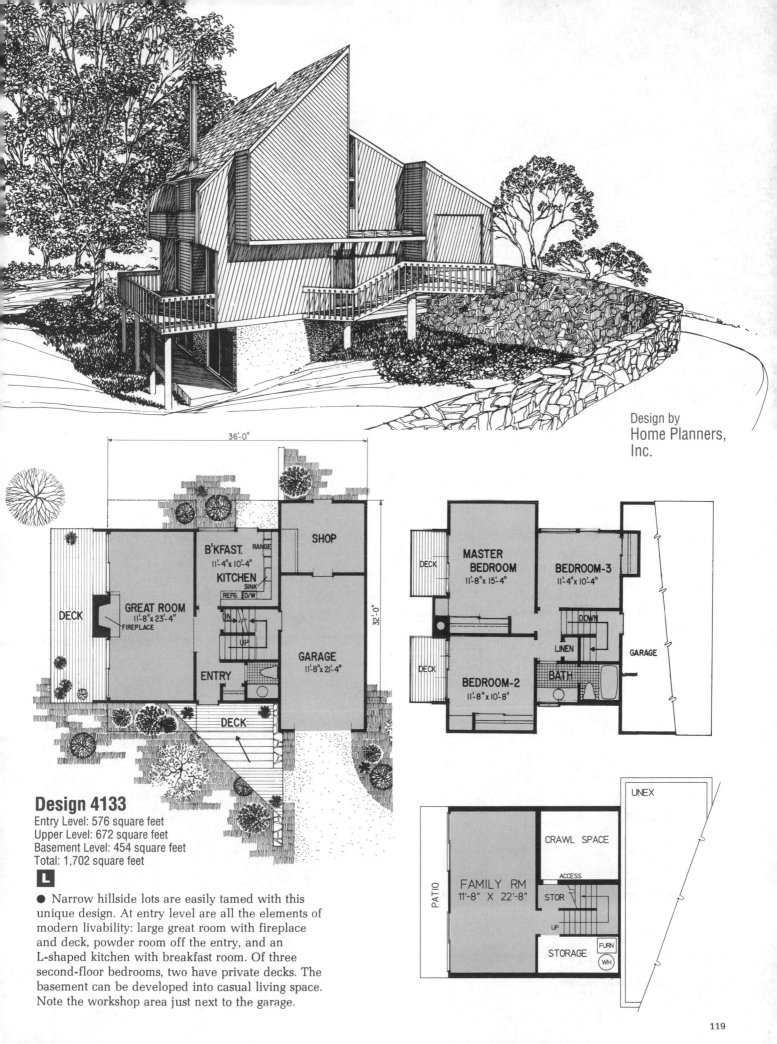

Design by
**Home Planners,
Inc.**

36'-0"

| B'KFAST. 11'-4" x 10'-4" | SHOP |

KITCHEN

RANGE

SINK

REFG. D/W

GREAT ROOM 11'-8" x 23'-4"
FIREPLACE

DECK

DN

UP

GARAGE 11'-8" x 21'-4"

32'-0"

ENTRY

DECK

MASTER BEDROOM 11'-8" x 15'-4"

BEDROOM-3 11'-4" x 10'-4"

DECK

DECK

DOWN

LINEN

GARAGE

BEDROOM-2 11'-8" x 10'-8"

BATH

UNEX

CRAWL SPACE

PATIO

FAMILY RM 11'-8" X 22'-8"

ACCESS

STOR

UP

STORAGE

FURN

WH

Design 4133

Entry Level: 576 square feet
Upper Level: 672 square feet
Basement Level: 454 square feet
Total: 1,702 square feet

L

● Narrow hillside lots are easily tamed with this
unique design. At entry level are all the elements of
modern livability: large great room with fireplace
and deck, powder room off the entry, and an
L-shaped kitchen with breakfast room. Of three
second-floor bedrooms, two have private decks. The
basement can be developed into casual living space.
Note the workshop area just next to the garage.

● There's a lot to love in this wood-and-stone contemporary. From three wood decks to the second-floor balcony overlook, the planning is just right. The split-bedroom design puts the master bedroom on the first floor. It is luxuriously appointed with a sloped ceiling, fireplace, walk-in closet, and deck access. A U-shaped kitchen serves both breakfast room and dining room. On the basement level is a large playroom, a washroom, and shop area that could be converted to a fourth bedroom with full bath.

Design by
Home Planners,
Inc.

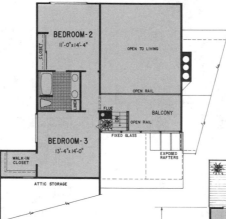

BEDROOM-2
11'-0"x14'-4"

OPEN TO LIVING

OPEN RAIL

BALCONY

OPEN RAIL

FIXED GLASS

BEDROOM-3
13'-4"x14'-0"

WALK-IN CLOSET

ATTIC STORAGE

EXPOSED RAFTERS

FLUE

Design 4331

First Floor: 1,580 square feet
Second Floor: 730 square feet
Basement Level: 1,323 square feet
Total: 3,633 square feet

[L]

WOOD RAIL

WOOD DECK

WOOD DECK

DINING
13'-4"x12'-4"

LIVING
17'-4"x23'-0"

MASTER BEDROOM
15'-8"x15'-0"

KITCHEN
12'-10"x10'-0"

SLOPE CLG TO 2ND FL

LINE OF BALCONY

D/W

WOOD DECK

BREAKFAST
13'-4"x9'-0"

PANTRY

1/2 BATH

DRESS ROOM

WALK-IN CLOSET

STORAGE

WASH. DRY.

LAUNDRY

ENTRY

FOYER

ENTRY DECK

STONE VENEER

GARAGE
21'-4"x21'-8"

OVERHEAD GARAGE DOOR

STONE VENEER

60'-0"

58'-0"

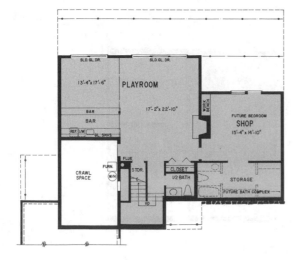

SLD. GL. DR.

SLD. GL. DR.

13'-4"x17'-6"

PLAYROOM

17'-2"x22'-10"

BAR

BAR

REF L/M

GL SHVS

WORK BENCH

FUTURE BEDROOM
SHOP
15'-4"x14'-0"

CRAWL SPACE

FURN.
W/H

FLUE

STOR.

CLOSET

1/2 BATH

STORAGE

FUTURE BATH COMPLEX

UP

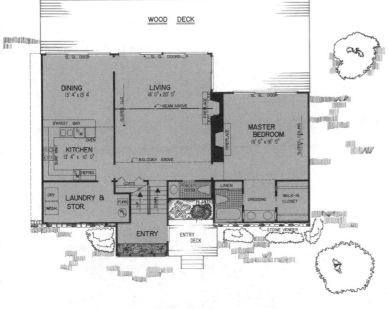

WOOD DECK

DINING
13' 4" x 13' 4"

LIVING
16' 0" x 20' 0"

B'KFAST BAR

KITCHEN
13' 4" x 10' 0"

MASTER
BEDROOM
16' 0" x 16' 0"

BALCONY ABOVE

LAUNDRY &
STOR.

POWDER
ROOM

LINEN

DRESSING

WALK-IN
CLOSET

DRY

WASH.

FURN.

ENTRY

ENTRY
DECK

STONE VENEER

Width 50'-8"
Depth 47'-8"

Design 4115

Main Level: 1,494 square feet
Upper Level: 597 square feet
Total: 2,091 square feet

Design by
**Home Planners,
Inc.**

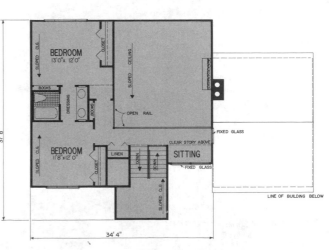

BEDROOM
13' 0" x 12' 0"

BEDROOM
11' 8" x 12' 0"

DRESSING

SITTING

LINEN

OPEN RAIL

CLEAR STORY ABOVE

FIXED GLASS

FIXED GLASS

LINE OF BUILDING BELOW

37' 8"

34' 4"

● Here is a home that's moderately sized without sacrificing livability. Just off the entry is a large, two-story living room. There's also a dining room with a breakfast bar/pass-through to the kitchen. To the rear is an enormous deck for sunning and relaxing. A split-sleeping area features two upper-level bedrooms and a main-level master bedroom. Notice the fireplace and sloped ceilings.

Design by
Home Planners, Inc.

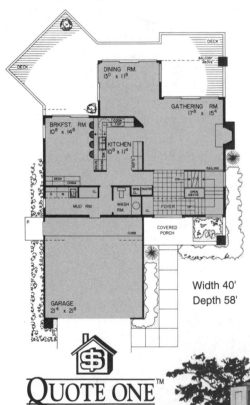

Width 40'
Depth 58'

Quote One™

Cost to build? See page 214
to order complete cost estimate
to build this house in your area!

Design 2937 Main Level: 1,096 square feet

Lower Level: 1,104 square feet; Upper Level: 1,115 square feet; Total: 3,315 square feet

L

● This contemporary multi-level home features an extended rear balcony that covers a rear patio, plus a master bedroom suite, complete with whirl-pool and raised-hearth pass-thru. Two other bedrooms and a second bath are on the upper level.

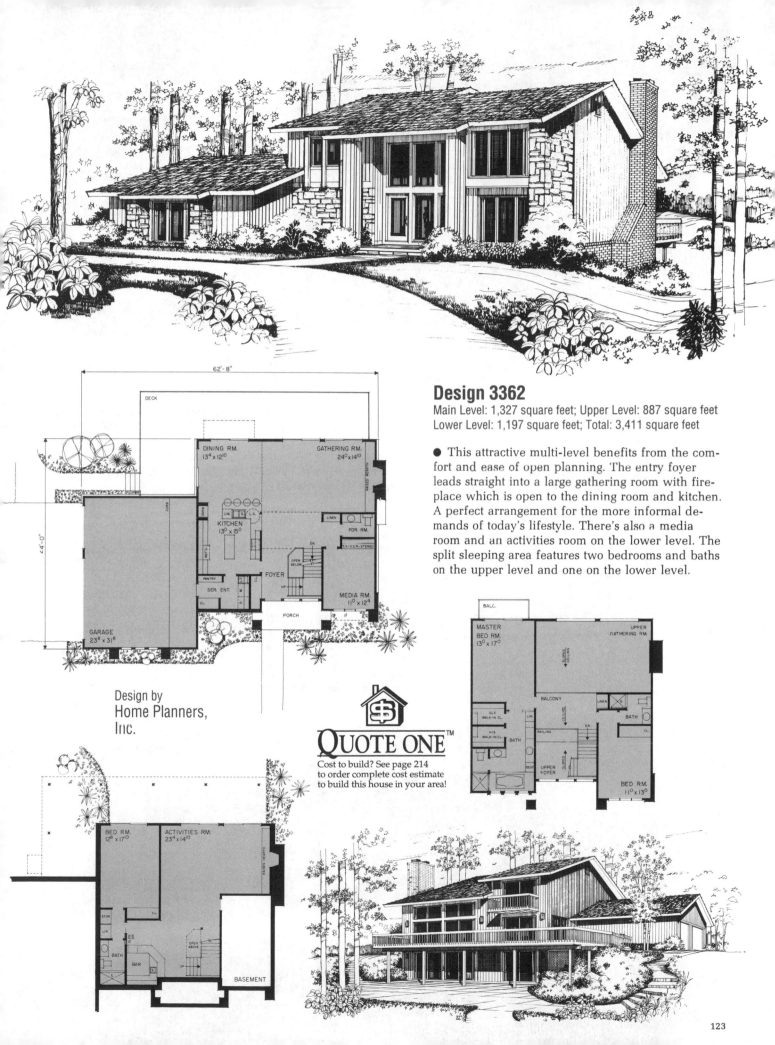

Design 3362

Main Level: 1,327 square feet; Upper Level: 887 square feet
Lower Level: 1,197 square feet; Total: 3,411 square feet

● This attractive multi-level benefits from the comfort and ease of open planning. The entry foyer leads straight into a large gathering room with fireplace which is open to the dining room and kitchen. A perfect arrangement for the more informal demands of today's lifestyle. There's also a media room and an activities room on the lower level. The split sleeping area features two bedrooms and baths on the upper level and one on the lower level.

Design by
Home Planners, Inc.

QUOTE ONE™

Cost to build? See page 214 to order complete cost estimate to build this house in your area!

Design 2716 Main Level: 1,013 square feet
Upper Level: 885 square feet; Lower Level: 1,074 square feet; Total: 2,972

L

● A genuine master suite! It overlooks the gathering room through shuttered windows and includes a private balcony. A 9' x 9' sitting/dressing room and a full bath. There's more, a two-story gathering room with a raised-hearth fireplace, sloped ceiling and sliding glass doors onto the main balcony. Plus, a family room and a study both having a fireplace. A kitchen with lots of built-ins and a separate dining nook.

Design by
Home Planners, Inc.

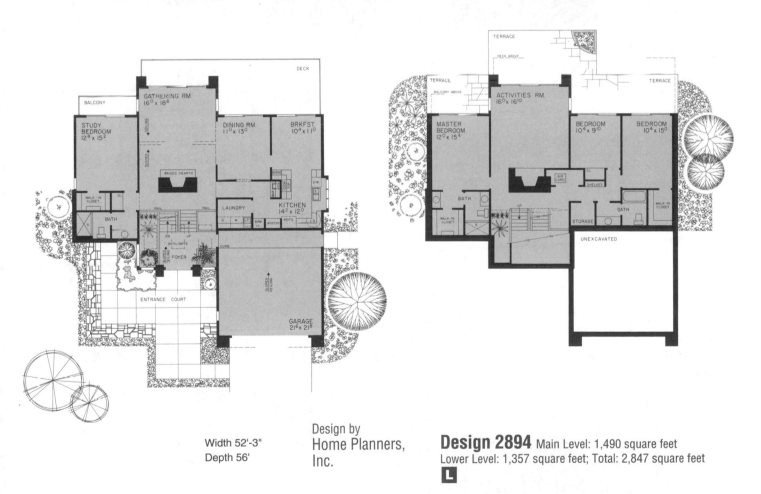

Width 52'-3"
Depth 56'

Design by
Home Planners,
Inc.

Design 2894 Main Level: 1,490 square feet
Lower Level: 1,357 square feet; Total: 2,847 square feet

L

● Contemporary, bi-level living will be enjoyed by all members of the family. Upon entering the foyer, complimented by skylights, stairs will lead you to the upper and lower levels. Up a few steps, you will find yourself in the large gathering room. The fire- place, sloped ceiling and the size of this room will make this a favorite spot. To the left is a study/bedroom with a full bath and walk-in closet. Notice the efficient kitchen and break- fast room with nearby wet bar. The lower level houses two bedrooms and a bath to one side; and a master bed- room suite to the other. Centered is a large activity room with raised-hearth fireplace. It will be enjoyed by all. Note - all of the rear rooms on both levels have easy access to the outdoors for excellent indoor-outdoor livability.

Design 2511 Main Level: 1,043 square feet
Upper Level: 703 square feet; Lower Level: 794 square feet
Total: 2,540 square feet

L **D**

● Study this outstanding multi-level with its dramatic outdoor deck and balconies. This home is ideal if you are looking for a home that is new and exciting. The livability that it offers will efficiently serve your family.

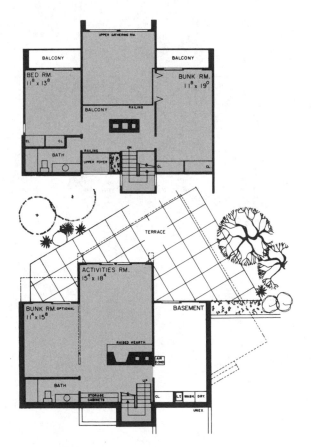

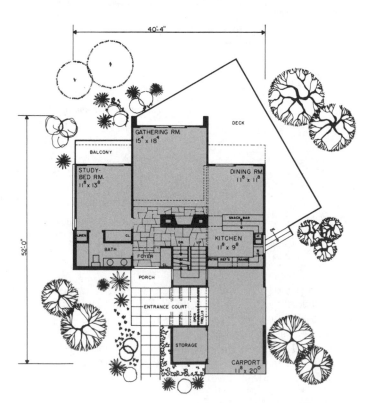

QUOTE ONE™
Cost to build? See page 214
to order complete cost estimate
to build this house in your area!

Design by
Home Planners,
Inc.

Design by
Home Planners, Inc.

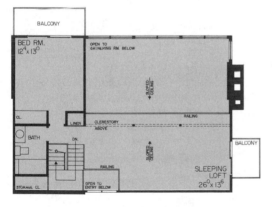

Design 2548

Main Level: 1,109 square feet
Upper Level: 739 square feet
Lower Level: 869 square feet
Total: 2,717 square feet

● Go contemporary with this multi-level home. The entry level features a huge gathering room with deck access. The kitchen passes through to this area for easy service. The dining room links to an outdoor terrace for more versatility in living patterns. A bedroom or study utilizes a hall bath. On the upper level, a sleeping loft will also make a fine play room or studio. The bedroom here opens to an outdoor balcony. The lower level reserves space for a large laundry room, an activities room and another bedroom.

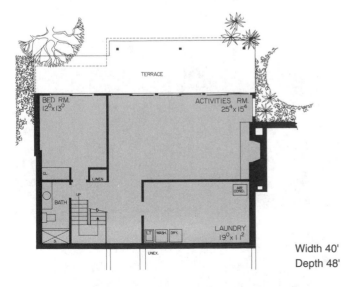

Width 40'
Depth 48'

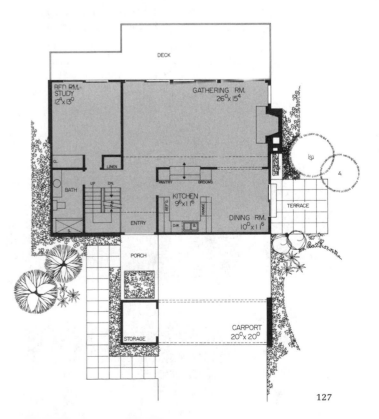

Design 2392

Main Level: 1,691 square feet
Lower Entry Level: 1,127 square feet
Upper Level: 396 square feet
Lower Level: 844 square feet
Total: 4,058 square feet

Design by
Home Planners,
Inc.

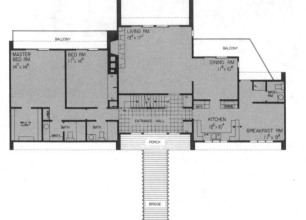

Width 78'
Depth 40'

● Here is a home with a bold contemporary facade. Its variety of balconies and natural-looking wood siding provide admirable flair. The interior floor plan holds living, working and sleeping space for the most active of families. Notice the different levels of living: a main-level living room and dining room and lower-entry level family room. Recreation and hobby rooms are found on the lowest level. Bedrooms are split — master and one family bedroom on the main level; two family bedrooms on the lower-entry level. The upper level has a lounge area and studio space.

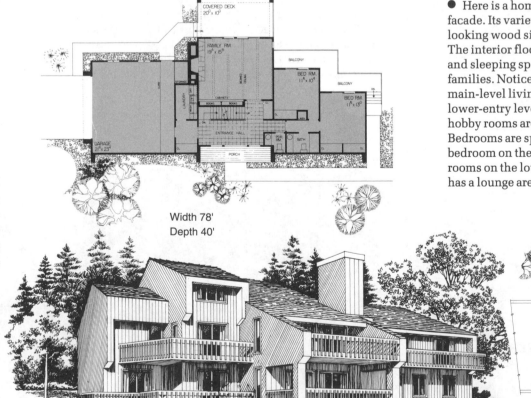

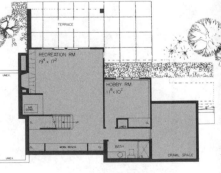

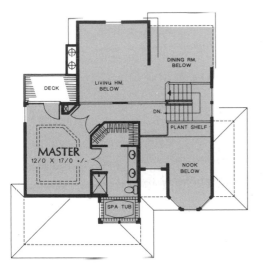

Design 9510

Main Level: 800 square feet
Upper Level: 462 square feet
Lower Level: 732 square feet
Total: 1,994 square feet

● With undeniable style, this home would easily serve steep, daylight-basement lots. The lower level houses two bedrooms and the family room where sliding glass doors provide outdoor access. A utility area is tucked away near the full bath here. On the main level, the foyer opens to a two-story kitchen which affords room enough for a dinette set. A formal living room/dining room combination speaks for the rest of this level. Notice that the dining room is vaulted and enjoys a balcony overlooking the backyard. With true flair, the master bedroom impresses with its private upper-level location. A deck opens off the back of the room. The bath spoils with its dual lavatories and bumped-out spa tub.

Design by
Alan Mascord
Design Associates, Inc.

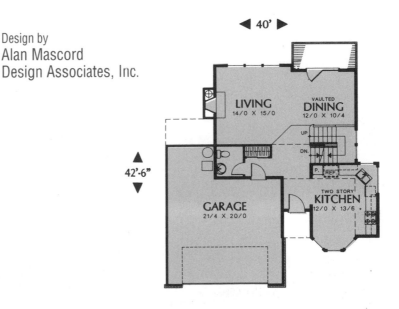

Design 2579

First Floor: 2,383 square feet
Second Floor: 1,716 square feet
Total: 4,099 square feet

Design by
**Home Planners,
Inc.**

Width 87'-7"
Depth 42'

● A huge gathering room, almost 27'
with a raised hearth fireplace in the
center, sloped ceilings and separate
areas for dining and games. Plus balconies on two sides and a deck on
the third. A family room on the lower
level of equal size to the gathering
room with its own center fireplace
and adjoining terrace. An activities
room to enjoy more living space. A
room both youngsters along with
adults can utilize. There is an efficient kitchen and dining nook with a
built-in desk. Four bedrooms, including a master suite with private bath,
two walk-in closets and a private balcony. In fact, every room in the house
opens onto a terrace, a deck or a balcony. Sometimes more than one!
Indoor-outdoor living will be enjoyed
to the maximum. With a total of over
4,000 square feet, there are truly
years of gracious living ahead.

Plans With Livable Basements

◀ 62' ▶

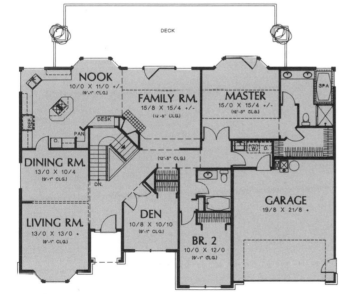

▲
45'
▼

Design 9568

Main Level: 1,972 square feet
Lower Level: 837 square feet
Total: 2,809 square feet

● A gracious facade welcomes all into this delightful family plan. A formal zone, consisting of living and dining rooms, greets you at the foyer. To the right, a double-doored den provides a peaceful place to work or relax. The spacious kitchen has a cooktop island, a pantry and a window-laden breakfast nook. The family room offers passage to the rear deck. The master suite does the same. You'll also find a private bath and a walk-in closet here. Bedroom 2 is nestled in front by a full hall bath. Downstairs, two bedrooms flank a games room. A two-car garage opens to a laundry room.

Design by
Alan Mascord
Design Associates, Inc.

Design 7277

Main Level: 962 square feet
Lower Level: 668 square feet
Total: 1,630 square feet

● Efficient site utilization is paramount in this dapper home. In the expansive great room, a sloped ceiling and a warming hearth combine for the best in both formal and informal living. The kitchen forms a snack bar for impromptu dining. The master bedroom views the rear grounds through two windows. A secondary bedroom also overlooks this area. Downstairs, a family room provides extra room to grow. Bedrooms 3 and 4 share a full bath. A laundry room and a one-car garage with built-in shelves finish the plan.

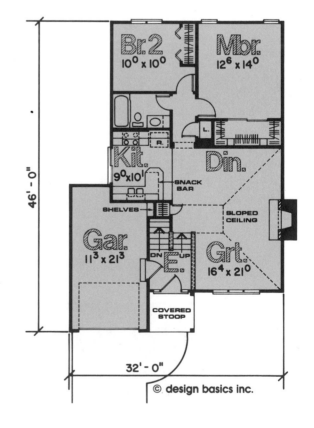

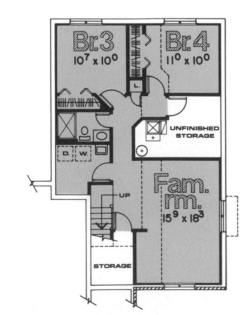

Design by
Design
Basics,
Inc.

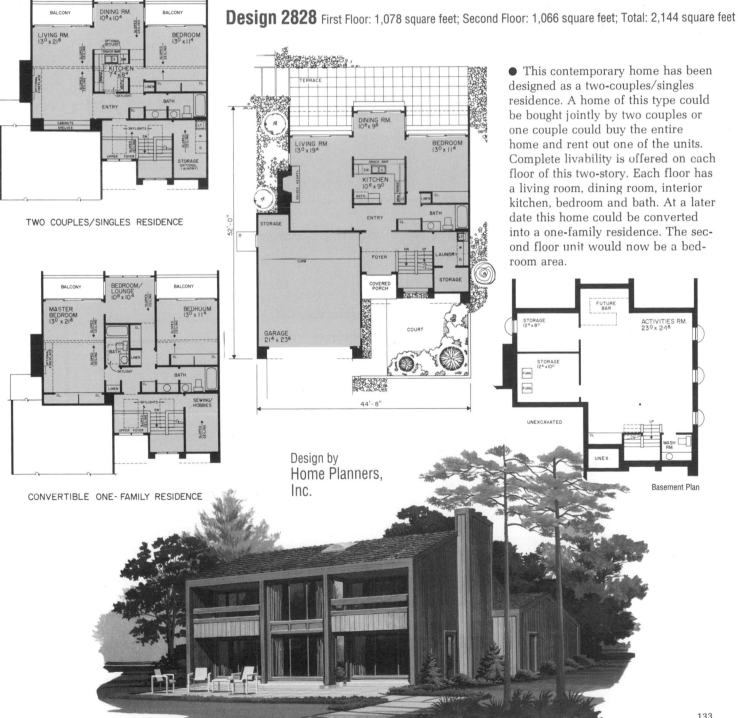

Design 2828 First Floor: 1,078 square feet; Second Floor: 1,066 square feet; Total: 2,144 square feet

TWO COUPLES/SINGLES RESIDENCE

CONVERTIBLE ONE-FAMILY RESIDENCE

Design by
Home Planners,
Inc.

● This contemporary home has been designed as a two-couples/singles residence. A home of this type could be bought jointly by two couples or one couple could buy the entire home and rent out one of the units. Complete livability is offered on each floor of this two-story. Each floor has a living room, dining room, interior kitchen, bedroom and bath. At a later date this home could be converted into a one-family residence. The second floor unit would now be a bedroom area.

Basement Plan

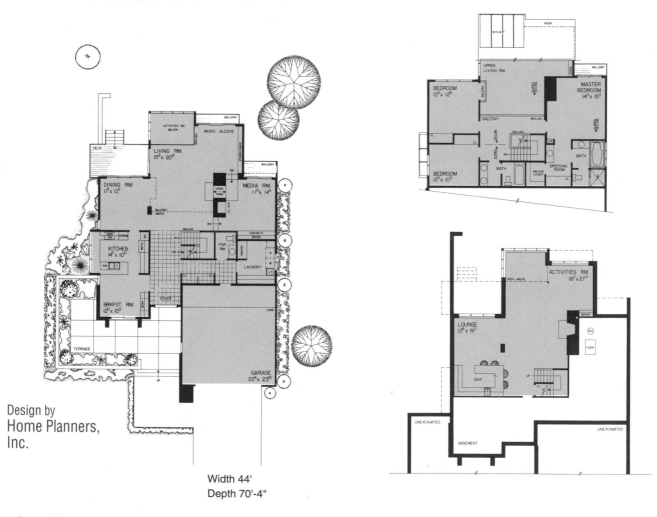

Design by
Home Planners,
Inc.

Width 44'
Depth 70'-4"

Design 2944 Main Level: 1,545 square feet; Upper Level: 977 square feet; Lower Level: 933 square feet; Total: 3,455 square feet

● This eye-catching contemporary features three stacked levels of livability. And what livability it will truly be! The main level has a fine U-shaped kitchen which is flanked by the informal breakfast room and formal dining room. The living room will be dramatic, indeed. Its sloping ceiling extends through the upper level. It overlooks the lower level activities room and has wonderfully expansive window areas for full enjoyment of surrounding vistas. A two-way fireplace can be viewed from dining, living and media rooms. A sizable deck and two cozy balconies provide for flexible outdoor living. Don't miss the music alcove with its wall for stereo equipment. Upstairs, the balcony overlooks the living room. It serves as the connecting link for the three bedrooms. The lower level offers more cheerful livability with the huge activities room plus lounge area. Note bar, fireplace.

Design 2827 Main Level: 1,618 square feet
Lower Level: 1,170 square feet; Total: 2,788 square feet

L

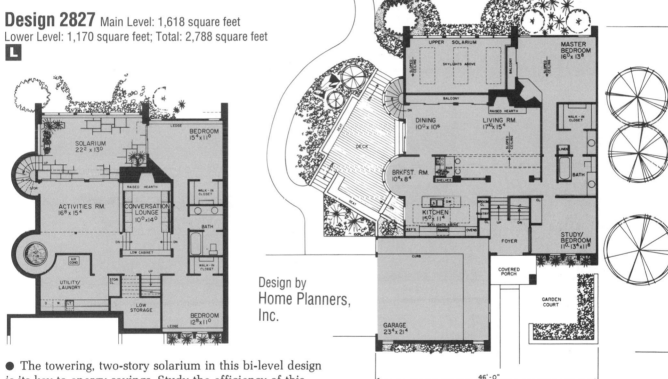

Design by
Home Planners, Inc.

● The towering, two-story solarium in this bi-level design is its key to energy savings. Study the efficiency of this floor plan. The conversation lounge on the lower level is a unique focal point.

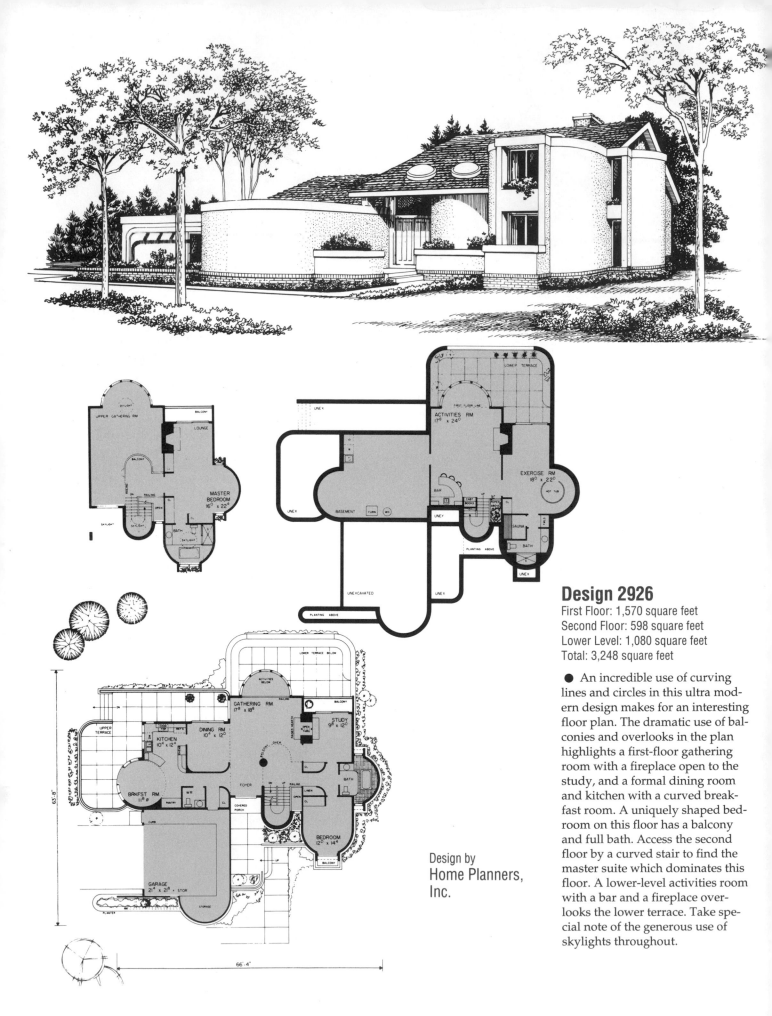

Design 2926

First Floor: 1,570 square feet
Second Floor: 598 square feet
Lower Level: 1,080 square feet
Total: 3,248 square feet

● An incredible use of curving lines and circles in this ultra modern design makes for an interesting floor plan. The dramatic use of balconies and overlooks in the plan highlights a first-floor gathering room with a fireplace open to the study, and a formal dining room and kitchen with a curved breakfast room. A uniquely shaped bedroom on this floor has a balcony and full bath. Access the second floor by a curved stair to find the master suite which dominates this floor. A lower-level activities room with a bar and a fireplace overlooks the lower terrace. Take special note of the generous use of skylights throughout.

Design by
Home Planners,
Inc.

Width 70'-4"
Depth 51'-8"

Design 2913
Square Footage: 1,835

D

Design by
**Home Planners,
Inc.**

● This smart design features multi-gabled ends, varied roof lines, and vertical windows. It also offers efficient zoning by room functions and plenty of modern comforts for Contemporary family lifestyle. A covered porch leads through a foyer to a large central gathering room with fireplace, sloped ceiling, and its own special view of a rear terrace. A modern kitchen with snack bar has a pass-thru to a breakfast room with view of the terrace. There's also an adjacent dining room. A media room isolated along with bedrooms from the rest of the house offers a quiet private area for listening to stereos or VCRs. A master bedroom suite includes its own whirlpool. A large garage includes extra storage.

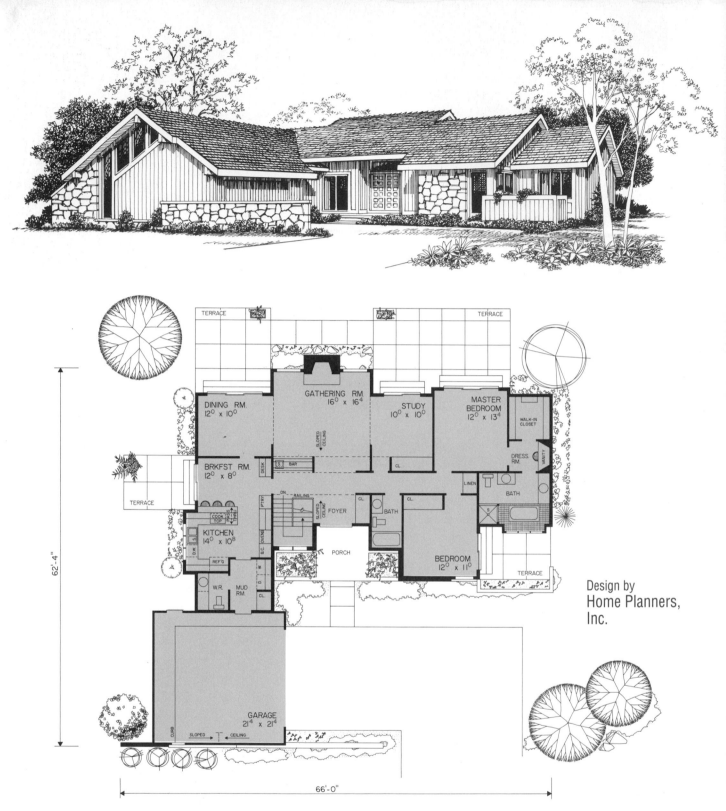

TERRACE

GATHERING RM.
16⁰ x 16⁴

STUDY
10⁰ x 10⁰

MASTER BEDROOM
12⁰ x 13⁴

WALK-IN CLOSET

DINING RM.
12⁰ x 10⁰

SLOPED CEILING

DRESS. RM.

VANITY

BRKFST RM.
12⁰ x 8⁰

DESK

BAR

CL.

LINEN

BATH

ON RAILING

SLOPED CEILING

FOYER

CL.

BATH

CL.

KITCHEN
14⁰ x 10⁸

COOK TOP

PTRY.

OVENS

B.C.

TERRACE

REF'G

D W

W.R.

MUD RM.

CL.

PORCH

BEDROOM
12⁰ x 11⁰

TERRACE

62'-4"

GARAGE
21⁴ x 21⁴

CURB

SLOPED CEILING

66'-0"

Design by
Home Planners,
Inc.

Design 2918

Square Footage: 1,693

D

● Alternating use of stone and wood gives a textured look to this striking contemporary home with wide overhanging roof lines and a built-in planter box. The design is just as exciting on the inside, with two bedrooms, including a master suite, a study (or optional third bedroom), a rear gathering room with a fireplace and a sloped ceiling, a rear dining room and an efficient U-shaped kitchen with a pass-through to an adjoining breakfast room. An open staircase leads to the lower level. A mud room and wash- room are located between the kitchen and the spacious two-car garage.

California Engineered Plans and California Stock Plans are available for this home. Call 1-800-521-6797 for more information.

Photos by Bob Greenspan

Design 2920

First Floor: 3,067 square feet
Second Floor: 648 square feet
Total: 3,715 square feet

L **D**

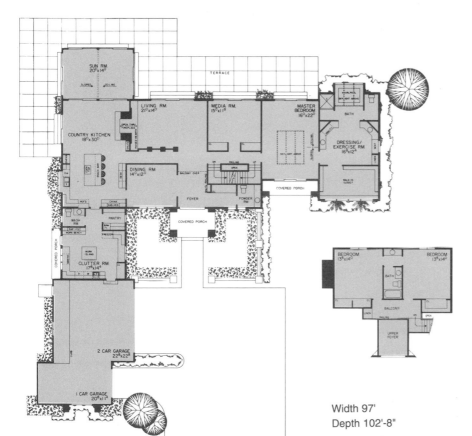

Width 97'
Depth 102'-8"

● This contemporary design has a great deal to offer. A fireplace opens up to both the living room and country kitchen. Privacy is the key word when describing the sleeping areas. The first floor master bedroom is away from the traffic of the house and features a dressing/exercise room, a whirlpool tub and shower, and a spacious walk-in closet. Two more bedrooms and a full bath are on the second floor. The three-car garage is arranged so that the owners have use of a double-garage with an attached single on reserve for guests. The cheerful sun room adds 296 square feet to the total.

California Engineered Plans and California Stock Plans are available for this home. Call 1-800-521-6797 for more information.

QUOTE ONE™
Cost to build? See page 214
to order complete cost estimate
to build this house in your area!

Design by
Home Planners,
Inc.

Design 1783

First Floor: 2,412 square feet
Second Floor: 640 square feet
Total: 3,052 square feet

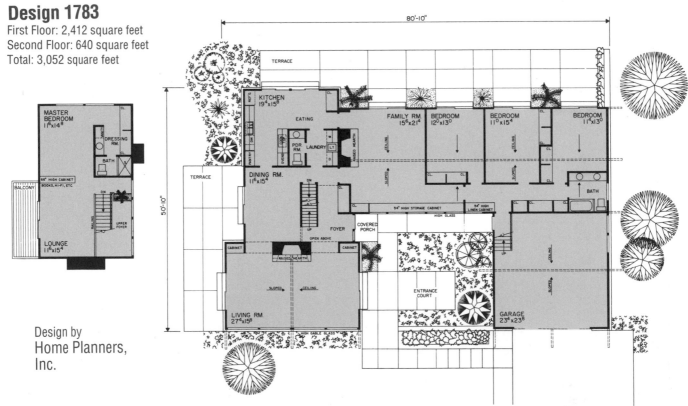

Design by
Home Planners,
Inc.

● This U-shaped home design features a central entrance court and an upper-story lounge with a balcony. There are four bedrooms in all, including a master bedroom with its own balcony on the second floor. There's a spacious front living room with its own raised-hearth fireplace, in addition to a rear family room with its own raised-hearth fireplace. A modern L-shaped kitchen features a casual eatery area and handy access to a laundry room nearby. In addition to the casual eatery area in the kitchen, there's a more formal dining room just off the kitchen area. Stairs to the upper lounge and master bedroom are located just off the foyer. A two-car garage allows extra storage room. This elegant Contemporary design with stylish stone exterior and overhanging gable roof lines provides the modern family with excellent traffic patterns and indoor-outdoor relationships. Study this fine floor plan carefully.

Design 2879
Living Area including Atrium: 3,173 square feet
Upper Lounge/Balcony: 267 square feet; Total: 3,440 square feet

● This plush modern design seems to have it all, including an upper lounge, upper family room, and upper foyer. There's also an atrium with skylight centrally located downstairs. A modern kitchen with snack bar service to a breakfast room also enjoys its own greenhouse window. A deluxe master bedroom includes its own whirlpool and bay window. Three other bedrooms also are isolated at one end of the house downstairs to allow privacy and quiet. A spacious family room in the rear enjoys its own raised-hearth fireplace and view of a rear covered terrace. A front living room with its own fireplace looks out upon a side garden court and the central atrium. There's also a formal dining room situated between the kitchen and living room, plus a three-car garage, covered porches, and sizable laundry with washroom just off the garage.

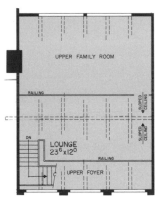

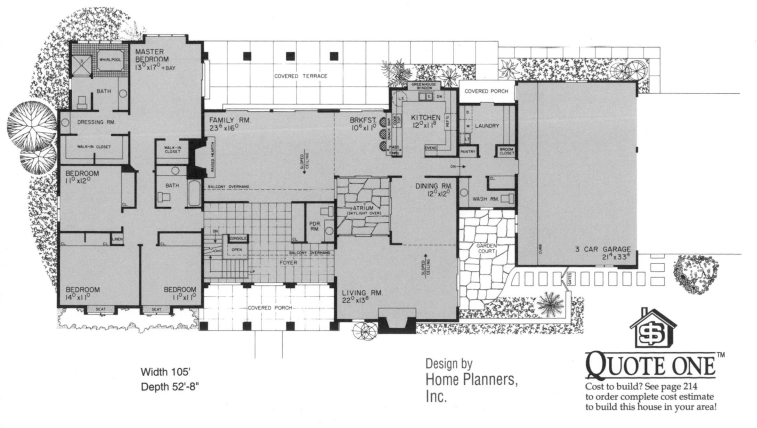

Width 105'
Depth 52'-8"

Design by
Home Planners,
Inc.

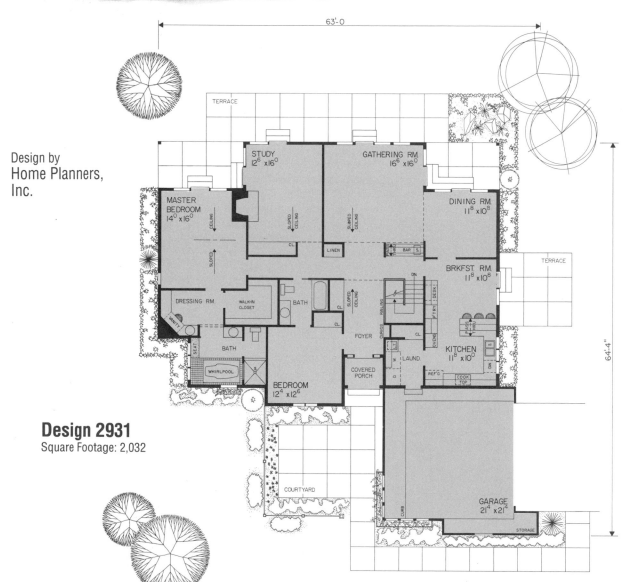

Design by
Home Planners,
Inc.

Design 2931
Square Footage: 2,032

● Little details make the difference. Consider these that make this such a charming showplace: Picket-fenced courtyard, carriage lamp, window boxes, shutters, muntined windows, multi-gabled roof, cornice returns, vertical and horizontal siding with corner boards, front door with glass side lites, etc. Inside this appealing exterior there is a truly outstanding floor plan for the small family or empty-nesters. The master bedroom suite is long on luxury, with a separate dressing room, private vanities, and whirlpool bath. An adjacent study is just the right retreat. There's room to move and — what a warm touch! — it has its own fireplace. Other attractions: roomy kitchen and breakfast area, spacious gathering room, rear and side terraces, and an attached two-car garage with storage.

70'-0

TERRACE

TERRACE

GATHERING RM.
18⁰ x 15⁰

COUNTRY KITCHEN
12⁰ x 27⁸

MASTER BEDROOM
13⁰ x 13⁴

VANITY

DRESS. RM.

BATH

TERRACE

SLOPED ← → CEILING

EATING

WALK-IN CLOSET

BATH

BAR

CL.

DINING RM.
11⁸ x 10⁴

FOYER

DN.

OPEN

CL.

CL.

LIN

CL.

COOK TOP

66'-8

BEDROOM
10⁴ x 12⁴

BEDROOM
12⁰ x 14⁰

B.C.

CL.

COVERED PORCH

MUD RM.

W.R.

D. W. LT.

SEAT

CURB

GARAGE
21⁴ x 21⁴

STORAGE

Design 2916
Square Footage: 2,129

L

Quote One™
Cost to build? See page 214
to order complete cost estimate
to build this house in your area!

● Pride of ownership will be forever yours as the occupant of this Early American styled one-story house. The covered front porch provides a shelter for the inviting panelled front door with its flanking side lites. Designed for fine family living, this three-bedroom, 2½-bath home offers wonderful formal and informal living patterns. The 27-foot country kitchen has a beamed ceiling and a fireplace. The U-shaped work center is efficient. It is but a step from the mud room area with its laundry equipment, clos-ets, cupboards, counter space and washroom. There are two dining areas — an informal eating space and a for-mal separate dining room. The more formal gathering room is spacious with a sloping ceiling and two sets of sliding glass doors to the rear terrace.

Design by
**Home Planners,
Inc.**

Design 2941
Square Footage: 1,842

D

● Here is a basic floor plan which goes with each of the differently styled exteriors. The Early American version above is charming, indeed. Horizontal siding, stone, window boxes, a dovecote, a picket fence and a garden court enhance its appeal. Note the covered entrance.

Design 2942
Square Footage: 1,834

D

● The Tudor exterior above will be the favorite of many. Stucco, simulated timber work and diamond-lite windows set its unique character. Each of the delightful exteriors features eye-catching roof lines. Inside, there is an outstanding plan to cater to the living patterns of the small family, empty nesters, or retirees.

Design 2943
Square Footage: 1,834

D

● The Contemporary optional exterior above features vertical siding and a wide-overhanging roof with exposed rafter ends. The foyer is spacious with sloped ceiling and dramatic open staircase to the basement recreation area. Other ceilings in the house are also sloped. The breakfast, dining and media rooms are highlights, along with the laundry, the efficient kitchen, the snack bar and the master bath. Quote One™ cost estimating service is available for this plan.

QUOTE ONE™
Cost to build? See page 214
to order complete cost estimate
to build this house in your area!

Width 58'-2"
Depth 59'-9"

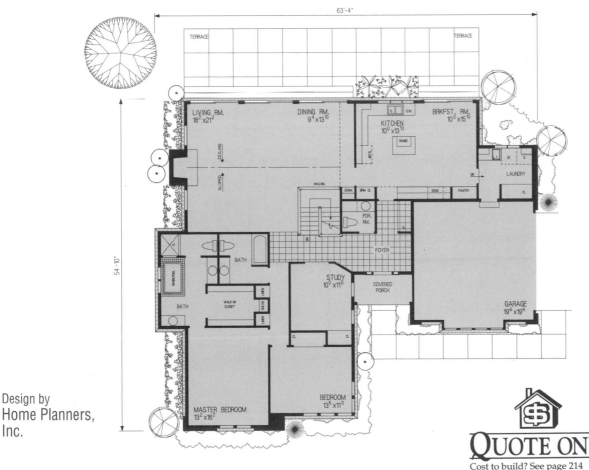

Design by
**Home Planners,
Inc.**

Design 2962
Square Footage: 2,112

● A Tudor exterior with an efficient floor plan favored by many. Each of the three main living zones — the sleeping zone, living zone, and the working zone — are but a couple steps from the foyer. This spells easy, efficient traffic patterns. Open planning, sloping ceiling and plenty of glass create a nice environment for the living-dining area. Its appeal is further enhanced by the open staircase to the lower level recreation/hobby area. The L-shaped kitchen with its island range and work surface is delightfully opened to the large breakfast room. Again, plenty of glass area adds to the feeling of spaciousness. Nearby is the step-saving first floor laundry. The sleeping zone has the flexibility of functioning as a two or three bedroom area. Notice the economical back-to-back plumbing.

● Every detail of this plan speaks of modern design. The exterior is simple yet elegant, while interior floor planning is thorough yet efficient. The formal living and dining rooms are to the left of the home, separated by columns. The living room features a wall of windows and a fireplace. The kitchen with island cooktop is adjacent to the large family room with terrace access. A study with additional terrace access completes the first floor. The master bedroom includes a balcony and a spectacular bath with whirlpool tub, shower with seat, separate vanities and a walk-in closet. Two family bedrooms share access to a full bath. Also notice the three-car garage.

Design 3565

First Floor: 1,248 square feet
Second Floor: 1,012 square feet
Total: 2,260 square feet

L **D**

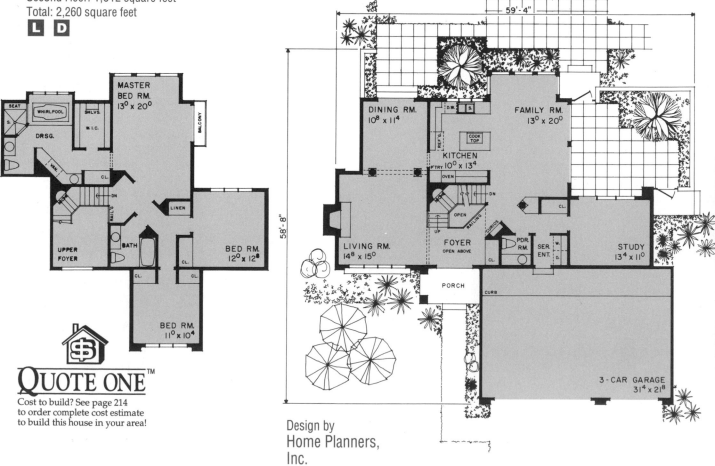

Quote One™

Cost to build? See page 214
to order complete cost estimate
to build this house in your area!

Design by
Home Planners,
Inc.

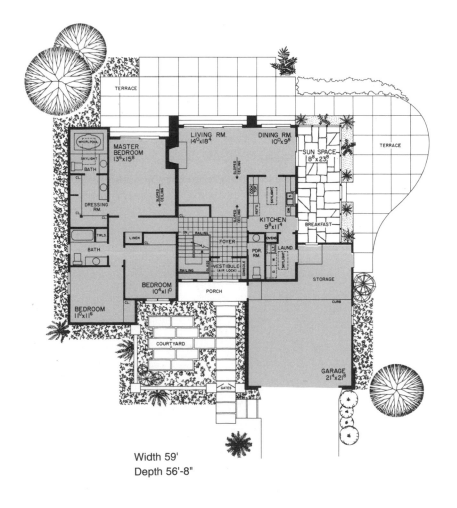

Width 59'
Depth 56'-8"

Design 2902

Square Footage: 1,632

L

● A sun space highlights this passive solar design. It has access from the kitchen, dining room and garage. The location makes it a great place to enjoy meals. Three skylights brighten the interior—one in the kitchen, laundry room and master bath. An air-locked vestibule helps this design's energy efficiency. Interior livability is enhanced with a living/dining room that features a sloped ceiling, a fireplace and two sets of sliding glass doors that open onto the terrace. This area—as well as the basement— will cater to family activities. Three bedrooms that include a spacious master suite are located in the left wing of the plan. The square footage of the sun space—216 square feet—is not included in the above figure.

Cost to build? See page 214
to order complete cost estimate
to build this house in your area!

Design 2940 First Floor: 4,786 square feet; Second Floor: 1,842 square feet; Total: 6,628 square feet

L D

● Graceful window arches soften the massive chimneys and steeply gabled roof of this grand Norman manor. A two-story gathering room is two steps down from the adjacent lounge with impressive wet bar and semi-circular music alcove perfect for private concerts. The highly efficient galley-style kitchen overlooks the family room fireplace and spectacular windowed breakfast room. Bookshelves line an entire wall of the media room. The master suite is a private retreat equal to any of the best hotels. A fireplace and woodbox are tucked into a corner of the curved sitting room. Separate His and Hers baths and dressing rooms guarantee plenty of space and privacy while bathing and dressing. A large, built-in whirlpool tub adds the final touch of luxury to this personal spa. Upstairs, a second-floor balcony overlooks the gathering room below. Four additional bedrooms, each with a private bath, are located on the second floor, making every room of this house unique and memorable.

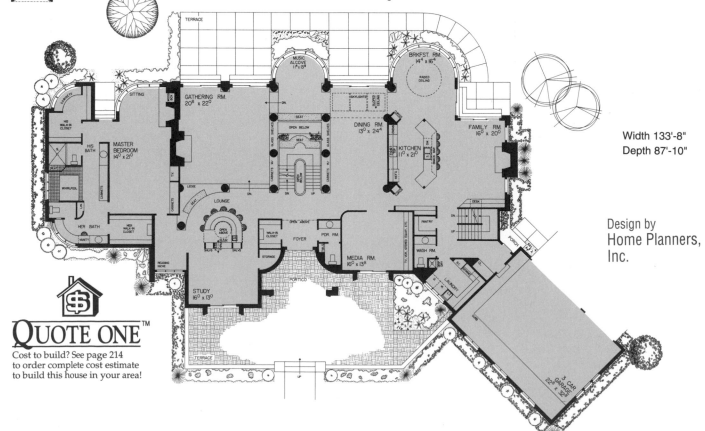

Width 133'-8"
Depth 87'-10"

Design by
Home Planners, Inc.

QUOTE ONE™

Cost to build? See page 214 to order complete cost estimate to build this house in your area!

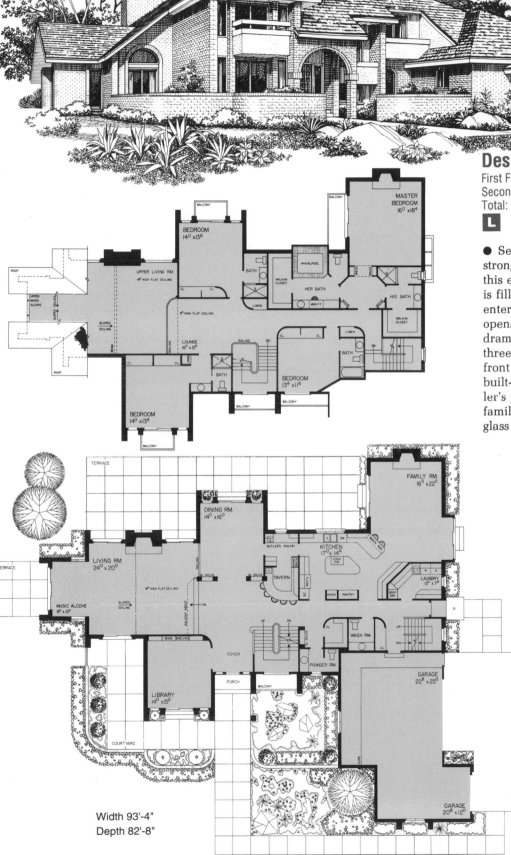

Design 2952

First Floor: 2,870 square feet
Second Floor: 2,222 square feet
Total: 5,092 square feet

L

● Semi-circular arches complement the strong linear roof lines and balconies of this exciting contemporary. The first floor is filled with well-planned amenities for entertaining and relaxing. The foyer opens to a step-down living room with a dramatic sloped ceiling, fireplace, and three sliding glass doors that access the front courtyard and terrace. A tavern with built-in wine rack and an adjacent butler's pantry are ideal for entertaining. The family room features a fireplace, sliding glass door, and a handy snack bar. The kitchen allows meal preparation, cooking and storage within a step of the central work island. Three second-floor bedrooms, each with a private bath and balcony, are reached by either of two staircases. The master suite, with His and Hers baths and walk-in closets, whirlpool, and fireplace, adds the finishing touch to this memorable home.

Width 93'-4"
Depth 82'-8"

Design by
Home Planners,
Inc.

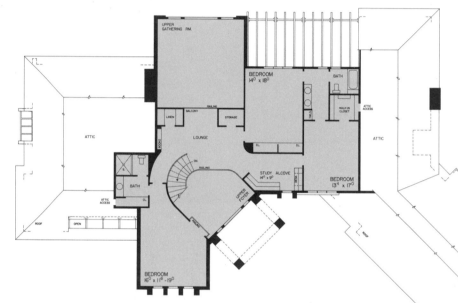

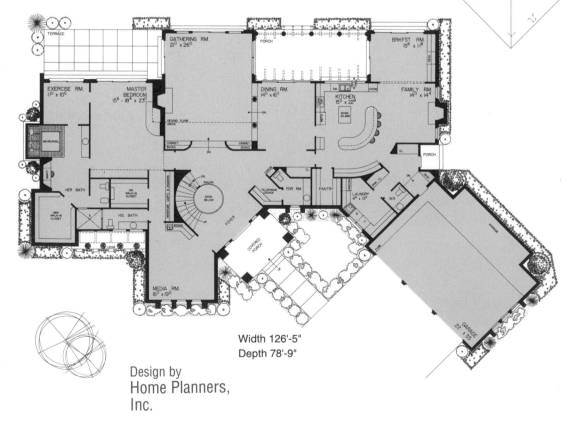

Width 126'-5"
Depth 78'-9"

Design by
**Home Planners,
Inc.**

Design 2956

First Floor: 4,222 square feet
Second Floor: 1,726 square feet
Total: 5,948 square feet

● Tall windows and two-story arches emphasize the soaring height of this elegant, northwest contemporary. A curved staircase is the focal point of the foyer. Two steps down from the foyer or dining room is the comfortable, two-story gathering room featuring a fireplace and two sliding glass doors. A large walk-in pantry, work island, snack bar, and view of the family room fireplace make the kitchen functional and comfortable. The master suite is secluded in its own wing. The bedroom, with a curved-hearth fireplace, and exercise room open to the terrace through sliding glass doors. His and Hers walk-in closets and baths (Hers with whirlpool tub) are added luxuries. A media room with wet bar, accessible from master bedroom and foyer, is the perfect place to relax. The second floor stairs open to a lounge which overlooks the gathering room. Three additional bedrooms and a quiet study alcove on the second floor round out the living area of this gracious and functional home.

Design 2966

Main Level: 3,403 square feet
Lounge: 284 square feet
Total: 3,687 square feet

● This Tudor adaptation is as dramatic inside as it is outside. As a visitor approaches the front courtyard there is much that catches the eye. The interesting roof lines, the appealing window treatment, the contrasting exterior materials and their textures, the inviting panelled front door and the massive twin chimneys with their protruding clay pots. Inside, the spacious foyer with its sloping ceiling looks up into the balcony-type lounge. It also looks down the open stairwell to the lower level area. From the foyer, traffic flows conveniently to other areas. The focal point of the living zone is the delightful atrium. Both the formal living room and the informal family room feature a fireplace. Each of the full baths highlights a tub and shower, a vanity and twin lavatories. Note the secondary access to the basement adjacent to the door to three car garage. Lounge adds an additional 284 sq. ft.

Design by
**Home Planners,
Inc.**

Design 2928 First Floor: 1,917 square feet
Second Floor: 918 square feet; Total: 2,835 square feet

● This handsome gambrel-roof design with Early American front window treatment and contemporary view windows in the rear is certain to turn heads wherever built! Its many highlights include a second-floor lounge, country kitchen, 74-sq. ft. greenhouse (not included in above total footage), and large gathering room with music alcove. Note fireplaces in both the country kitchen and gathering room!

Design by
Home Planners, Inc.

Bi-Level, Split-Level & Split-Foyer Designs

Design 3493

First Floor: 2,024 square feet
Second Floor: 717 square feet
Total: 2,741 square feet

L

● As you enter this traditional plan, you are greeted with warmth and livability. The dining room, to the left of the entry, includes a comfortable window seat and connects conveniently to the efficient kitchen with its snack bar to the breakfast area and to the large family room beyond. The family room features a central fireplace, a sloped ceiling and access to the back terrace. Beyond the formal living room are two family bedrooms with access to the terrace and to a covered patio, a shared full bath, and a strategically placed laundry room. The luxurious master bedroom is located on the second floor for privacy and features a separate study and sitting area, a private deck, and an amenity-filled master bath.

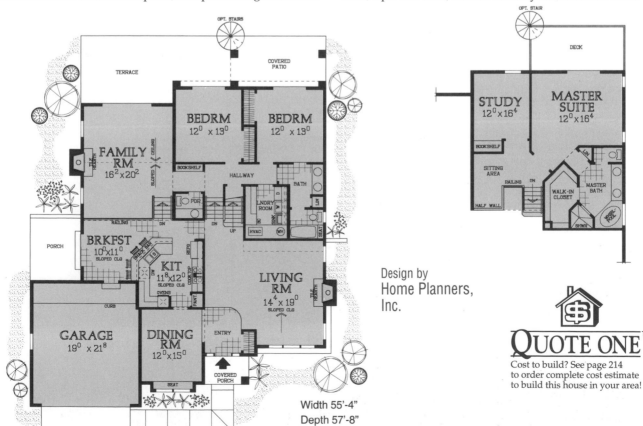

Design by
Home Planners,
Inc.

QUOTE ONE™

Cost to build? See page 214
to order complete cost estimate
to build this house in your area!

Width 55'-4"
Depth 57'-8"

Design 9914

Square Footage: 1,770

● Perfect for sloping lots, this European-style plan includes living areas on one level and bedrooms on another. The great room contains a fireplace and access to the rear deck. Close by are the U-shaped kitchen and breakfast room with a boxed window. The formal dining room completes the living areas and is open to the entry foyer. Bedrooms are a few steps up from the living areas and include a master suite with two walk-in closets and a sumptuous bath with a compartmented toilet. Secondary bedrooms share a full bath with a double-bowl vanity. On the lower level is garage space and bonus space that may be used later for additional bedrooms or casual gathering areas. This home is designed with a basement foundation.

Design by
Design Traditions

Quote One®

Cost to build? See page 214 to order complete cost estimate to build this house in your area!

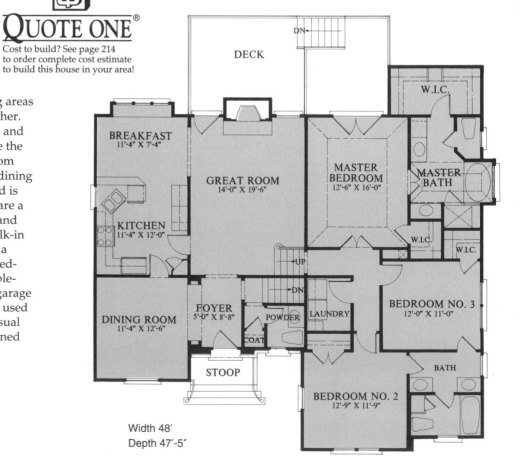

Width 48'
Depth 47'-5"

BREAKFAST
10'-10" X 9'-4"

FAMILY ROOM
14'-0" X 19'-0"

KITCHEN
0'-10" X 11'-0"

MASTER BEDROOM
13'-0" X 15'-6"

MASTER BATH

W.I.C.

DINING ROOM
13'-6" X 10'-6"

FOYER
7'-6" X 18'-0"

BATH

BEDROOM NO.2
12'-0" X 10'-6"

BEDROOM NO.1
12'-0" X 10'-0"

STOOP

Design by
Design Traditions

Design 9897
Square Footage: 1,770

● Perfect for a hillside lot, this split-level plan has three distinct levels: basement, sleeping and living. The basement is undeveloped space but could be used for any number of activities if needed. The sleeping level holds two family bedrooms and a master suite with plenty of amenities. Its bath is truly opulent with corner tub, double vanity, walk-in closet and separate shower. The family bedrooms each have a walk-in closet and share a full bath. The living areas include a formal dining room, family room and kitchen with breakfast nook. Special items include the fireplace in the family room and the columns that separate the dining and family rooms. This home is designed with a basement foundation.

Width 49'-6"
Depth 47'

Copyright 1992 Stephen S. Fuller, Inc.

DECK

BREAKFAST
11'-4" X 7'-6"

GREAT ROOM
14'-0" X 16'-0"

MASTER
BEDROOM
12'-6" X 16'-0"

W.I.C.

MASTER
BATH

KITCHEN
11'-4" X 12'-0"

W.I.C.

W.I.C.

UP

DN.

LNDR.

FOYER
5'-0" X
8'-6"

POWDER

BEDROOM NO. 3
12'-0" X 11'-0"

DINING ROOM
11'-4" X 13'-6"

BATH

BEDROOM NO. 2
12'-4" X 11'-4"

Width 48'
Depth 47'-5"

Design by
Design Traditions

Design 9949
Square Footage: 1,770

● Wood frame, weatherboard siding and stacked stone give this home its country cottage appeal. The concept is reinforced by the double elliptical-arched front porch, the Colonial balustrade and the roof-vent dormer. Inside, the foyer leads to the great room and the dining room. The well-planned kitchen easily serves the breakfast room. A rear deck makes outdoor living extra enjoyable. The bi-level nature of the home puts three bedrooms upstairs. They include a master suite with a tray ceiling and a luxurious bath. The two secondary bedrooms share a compartmented bath. A basement foundation provides extra storage.

FAMILY ROOM
14'-0" X 19'-0"

BREAKFAST
10'-10" X 9'-4"

KITCHEN
0'-10" X 11'-0"

MASTER
BEDROOM
13'-0" X 15'-6"

MASTER BATH

W.I.C.

DN

FOYER
7'-6" X 18'-0"

UP

BATH

BEDROOM NO.2
12'-0" X 10'-6"

DINING ROOM
13'-6" X 10'-6"

Width 49'-6"
Depth 47'

STOOP

BEDROOM NO.1
12'-0" X 10'-0"

Design by
Design Traditions

Design 9917

Square Footage: 1,770

● This fine family home will delight for years to come. It utilizes the contours of your lot to the best advantage. A recessed front door opens to a columned dining room that shares space with the family room. A bayed breakfast nook enjoys expansive rear views and direct service from the kitchen. Up a short flight of stairs, three bedrooms include two family bedrooms and a master suite. Bedroom 2 gains access to the compartmented hall bath. Bedroom 1 has a raised ceiling. In the master suite, French doors lead to a private deck. An expansive, secluded bath offers dual lavatories, a corner garden tub and a walk-in closet. This home is designed with a basement foundation.

Design 7285

First Floor: 968 square feet
Second Floor: 1,018 square feet
Total: 1,986 square feet

● Brick and lap siding give appeal to this elevation. An inviting entry leads directly to the great room and the dining room. The spacious great room features a raised-hearth fireplace and sunny windows. The kitchen and dinette area has outdoor access, wrapping counters, two Lazy Susans, a built-in desk and a snack bar. The unfinished family room, a half bath and a laundry—all sunken a few steps off the great room—can be completed in future expansion. Three comfortable secondary bedrooms are upstairs. This is where you'll also find the master suite and its vaulted ceiling. In the master bath, a whirlpool and dual lavatories complement the compartmented toilet and shower. A walk-in closet finishes the suite.

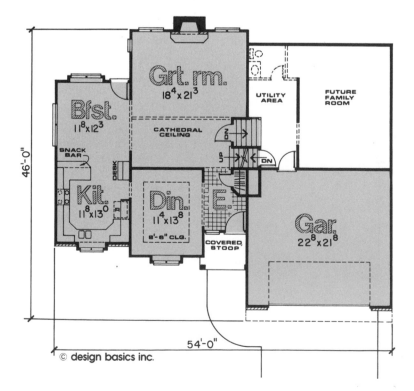

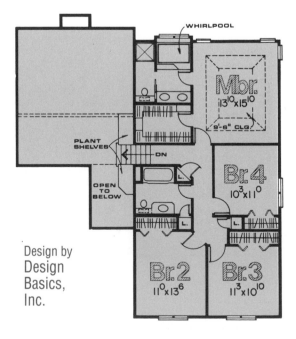

Design by
Design Basics, Inc.

Design 7282

First Floor: 1,015 square feet
Second Floor: 675 square feet
Total: 1,690 square feet

● This home's comfortable living room with bayed window and vaulted ceiling opens to the formal dining room. The efficient kitchen overlooks the sunken family room with its raised-hearth fireplace. The bayed breakfast area has a planning desk. On the upper level, the secondary bedrooms share a functional hall bath. The master bedroom's vaulted ceiling, window seat, walk-in closet and private bath are fine features. Storage space in the garage and a full basement assure room for everything.

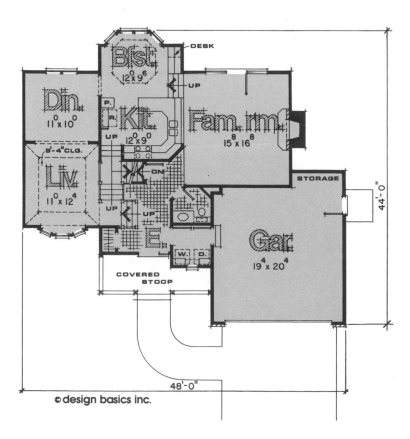

Design by
Design
Basics,
Inc.

Design 7284

First Floor: 1,195 square feet
Second Floor: 789 square feet
Total: 1,984 square feet

● A covered porch and window detailing add excitement to this home's elevation. Step up to the living room, which contains a lovely boxed ceiling and is open to the dining room with angled windows. Entertaining will be a pleasure in these areas. The kitchen and sunny breakfast room showcase lots of counter space, a Lazy Susan, a pantry and skylights. The family room—a few steps down from the kitchen—offers a cozy raised-hearth fireplace, access to the outside and large corner windows. Upstairs, secondary bedrooms share a conventional hall bath. The master suite features a vaulted ceiling and two closets.

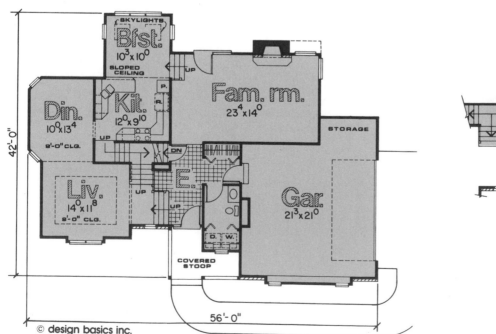

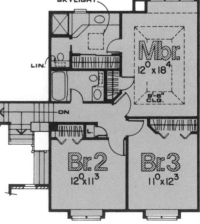

Design by
Design
Basics,
Inc.

Design 7283

Main Level: 1,291 square feet
Lower Level: 408 square feet
Total: 1,699 square feet

● Formal entertaining is accomplished beautifully on the main level in this home's living room. The lower-level family room accommodates casual pursuits. In the efficient kitchen, a desk and a walk-in pantry add to convenience. A breakfast room adjoins the kitchen and is accented with special ceiling detail. The master bed-room suite has a skylit dressing/bath area with a double vanity, a walk-in closet and a whirlpool tub. Secondary bedrooms share a convenient hall bath. The laundry room includes a sink and a pull-out iron, as well as access to the outdoors.

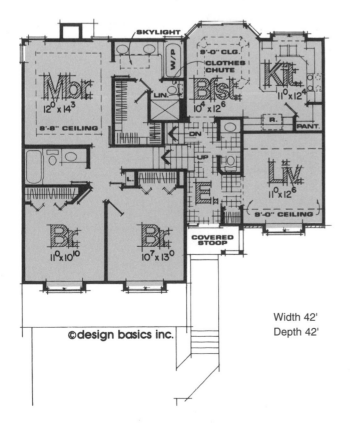

Width 42'
Depth 42'

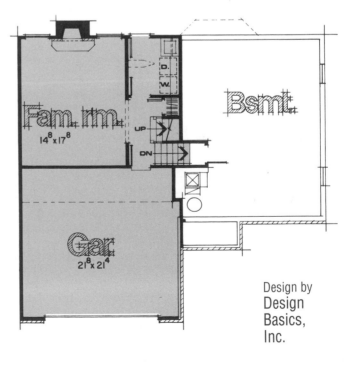

Design by
Design
Basics,
Inc.

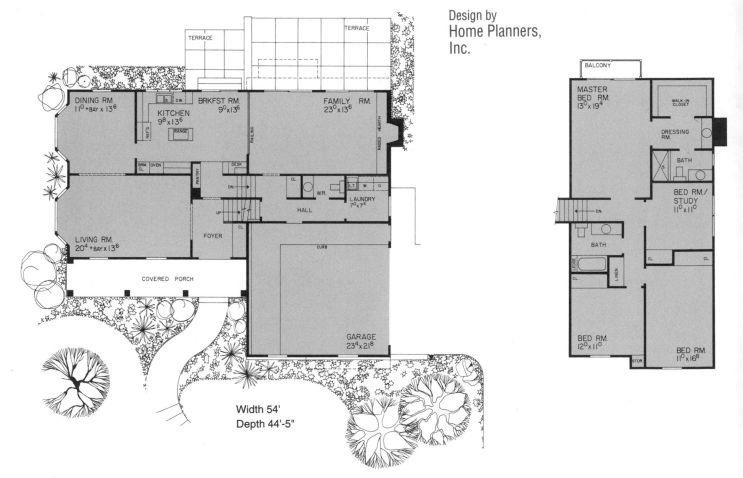

Design by
**Home Planners,
Inc.**

Width 54'
Depth 44'-5"

Design 2786 Main Level: 871 square feet; Upper Level: 1,132 square feet; Lower Level: 528 square feet; Total: 2,531 square feet

● A bay window in each the formal living room and dining room. A great interior and exterior design feature to attract attention to this tri-level home. The exterior also is enhanced by a covered front porch to further the Colonial charm. The interior livability is outstanding, too. An abundance of built-ins in the kitchen create an efficient work center. Features include an island range, pantry, broom closet, desk and breakfast room with sliding glass doors to the rear terrace. The lower level houses the informal family room, wash room and laundry. Further access is available to the outdoors by the family room to the terrace and laundry room to the side yard.

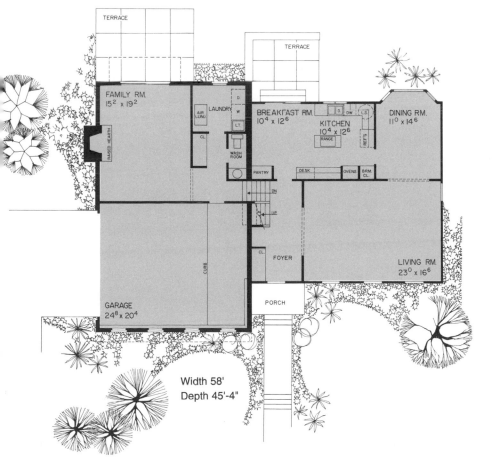

TERRACE

TERRACE

FAMILY RM.
15² x 19²

LAUNDRY

AIR COND

BREAKFAST RM.
10⁴ x 12⁶

KITCHEN
10⁴ x 12⁶

RANGE

DINING RM.
11⁰ x 14⁶

WASH ROOM

PANTRY

DESK

OVENS

B.RM. CL.

DN

UP

RAISED HEARTH

CURB

CL.

FOYER

LIVING RM.
23⁰ x 16⁶

GARAGE
24⁸ x 20⁴

PORCH

Width 58'
Depth 45'-4"

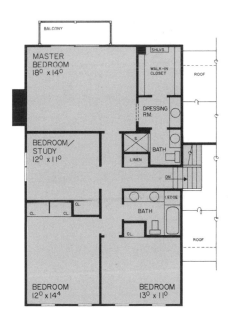

BALCONY

MASTER BEDROOM
18⁰ x 14⁰

SHLVS.

WALK-IN CLOSET

ROOF

DRESSING RM.

BEDROOM/ STUDY
12⁰ x 11⁰

BATH

LINEN

CL.

CL.

DN

LEDGE

BATH

ROOF

BEDROOM
12⁰ x 14⁴

BEDROOM
13⁰ x 11⁰

Design by
Home Planners,
Inc.

Design 2787 Main Level: 976 square feet; Upper Level: 1,118 square feet; Lower Level: 524 square feet; Total: 2,618 square feet

L D

● Three level living! Main, upper and lower levels to serve you and your family with great ease. Start from the bottom and work your way up. Family room with raised hearth fireplace, laundry and wash room on the lower level. Formal living and dining rooms, kitchen and breakfast room on the main level. Stop and take note at the efficiency of the kitchen with its many outstanding extras. The upper level houses the three bedrooms, study (or fourth bedroom if you prefer) and two baths. This design has really stacked up its livability to serve its occupants to their best advantage. This design has great interior livability and exterior charm.

Design 1324

Main Level: 682 square feet; Upper Level: 672 square feet
Lower Level: 656 square feet; Total: 2,010 square feet

● Wonderfully proportioned, this tri-level
has delightful symmetry. Designed to satisfy the requirements of the medium-sized
building budget, the exterior houses an
extremely practical floor plan. Although the
upper-level sleeping area features three bedrooms and two full baths, this home could
function admirably as a four-bedroom
home. The fourth bedroom is acquired by
utilizing the extra bedroom on the lower
level. In addition to the study/bedroom of
the lower level, there is a separate laundry,
an extra wash room and a multi-purpose
family room.

Design by
Home Planners,
Inc.

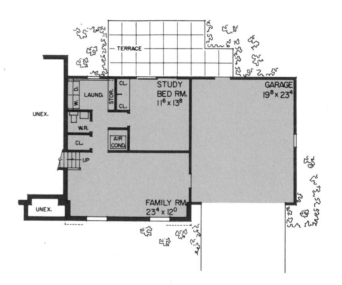

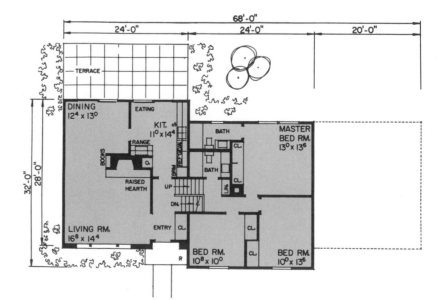

TERRACE   TERRACE

STUDY - B.R.
10⁴ x 11⁰

KIT.
12⁰ x 11⁶

DINING
11⁴ x 11⁶

RANGE

W.R.

AIR COND.

CL.

REF'G

BRM.

DN.

CL.

UP

LOCATION OF
OPTIONAL
BSMT. STAIR

CL.

5' HIGH
BOOKCASE

UP

CL.

LIVING RM.
18⁰ x 13⁶

ENTRY

GARAGE
11⁶ x 20⁰

FAMILY RM.
11⁶ x 20⁰

R.

Width 48'
Depth 32'

Design by
Home Planners,
Inc.

Design 1770

Main Level: 636 square feet
Upper Level: 672 square feet
Lower Level: 528 square feet
Total: 1,836 square feet

● This delightfully proportioned
split-level is highlighted by fine
window treatment, interesting roof
lines, an attractive use of materials
and an inviting front entrance. The
main level offers a front living
room with a built-in bookcase, a
kitchen and a formal dining area
with access to a terrace. The lower
level provides a 20-foot family
room, a study or bedroom, a laundry room, a wash room and a
garage. Three bedrooms and two
full baths occupy the upper level.

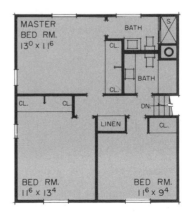

MASTER
BED RM.
13⁰ x 11⁶

BATH

CL.

BATH

CL.   CL.

DN.

CL.

LINEN

BED RM.
11⁶ x 13⁴

BED RM.
11⁶ x 9⁴

Design 2125

Main Level: 728 square feet
Upper Level: 672 square feet
Lower Level: 656 square feet
Total: 2,056 square feet

● A long list of features is available to recommend this four-level, traditional home. First of all, it is a real beauty. The windows, shutters, doorway, horizontal siding and stone all go together with great proportion to project an image of design excellence. Inside, the livability is outstanding. There are three bedrooms plus a study that may convert to a fourth bedroom. A kitchen with a breakfast area and a formal dining room make mealtimes enjoyable. An all-purpose family room is large.

Design by
Home Planners,
Inc.

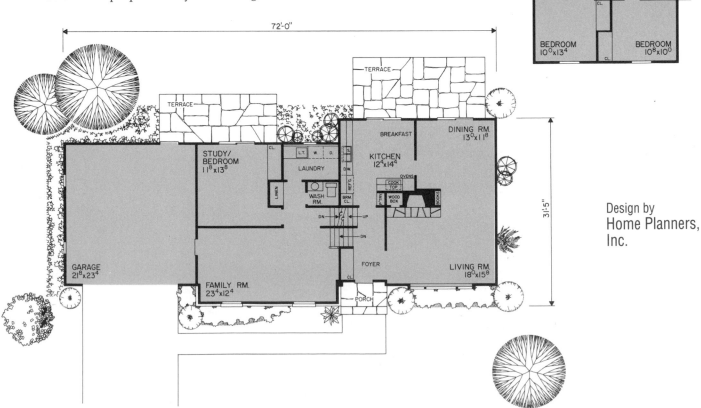

Design 1981

Main Level: 785 square feet
Upper Level: 912 square feet
Lower Level: 336 square feet
Total: 2,033 square feet

L **D**

● Here is a multi-level design ideal for those who wish to build on a relatively narrow site. A delightful exterior conceals a floor plan with exceptional family livability. Formal and informal areas are accompanied by efficiently planned work centers. Outdoor areas are easily accessible from various rooms. The upper level provides four bedrooms, including a master bedroom with a walk-in closet, dressing room and a balcony. The lower-level family room features a raised-hearth fireplace and a beamed ceiling. A railing separates the family room from the breakfast room and kitchen on the main level.

Design by
Home Planners,
Inc.

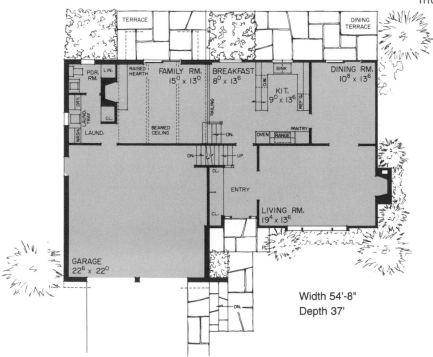

Width 54'-8"
Depth 37'

Design 2628

Main Level: 649 square feet
Upper Level: 672 square feet
Lower Level: 624 square feet
Total: 1,945 square feet

L **D**

● For a growing family on a budget, this plan has a good-looking face and plenty of affordable space—plus a few extras. Open to the dining room, the living room has a fireplace with bookshelves built in. The L-shaped kitchen has just enough room for a nook, which, like the dining room, leads out to a rear terrace. On the lower level are a large family room with beamed ceiling and wet bar, fourth bedroom (or quiet study), and extra storage. The upper level has three bedrooms, including a cozy master suite.

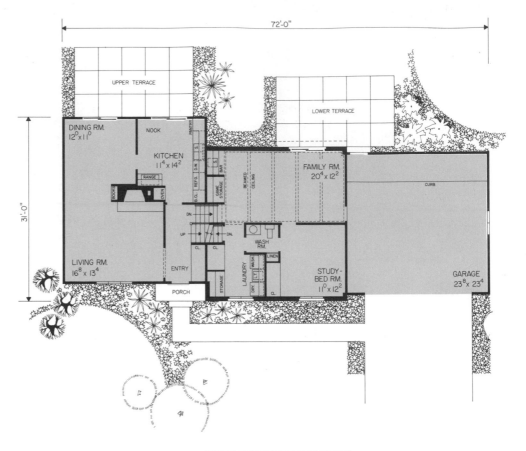

Design by
Home Planners,
Inc.

Design 2608

Main Level: 728 square feet
Upper Level: 874 square feet
Lower Level: 310 square feet
Total: 1,912 square feet

L **D**

● Here is tri-level livability with a fourth basement level for bulk storage and, perhaps, a shop area. There are four bedrooms, a handy laundry, two eating areas, formal and informal living areas and two fireplaces. Sliding glass doors in the formal dining room and the family room open to a terrace. The U-shaped kitchen has a built-in range/oven and a storage pantry. The breakfast nook overlooks the family room. The sleeping quarters consist of three secondary bedrooms and a master bedroom. The master suite enjoys a private bath with a dressing area and a walk-in closet. There's also a balcony off this bedroom. The two-car garage will accommodate the family vehicles and storage.

Design by
Home Planners, Inc.

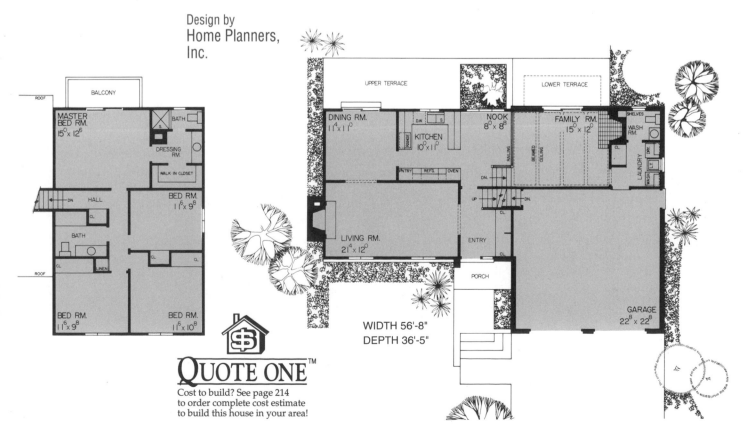

WIDTH 56'-8"
DEPTH 36'-5"

QUOTE ONE™
Cost to build? See page 214
to order complete cost estimate
to build this house in your area!

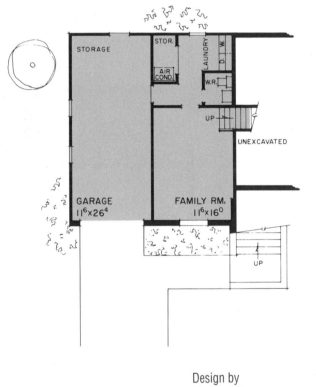

Design 1358

Main Level: 576 square feet
Upper Level: 672 square feet
Lower Level: 328 square feet
Total: 1,576 square feet

● Here is a charming split-level design for the modest budget. It will not require a large, expensive piece of property. The lower level includes a garage with storage space, a family room, a wash room and a laundry room. The kitchen with eating area, the living room and the formal dining room are on the main level. A rear terrace is accessible from the kitchen and dining room. The sleeping area occupies a level of its own, comprised of three bedrooms, including a master bedroom with private bath.

Design by
Home Planners,
Inc.

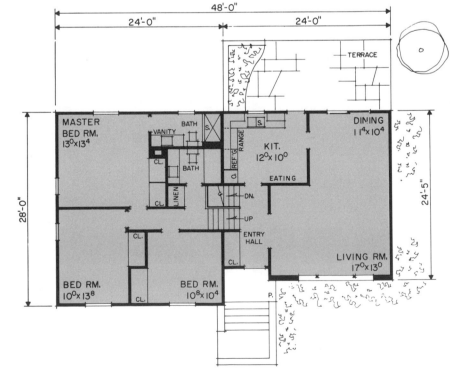

Design 1882

Main Level: 800 square feet
Upper Level: 864 square feet
Lower Level: 344 square feet
Total: 2,008 square feet

● This home will be most economical
to build. As the house begins to take
form, you'll appreciate even more all
the livable space you and your family
will enjoy. The basement, if finished,
provides a fourth level of livability.
The main level offers a living room
with a bowed window bay and a fireplace. The kitchen with eating area
and a formal dining room round out
this level. The three bedrooms and
two full baths are found on the upper
level. The lower level provides a study
or TV room, a laundry area and a
wash room.

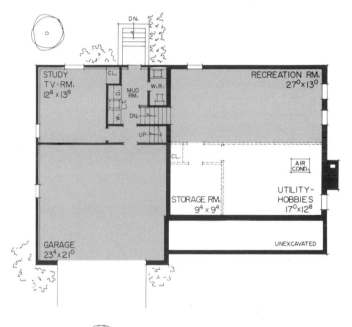

Width 54'-5"
Depth 36'

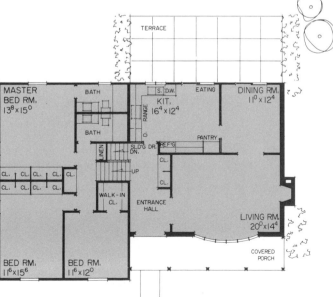

Design by
Home Planners,
Inc.

Design 1930

Main Level: 947 square feet
Upper Level: 768 square feet
Lower Level: 740 square feet
Total: 2,455 square feet

● The warmth of this inspiring Colonial adaptation is not restricted to the exterior. Its homey charm is readily apparent upon stepping through the front door. The sunken living room and the beamed-ceilinged family room with its raised-hearth fireplace are cozy living spaces. The kitchen, powder room and closet are situated near the garage. There are three bedrooms on the upper level, while a fourth is found on the lower level.

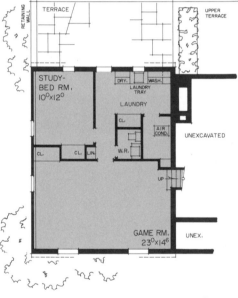

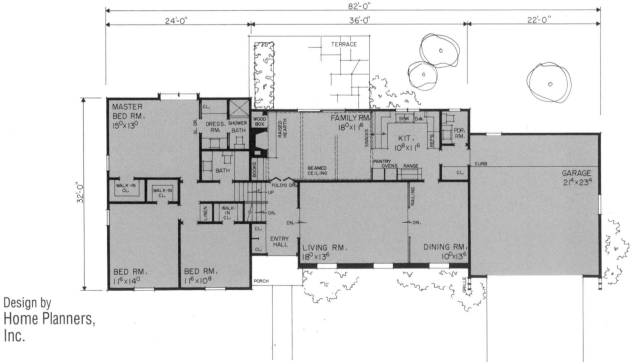

Design by
Home Planners,
Inc.

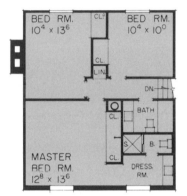

BED RM.
10⁴ x 13⁶

BED RM.
10⁴ x 10⁰

CL.

CL.

LIN.

DN.

BATH

CL.

S.

B.

CL.

MASTER
BED RM.
12⁸ x 13⁶

DRESS.
RM.

Design 1347

Main Level: 750 square feet
Upper Level: 672 square feet
Lower Level: 664 square feet
Total: 2,086 square feet

● This impressive split-level is as convenient to live in as it is beautiful. Gabled roofs, muntined windows with shutters, a covered front porch, paneled double doors and a cupola over the garage give a Colonial touch to the exterior. Inside, formal and informal areas include a living room and a family room. The kitchen passes through to an eating area. Three bedrooms upstairs and one downstairs accommodate family and guests.

Design by
Home Planners,
Inc.

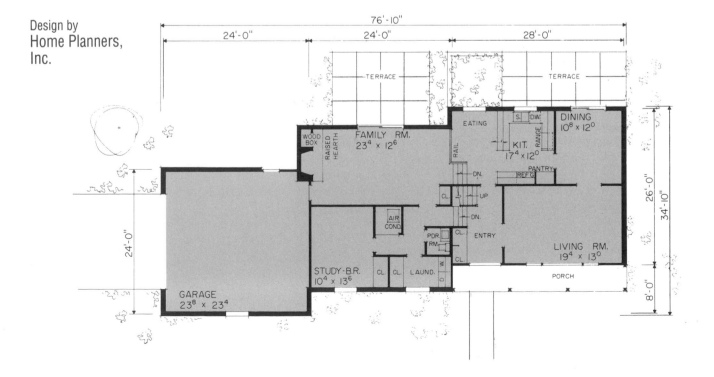

Design 1705

Main Level: 896 square feet
Upper Level: 896 square feet
Lower Level: 870 square feet
Total: 2,662 square feet

● Five bedrooms may become six if your family needs the room. Otherwise, this home's multi-purpose nature is a definite attention getter. The entry gives way to a large living room attached to a formal dining room. The U-shaped kitchen easily serves both formal and informal areas. In the family room, a fireplace and terrace enhance casual living. A dining porch located nearby features a built-in barbecue and doubles as space for a play area. Four bedrooms are contained on the second floor including a master suite that provides a private bath and a walk-in closet.

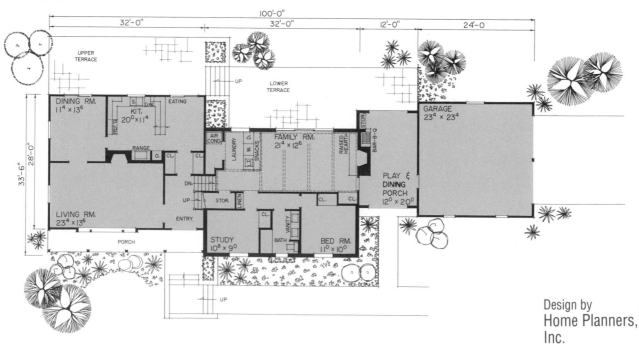

Design by
Home Planners,
Inc.

● Here are three optional elevations that function with the same basic floor plan. No need to decide now which is your favorite since the blueprints for this design include details for each optional exterior.

If yours is a restricted building budget, your construction dollar could hardly return greater dividends in the way of exterior appeal and interior livability. Also, you won't need a big, expensive site on which to build.

In addition to the four bedrooms and 2½ baths, there are two living areas, two places for dining, a fireplace and a basement. Notice the fine accessibility of the rear outdoor terrace.

Design by
Home Planners, Inc.

Design 2366

First Floor: 1,078 square feet
Second Floor: 880 square feet
Total: 1,958 square feet

D

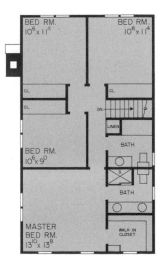

52'-0"

38'-0"

TERRACE

FAMILY RM.
21⁴ x 12⁸

BEAMED CEILING

CABINET

BOOKS

NOOK
8⁰ x 11⁶

KITCHEN
10⁶ x 11⁶

DINING RM.
11⁰ x 11⁶

DN.

DN.

UP

DN.

PANTRY

OVEN

WASH. DRY

PDR. RM.

CL.

CURB

ENTRY

LIVING RM.
19⁰ x 13⁶

GARAGE
21⁴ x 21⁰

PORCH

BED RM.
10⁶ x 11⁴

BED RM.
10⁶ x 11⁴

CL.

CL.

CL.

DN.

LINEN

BED RM.
10⁶ x 9⁰

BATH

BATH

MASTER
BED RM.
13¹⁰ x 13⁸

WALK-IN CLOSET

Design 1376

24-Foot-Depth Plan
Main Level: 960 square feet
Lower Level: 960 square feet
Total: 1,920 square feet

Design 1378

26-Foot-Depth Plan
Main Level: 1,040 square feet
Lower Level: 1,040 square feet
Total: 2,080 square feet

● The popularity of the bi-level can be traced to the tremendous amount of livable space that such a design provides per construction dollar. While the lower level is partially below grade, it enjoys plenty of natural light and, hence, provides a bright, cheerful atmosphere for total livability. While both the 24-foot-depth plan and the 26-foot-depth plan are essentially the same, it is important to note that the larger of the two features a private bath for the master bedroom. All three exteriors are available for the two different-sized plans.

Design by
Home Planners,
Inc.

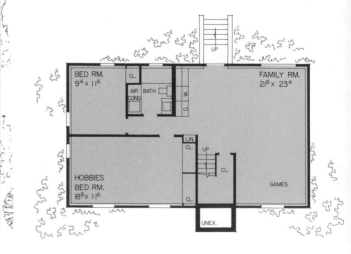

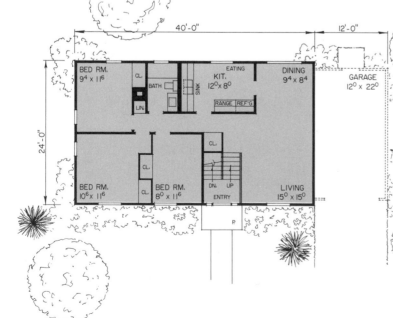

Design by
Home Planners,
Inc.

Design 1822

Main Level: 1,836 square feet
Lower Level: 1,150 square feet
Total: 2,986 square feet

● Here is a unique bi-level, not only in its delightful exterior appeal, but also in its practical planning. The covered porch has impressive columns that are enhanced by the traditional window and door detailing. The upper living level of this home is complete with three bedrooms and two baths. Separate living, dining and family rooms accommodate various living patterns. Downstairs, additional space includes an additional bedroom and bath, a laundry, a card room and a recreation room.

Design 1341

Upper Level: 1,248 square feet
Lower Level: 676 square feet
Total: 1,924 square feet

● Take a few steps up from the
entry of this Colonial home to the
formal living and dining area
with an optional fireplace located
to warm both areas. A deck is
accessible from the dining room.
The kitchen provides an informal
eating area. Also on the upper
level are the sleeping accommo-
dations: a master bedroom with
a private bath, two family bedrooms and another full bath. A
fourth bedroom or optional study
is on the lower level, along with
the family room, laundry and
wash room. The garage contains
a built-in work bench.

Design by
Home Planners,
Inc.

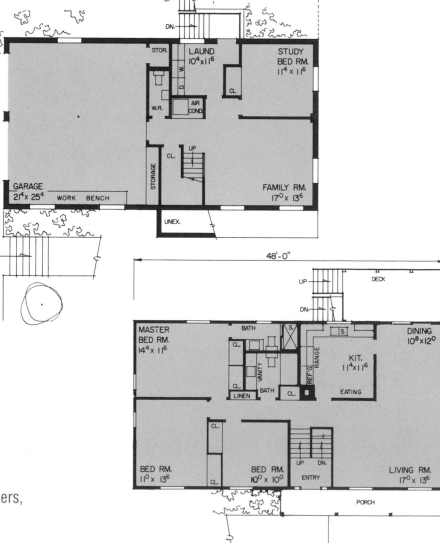

Design by
**Home Planners,
Inc.**

Design 1375

Main Level: 1,040 square feet
Lower Level: 1,040 square feet
Total: 2,080 square feet

● The bi-level or split-foyer design has become increasingly popular due to its efficient utilization of space and construction dollars. All of these traditional exteriors come with the plan. An optional garage is an added feature.

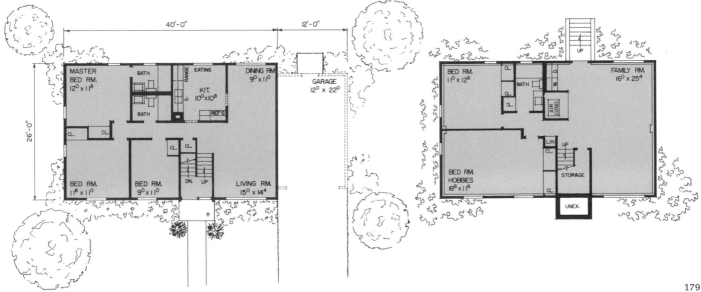

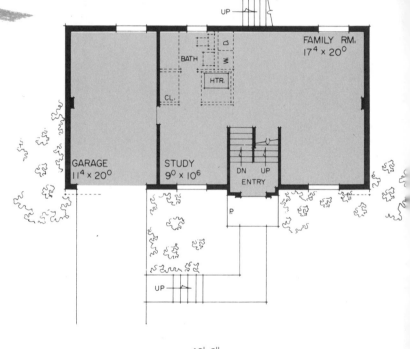

Design 1386 Main Level: 880 square feet
Lower Level: 596 square feet; Total: 1,476 square feet

● This design features traditional exterior styling with split-foyer, bi-level interior living. Great livability comes from such an economical plan without sacrificing any of the fine qualities of a much larger and more expensive plan. The entry leads up to a living room, which combines with a dining area for fine entertaining. Three bedrooms are situated near a full hall bath. The lower level includes a spacious family room and a study. You may choose to include a full bath on this level, too.

Design by
Home Planners,
Inc.

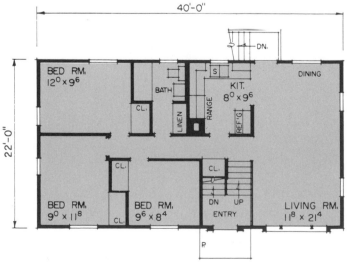

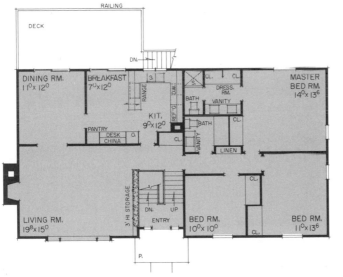

Design 1850

Main Level: 1,456 square feet
Lower Level: 728 square feet
Total: 2,184 square feet

● A perfect rectangle, this split-level is comparatively inexpensive to build and very appealing to live in. It features a large upper-level living room with fireplace, formal dining room, three bedrooms (with two full baths nearby), and an outdoor deck. Another fireplace warms the family room on the lower level, which also has a full bath and room for a study or fourth bedroom.

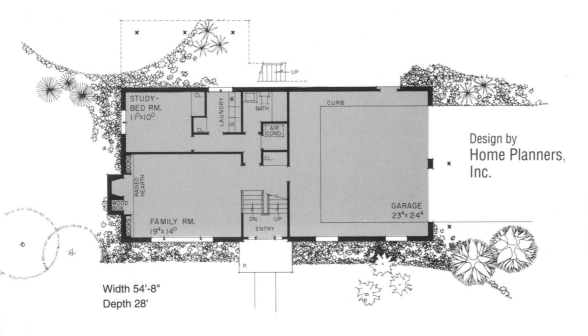

Design by
Home Planners, Inc.

Width 54'-8"
Depth 28'

QUOTE ONE™

Cost to build? See page 214
to order complete cost estimate
to build this house in your area!

Design 1935

Main Level: 904 square feet
Upper Level: 864 square feet
Lower Level: 840 square feet
Total: 2,608 square feet

● This design will adapt equally well to a flat or sloping site. There's no question about the family's ability to adapt to what the interior has to offer. Features include two fireplaces, a study, a family room with a beamed ceiling, a laundry room and lots of storage space. The blueprints for this home also provide non-basement details.

Design by
Home Planners,
Inc.

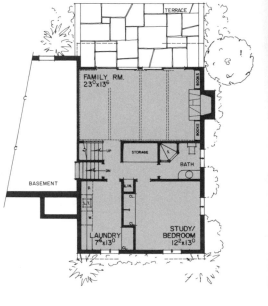

FAMILY RM.

UP

STORAGE   AIR COND.   BATH

LAUNDRY   LIN.   STUDY-BEDROOM

OPTIONAL   NON-BASEMENT

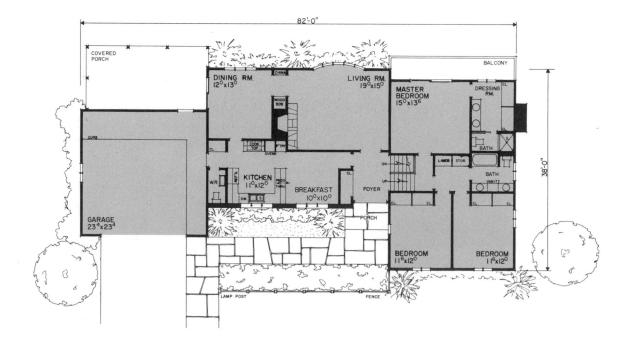

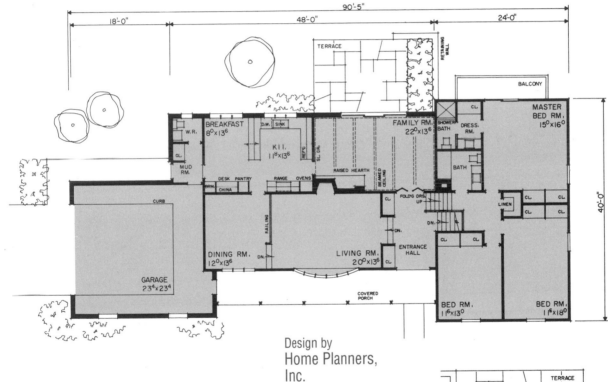

Design by
Home Planners,
Inc.

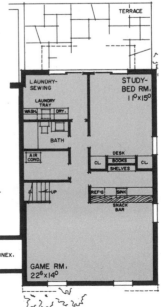

Design 1927

Main Level: 1,272 square feet; Upper Level: 960 square feet
Lower Level: 936 square feet; Total: 3,168 square feet

● Living in this traditional split level home will be a great experience. For here is a design that has everything. It has good looks and an abundance of livability features. The long, low appearance is accentuated by the large covered porch which shelters the bowed window and the inviting double front doors. Whatever your preference for exterior materials they will show well on this finely proportioned home. They start with four bedrooms and three full baths and continue with: beamed ceiling family room, sunken living room, formal dining room, informal breakfast room, extra wash room, outstanding kitchen and two attractive fireplaces.

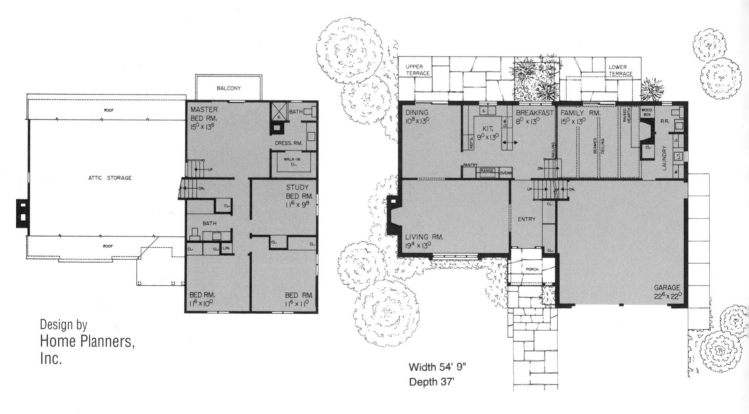

BALCONY

MASTER
BED RM.
15⁰ x 13⁶

BATH

ROOF

DRESS. RM.

ATTIC STORAGE

UP

WALK-IN
CL.

DN.

STUDY
BED RM.
11⁶ x 9⁸

CL.

BATH

ROOF

CL.   CL. LIN.

CL.

CL.

BED RM.
11⁶ x 10⁰

BED RM.
11⁶ x 11⁰

UPPER
TERRACE

LOWER
TERRACE

DINING
10⁸ x 13⁰

KIT.
9⁰ x 13⁰

BREAKFAST
8⁰ x 13⁰

FAMILY RM.
15⁰ x 13⁰

WOOD
BOX

R.R.

REF'G.

BEAMED CEILING

RAISED HEARTH

CL.

LAUNDRY

PANTRY

RANGE   OVENS

DN.

RAILING

UP   DN.

CL.

LIVING RM.
19⁴ x 13⁰

ENTRY

CL.

PORCH

GARAGE
22⁶ x 22⁰

Design by
Home Planners,
Inc.

Width 54' 9"
Depth 37'

Design 2171

Main Level: 795 square feet; Upper Level: 912 square feet; Lower Level: 335 square feet; Total: 2,042 square feet

L **D**

● This English Tudor split-level adaptation has much to recommend it. Perhaps, its most significant feature is that it can be built economically on a relatively small site. The width of the house is just over 52 feet. But its size does not inhibit it's livability features. There are many fine qualities: Observe the living room fireplace in addition to that in the family room with a wood box. Don't miss the balcony off the master bedroom. Also, worthy of note is the short flight of stairs leading to the huge attic storage area. For the development of even more space there is the basement below the main level. Access to this area is directly from the two-car garage. The breakfast room with its railing looks down into the lower level family room. Also it has a pass-thru to the kitchen.

Design 2624

Main Level: 904 square feet; Upper Level: 1,120 square feet
Lower Level: 404 square feet; Total: 2,428 square feet

L **D**

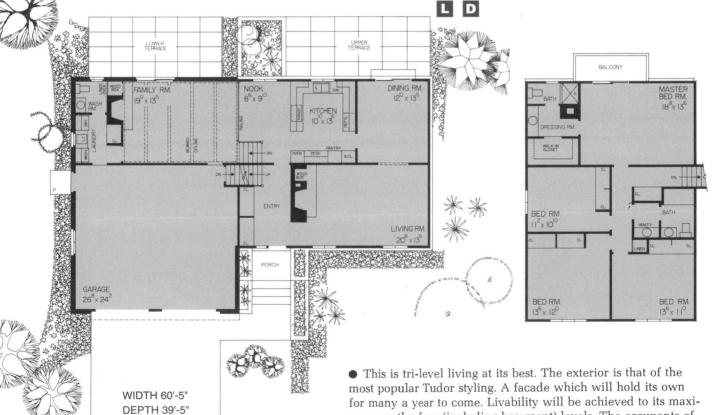

WIDTH 60'-5"
DEPTH 39'-5"

Design by
**Home Planners,
Inc.**

● This is tri-level living at its best. The exterior is that of the most popular Tudor styling. A facade which will hold its own for many a year to come. Livability will be achieved to its maximum on the four (including basement) levels. The occupants of the master bedroom can enjoy the outdoors on their private balcony. Additional outdoor enjoyment can be gained on the two terraces. That family room is more than 19' x 13' and includes a beamed ceiling and fireplace with wood box. Its formal companion, the living room, is similar in size and also will have the added warmth of a fireplace.

Design 2243

Main Level: 1,274 square feet; Upper Level: 960 square feet
Lower Level: 936 square feet; Total: 3,170 square feet

● An endearing Tudor exterior encloses a very livable
interior. The entrance hall provides passage to the living
and dining rooms, as well as the family room. The
kitchen and its breakfast nook are located nearby.
Downstairs, a game room and a bar will accommodate
fun with family and friends. A study and a laundry
room are also located here. The sleeping level contains
three bedrooms, including a master bedroom with a
private bath.

Design by
Home Planners,
Inc.

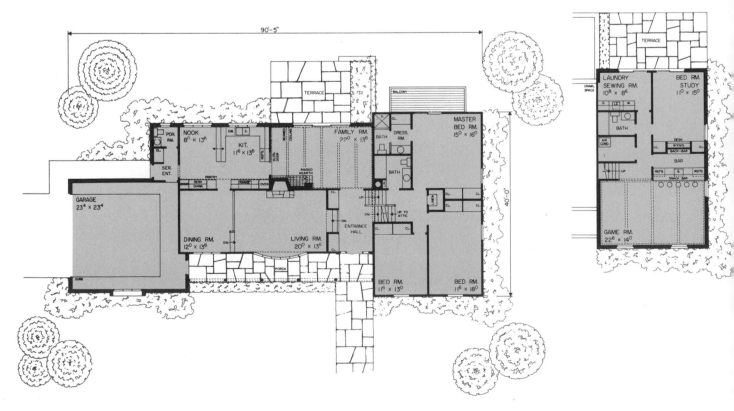

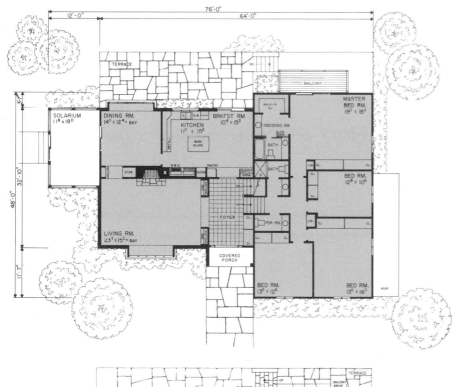

Design 2254

Main Level: 1,220 square feet
Upper Level: 1,344 square feet
Lower Level: 659 square feet
Total. 3,223 square feet

● Tudoresque down to the curved half timbers and diamond-paned windows, this multi-level is a classic design with a thoroughly modern floor plan. Centers of attention include a large foyer, a big kitchen and breakfast area, a splendidly large living room with a fireplace and a bay window, a formal dining room and a sun room. Upstairs are four bedrooms, one a master suite with a private balcony. The lower level has a family room, a built-in snack bar and access to a terrace out back.

Design by
**Home Planners,
Inc.**

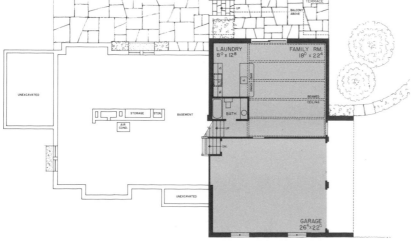

Design 2773

Main Level: 1,157 square feet
Upper Level: 950 square feet
Lower Level: 912 square feet
Total: 3,019 square feet

● Here is an exquisitely styled
Tudor tri-level which retains the
low-slung characteristics of a
one-story house. The contrasting
use of material surely makes the
exterior eye-catching. Another
outstanding feature will be the
covered front porch. A delightful
way to enter this home. Many
fine features also will be found
inside this design. Formal living
and dining room, U-shaped
kitchen with snack bar and family room find themselves located
on the main level. Two of the
three bedrooms are on the upper
level with two baths. Activities
room, third bedroom and hobby/
sewing room are on the lower
level — a real bonus. Notice the
built-in planter on the lower
level which is visible from the
other two levels. A powder room
and a washroom both are on the
main level. A study is on the
upper level which is a great
place for a quiet retreat. The
basement will be convenient
for storage of any bulk items.

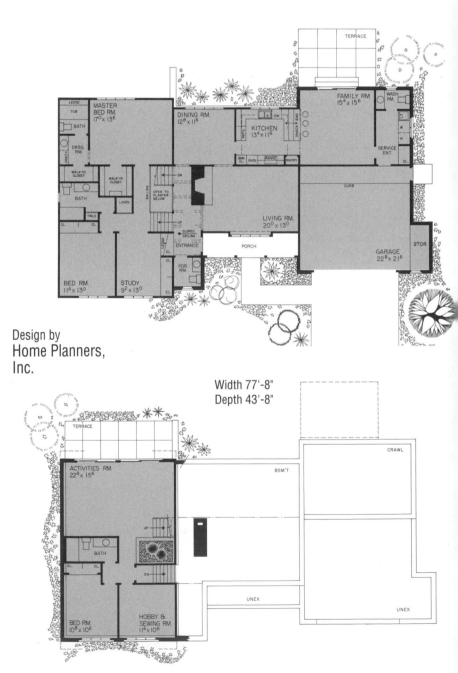

Design by
Home Planners,
Inc.

Width 77'-8"
Depth 43'-8"

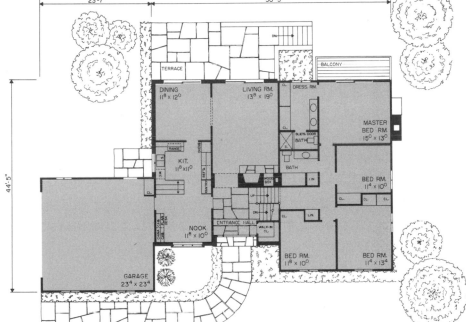

Design 2218

Main Level: 889 square feet; Upper Level: 960 square feet
Lower Level: 936 square feet; Total: 2,785 square feet

● Styled in the Tudor tradition, the warmth and charm of the exterior sets the tone for an exceptionally livable interior. Were you to ask each member of your family to choose his/her favorite feature there would be many outstanding highlights to consider.

Design 2375

Main Level: 993 square feet; Upper Level: 1,064 square feet
Lower Level: 335 square feet; Total: 2,392 square feet

● For those who like tri-level living, this contemporary design has much to offer. The low-pitched, overhanging roof, the effective use of contrasting exterior materials and raised planters create fine first impressions. The interior is dramatic with formal and casual living areas. Four bedrooms meet the needs of the family.

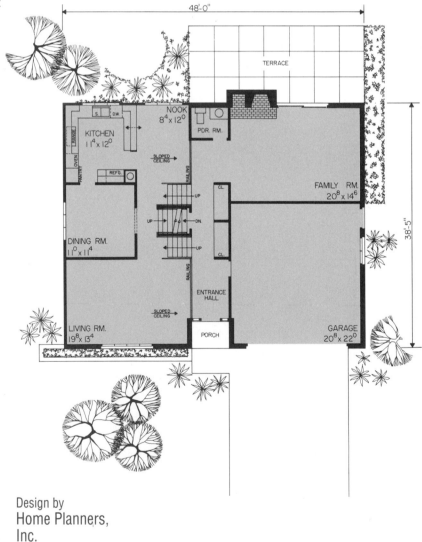

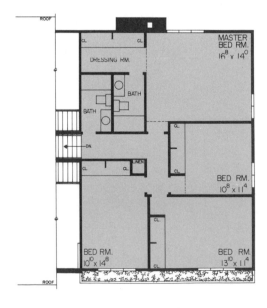

Design by
**Home Planners,
Inc.**

Design 1093

Main Level: 654 square feet; Upper Level: 768 square feet
Lower Level: 492 square feet; Total: 1,914 square feet

● This home is designed for active, family living. The kitchen conveniently serves a casual eating area and a dining room. The living room offers a fireplace and sliding glass doors to a terrace. Three bedrooms include two secondary bedrooms as well as a master suite with a private bath. On the lower level, a family room, hobby room and laundry room extend livability.

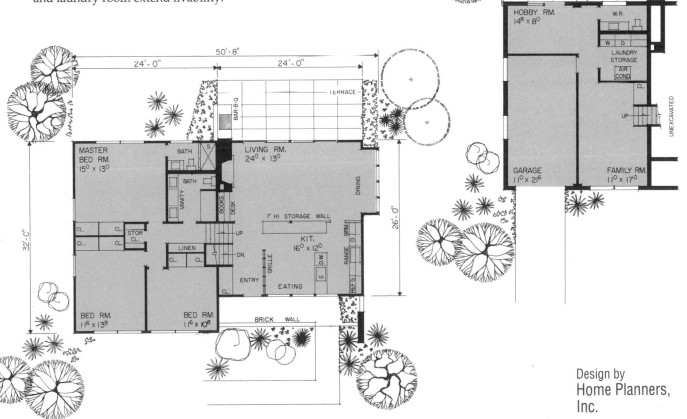

Design by
Home Planners, Inc.

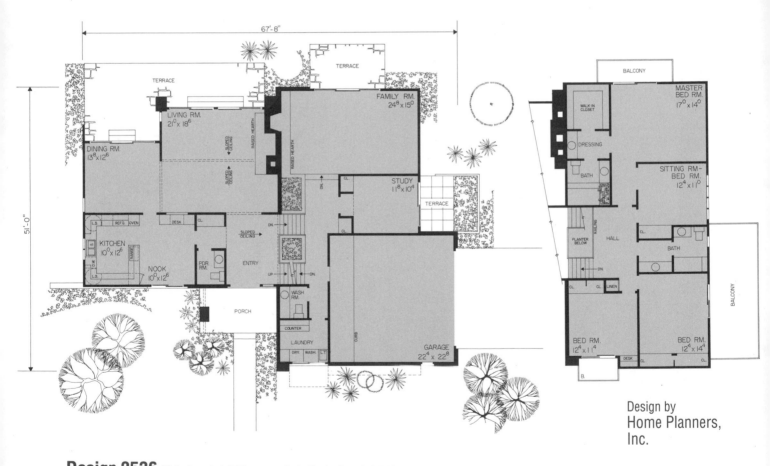

Design by
Home Planners,
Inc.

Design 2536 Main Level: 1,077 square feet; Upper Level: 1,319 square feet; Lower Level: 914 square feet; Total: 3,310 square feet

● Here are three levels of outstanding livability all packed in a delightfully contemporary exterior. The low pitched roof has a wide overhang with exposed rafter tails. The stone masses contrast effectively with the vertical siding and the glass areas. The extension of the sloping roof provides the

recessed feature of the front entrance with the patterned double doors. The homemaker's favorite highlight will be the layout of the kitchen. No crossroom traffic here. Only a few steps from the formal and informal eating areas, it is the epitome of efficiency. A sloping beamed ceiling, sliding glass doors and

a raised hearth fireplace enhance the appeal of the living room. The upper level offers the option of a fourth bedroom or a sitting room functioning with the master bedroom. Note the three balconies. On the lower level, the big family room, quiet study, laundry and extra washroom are present.

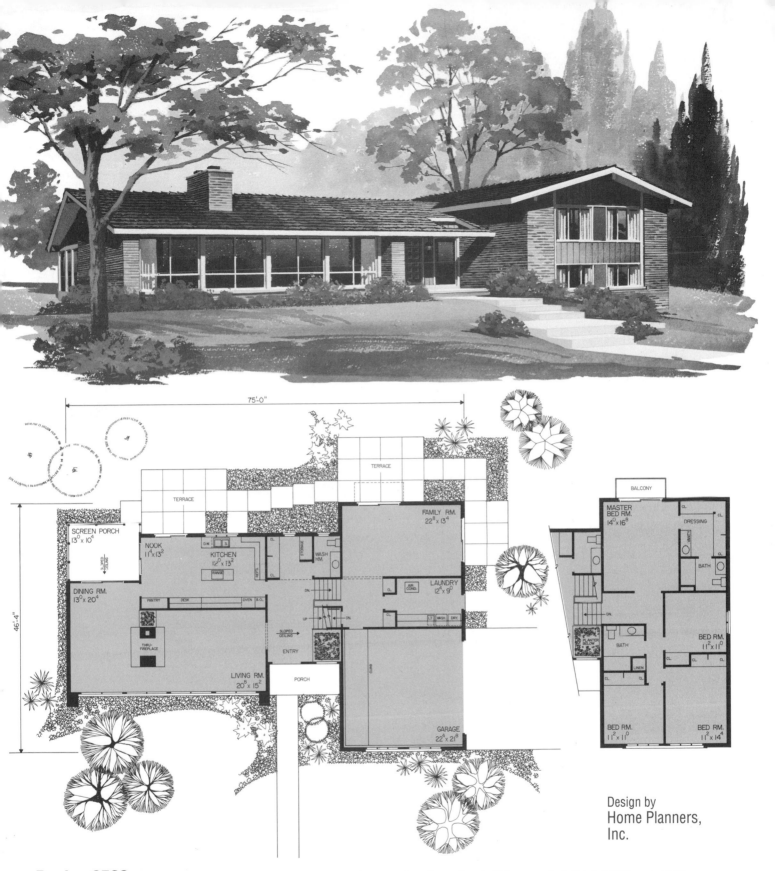

Design 2588 Main Level: 1,354 square feet; Upper Level: 1,112 square feet; Lower Level: 562 square feet; Total: 3,028 square feet

● A through-fireplace with an accompanying planter for the formal dining room and living room. That's old-fashioned good cheer in a contemporary home. The dining room has an adjacent screened-in porch for outdoor dining in the summertime. There are companions for these two formal areas, an informal breakfast nook and a family room. Each having sliding glass doors to separate rear terraces. Built-in desk, pantry, ample work space and is-land range are features of the L-shaped kitchen. The large laundry on the lower level houses the heating and cooling equipment. Three family bedrooms, bath and master bedroom suite are on the upper level.

Design 1220

Main Level: 1,456 square feet
Lower Level: 862 square feet
Total: 2,318 square feet

● A sleek, modern facade introduces ample living quarters. For entertaining, nothing will beat open living and dining rooms. The U-shaped kitchen and eating area are bright, efficient areas. Three bedrooms include a master suite with a balcony and private bath. On the lower level, another bedroom, a study and a family room further the appeal of this floor plan.

Design by
Home Planners, Inc.

Width 56'-9"
Depth 28'-10"

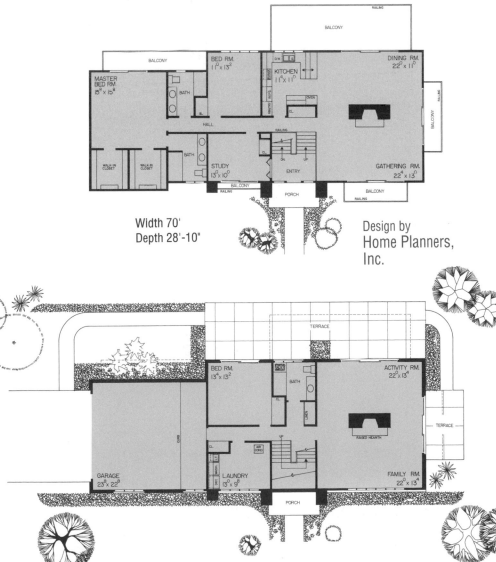

Width 70'
Depth 28'-10"

Design by
Home Planners, Inc.

Design 2580

Upper Level: 1,852 square feet
Lower Level: 1,297 square feet
Total: 3,149 square feet

● Indoor-outdoor living hardly could ask for more! And here's why. Imagine, five balconies and three terraces! These unique balconies add great beauty to the exterior while adding pleasure to those who utilize them from the interior. And there's more. This home has enough space for all to appreciate. Take note of the size of the gathering room, family room and activity room. There's also a large dining room. Four bedrooms too, for the large or growing family. Or three plus a study. Two fireplaces, one to service each of the two levels in this bi-level design. The rear terrace is accessible thru sliding glass doors from the lower level bedroom and activity room. The side terrace functions with the activity/family room area. The master suite has two walk-in closets and a private bath.

● This luxurious three-bedroom home offers comfort on many levels. Its modern design incorporates a rear garden room and conversation pit off a living room and dining room plus skylights in an adjacent family room with high sloped ceiling. Other features include an entrance court, activities room, modern kitchen, upper lounge, and master bedroom.

Design by
Home Planners, Inc.

Width 54'
Depth 63'-8"

Design 2901

Main Level: 1,449 square feet
Upper Level: 665 square feet
Master Bedroom Level: 448 square feet
Activities Room Level: 419 square feet
Total: 2,981 square feet

L

Design 2932
Main & Family Room Levels: 2,070 square feet
Upper Level: 680 square feet; Master Bedroom Level: 640 square feet
Total: 3,390 square feet

Design by
Home Planners, Inc.

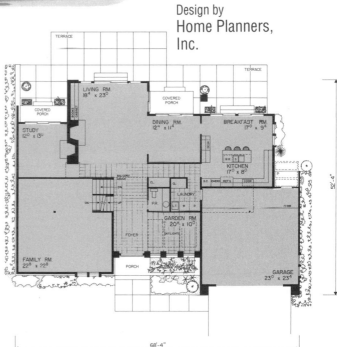

● This attractive split-level comtemporary home includes a garden room just off the foyer. Note also the master bedroom with whirlpool bath, large living room, and large family room.

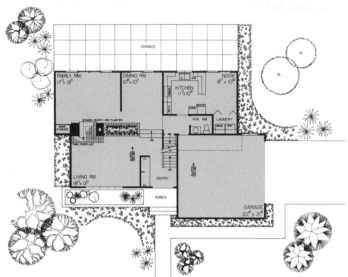

Design 2377 First Floor: 1,170 square feet
Second Floor: 815 square feet; Total: 1,985 square feet

● What an impressive, up-to-date home. Its refreshing configuration will command a full measure of attention. Note that all of the back rooms on the first floor are a couple steps lower than the entry and living room area. Separating the living room and the slightly lower level is a through-fireplace, which has a raised hearth in the family room. Four bedrooms, serviced by two full baths, comprise the second floor which looks down into the living room.

Width 55'
Depth 38'

Design by
Home Planners,
Inc.

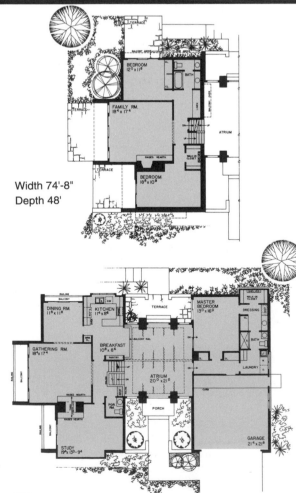

Width 74'-8"
Depth 48'

Design by
Home Planners,
Inc.

Design 2837
Main Level: 1,165 square feet; Atrium Level: 998 square feet
Lower Level; 1,090 square feet; Total: 3,253 square feet

● This split-level design presents fine traffic patterns. A highlight of the home, the atrium admits daytime solar warmth, which radiates into the other rooms for direct-gain heating. The master suite is outstanding with its dressing room, two large closets, bathroom and laundry access. The rear terrace is accessible by way of sliding glass doors.

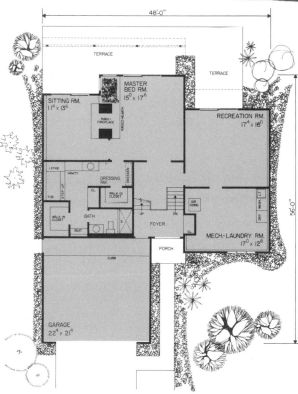

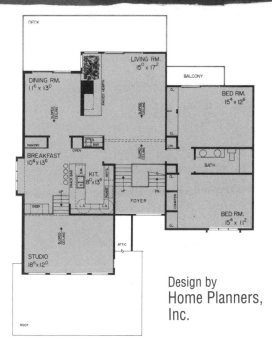

Design by
Home Planners,
Inc.

Design 2759 Upper Level: 1,747 square feet
Lower Level: 1,513 square feet; Total: 3,260 square feet

● A contemporary bi-level with a large bonus room on a third level over the garage. This studio will serve as a great room to be creative in or just to sit back in. The design also provides great indoor/outdoor living relationships with terraces and decks. The for-mal living/dining area has a sloped ceiling and built-in wet bar. The dra-matic beauty of a raised hearth fire-place and built-in planter will be en-joyed by those in the living room. Both have sliding glass doors to the rear deck. The breakfast area will serve as a pleasant eating room with ample space for a table plus the built-in snack bar. The lower level houses the recreation room, laundry and an out-standing master suite. This master suite includes a thru-fireplace, sitting room, tub and shower and more.

● This multi-level design will be ideal on a sloping site, both in the front and the rear of the house. The contemporary exterior is made up of vertical wood siding. The sloping roofline adds to the exterior appeal and creates a sloped ceiling in the formal living and dining rooms. An attractive bay window highlights the living room as will sliding glass doors in the dining room. The U-shaped kitchen and breakfast room also are located on this main level. The lower level houses the family room, wash room, laundry and access to the two-car garage. All of the sleeping facilities will be found on the upper level: three bedrooms and an exceptional master bedroom suite. Note two fireplaces, island range, two leveled terraces, covered porch, two balconies, etc.

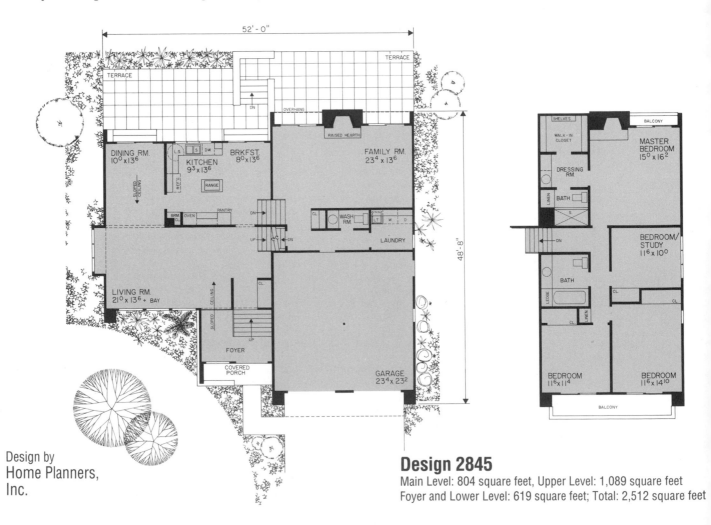

Design by
Home Planners, Inc.

Design 2845

Main Level: 804 square feet, Upper Level: 1,089 square feet
Foyer and Lower Level: 619 square feet; Total: 2,512 square feet

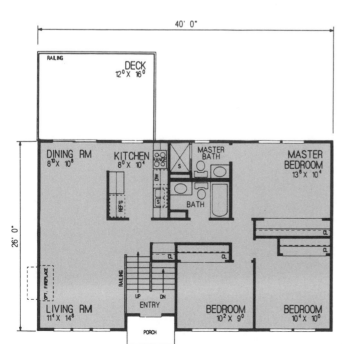

Rear

WEXFORD
Design 3713

Main Level: 1,028 square feet
Lower Level: 442 square feet
Total: 1,470 square feet

● The bi-level concept of living has understandably become popular for its convenient provision of the maximum amount of livable space within a basic floor plan. The main level offers a living room, dining room, kitchen, two baths and three bedrooms. The lower level, with a two-car garage, can be finished in the future to include a family room, powder room and utility room. The basic plan may be enhanced with a fireplace in the living room, brick veneer front, decorative louvers and a rear deck.

The blueprints for this house show how to build both the basic, low-cost version, and the enhanced, upgraded version. Blueprints and a complete limber and materials package are also available for this home at your local 84 Lumber dealer.

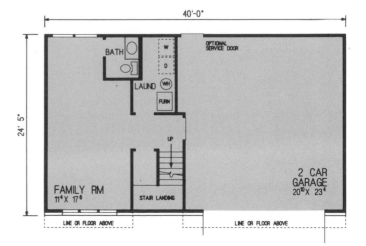

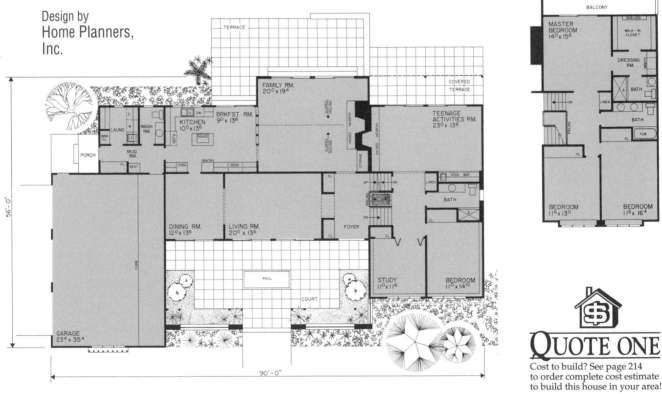

Design by
Home Planners,
Inc.

Cost to build? See page 214
to order complete cost estimate
to build this house in your area!

Design 2850

Main Level: 1,530 square feet; Upper Level: 984 square feet; Lower Level: 951 square feet; Total: 3,465 square feet

L **D**

● Entering through the entry court of this Spanish design is very impressive. Partially shielded from the street, this court features planting areas and a small pool. Enter into the foyer and this split-level interior will begin to unfold. Down six steps from the foyer is the lower level housing a bedroom and full bath, study and teenage activities room. Adults, along with teenagers, will enjoy the activities room which has a raised hearth fireplace, soda bar and sliding glass doors leading to a covered terrace. Six steps up from the foyer is the upper level bedroom area. The main level has the majority of the living areas. Formal living and dining rooms, informal family room, kitchen with accompanying breakfast room and mud room consisting of laundry and wash room. This home even has a three-car garage. Livability will be achieved with the greatest amount of comfort in this home.

Design 2843

Upper Level: 1,861 square feet
Lower Level: 1,181 square feet
Total: 3,042 square feet

L

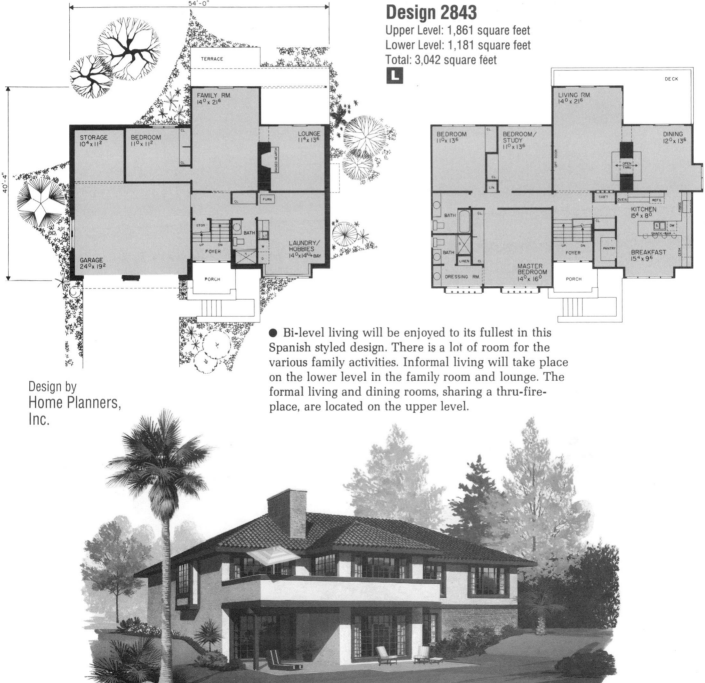

54'-0"

40'-4"

TERRACE

FAMILY RM.
14⁰ x 21⁶

LOUNGE
11⁴ x 13⁶

STORAGE
10⁴ x 11²

BEDROOM
11⁰ x 11²

GARAGE
24⁰ x 19²

CL

FURN

BATH

FOYER

UP DN

LAUNDRY/
HOBBIES
14⁰ x 14⁴ + BAY

PORCH

Design by
Home Planners,
Inc.

DECK

LIVING RM.
14⁰ x 21⁶

BEDROOM
11⁰ x 13⁶

BEDROOM/
STUDY
11⁰ x 13⁶

DINING
12⁰ x 13⁶

CL

LIN

KITCHEN
15⁴ x 8⁰

OVEN

REF'S

BATH

CAB'T

BATH

CL

PANTRY

BREAKFAST
15⁴ x 9⁶

LINEN

DRESSING RM.

MASTER
BEDROOM
14⁰ x 16⁰

FOYER

UP DN

PORCH

● Bi-level living will be enjoyed to its fullest in this Spanish styled design. There is a lot of room for the various family activities. Informal living will take place on the lower level in the family room and lounge. The formal living and dining rooms, sharing a thru-fire-place, are located on the upper level.

Design 4139

Main Level: 862 square feet
Upper Level: 920 square feet
Total: 1,782 square feet

D

● This home benefits from open, comfortable planning. Off the entry is a spacious great room with fireplace and access to a deck. Down a few steps is the country kitchen. There's enough room here for both a dining area and sitting area. Upstairs are three good-sized bedrooms and two baths. Notice the private deck off the master bedroom.

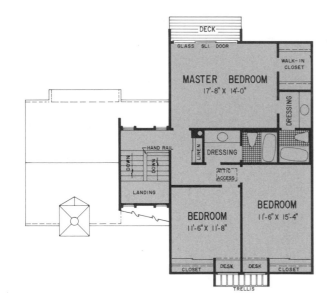

Design by
Home Planners, Inc.

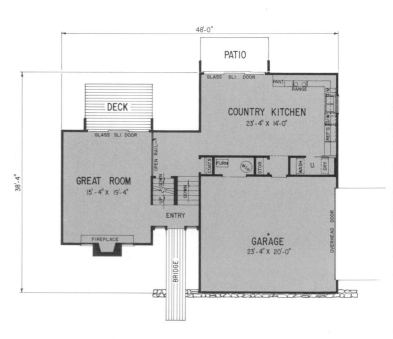

Homes With Raised Foundations

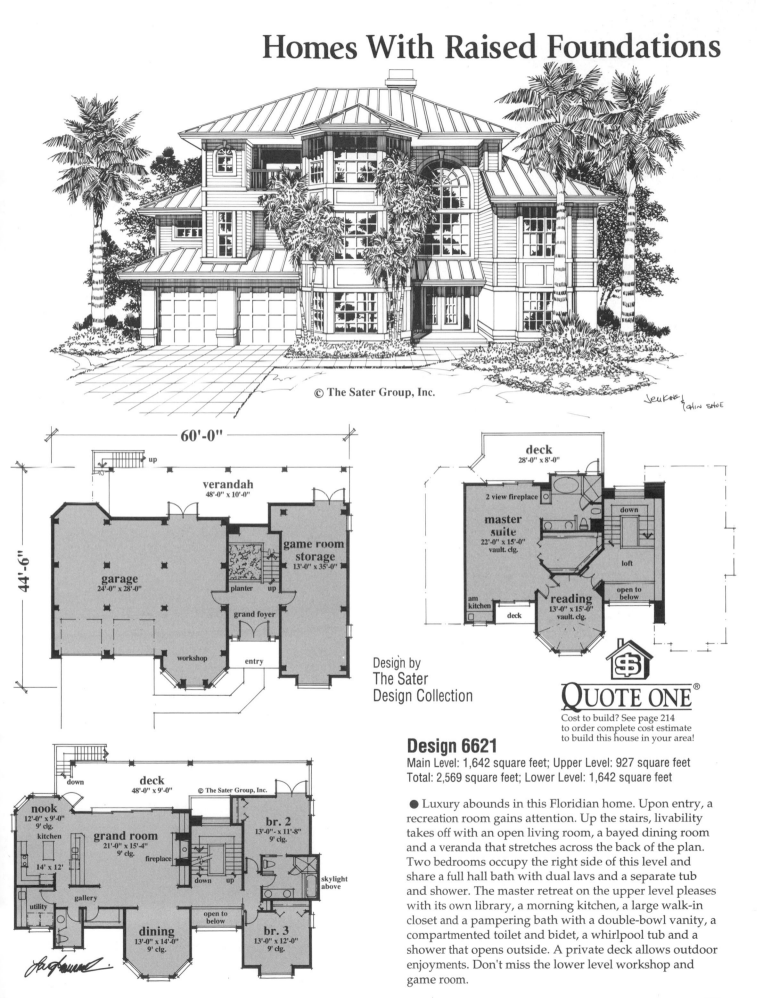

© The Sater Group, Inc.

verandah
48'-0" x 10'-0"

game room storage
13'-0" x 35'-0"

garage
24'-0" x 28'-0"

planter

up

grand foyer

workshop

entry

60'-0"

44'-6"

deck
28'-0" x 8'-0"

2 view fireplace

master suite
22'-0" x 15'-0"
vault. clg.

down

loft

am kitchen

deck

reading
13'-0" x 15'-0"
vault. clg.

open to below

Design by
The Sater
Design Collection

QUOTE ONE®
Cost to build? See page 214
to order complete cost estimate
to build this house in your area!

Design 6621

Main Level: 1,642 square feet; Upper Level: 927 square feet
Total: 2,569 square feet; Lower Level: 1,642 square feet

● Luxury abounds in this Floridian home. Upon entry, a recreation room gains attention. Up the stairs, livability takes off with an open living room, a bayed dining room and a veranda that stretches across the back of the plan. Two bedrooms occupy the right side of this level and share a full hall bath with dual lavs and a separate tub and shower. The master retreat on the upper level pleases with its own library, a morning kitchen, a large walk-in closet and a pampering bath with a double-bowl vanity, a compartmented toilet and bidet, a whirlpool tub and a shower that opens outside. A private deck allows outdoor enjoyments. Don't miss the lower level workshop and game room.

down

deck
48'-0" x 9'-0"

© The Sater Group, Inc.

nook
12'-0" x 9'-0"
9' clg.

kitchen

14' x 12'

grand room
21'-0" x 15'-4"
9' clg.

fireplace

br. 2
13'-0" - x 11'-8"
9' clg.

skylight above

down   up

utility

gallery

open to below

dining
13'-0" x 14'-0"
9' clg.

br. 3
13'-0" x 12'-0"
9' clg.

205

Design 6617

First Floor: 1,189 square feet
Second Floor: 575 square feet
Total: 1,764 square feet
Lower Level: 2,208 square feet

● An abundance of porches and a deck encourage year-round indoor/outdoor relationships in this classic two-story home. The spacious living room with its cozy fireplace and the adjacent dining room are perfect for formal or informal entertaining. An efficient kitchen and nearby laundry room make chores easy. The private master suite offers access to the screened porch and leads into a relaxing master bath complete with a walk-in closet, a tub and separate shower, double-bowl lavs and a compartmented toilet. A raised foundation makes this home easily adaptable to hilly sites.

Design by
The Sater
Design Collection

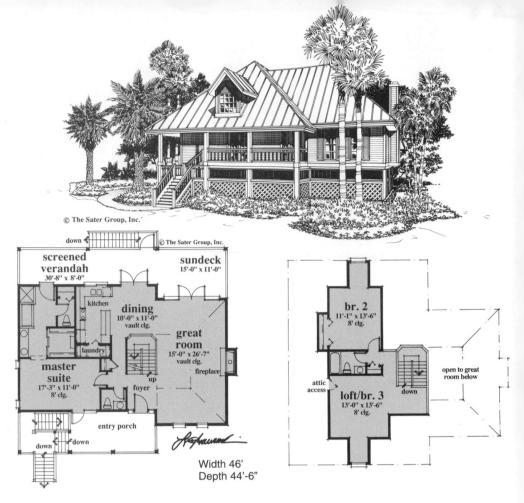

© The Sater Group, Inc.

Width 46'
Depth 44'-6"

Design 6615

Main Level: 1,736 square feet
Upper Level: 640 square feet
Total: 2,376 square feet
Lower Level: 840 square feet

● Lattice door panels, shutters, a balustrade, a metal roof and a raised foundation add character to this delightful coastal home. Double doors flanking a fireplace open to the sun deck from the spacious great room sporting a vaulted ceiling. An adjacent dining room provides views of the rear grounds and space for formal and informal entertaining. The glassed-in nook shares space with the L-shaped kitchen and a center work island. Bedrooms 2 and 3, a full bath and a utility room complete this floor. Upstairs, a sumptuous master suite awaits.

Cost to build? See page 214 to order complete cost estimate to build this house in your area!

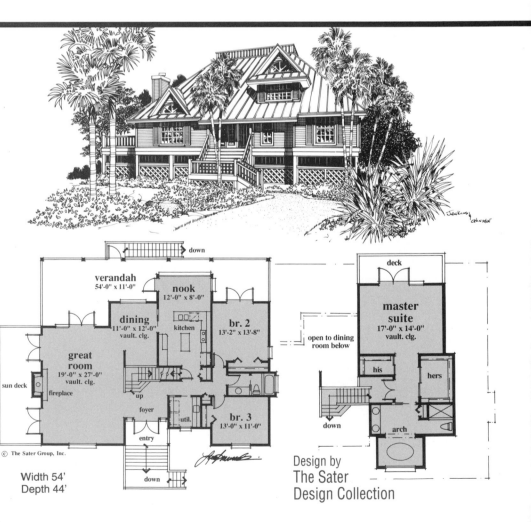

Design by
The Sater
Design Collection

Width 54'
Depth 44'

© The Sater Group, Inc.

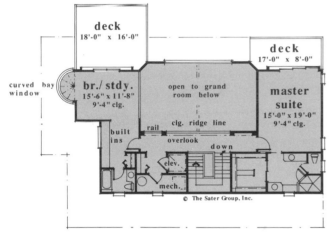

deck
18'-0" x 16'-0"

curved bay window

br./stdy.
15'-6" x 11'-8"
9'-4" clg.

deck
17'-0" x 8'-0"

open to grand room below

clg. ridge line

master suite
15'-0" x 19'-0"
9'-4" clg.

built ins

rail

overlook

down

elev.

mech.

© The Sater Group, Inc.

Design 6618

Main Level: 1,944 square feet
Upper Level: 1,196 square feet
Total: 3,140 square feet
Lower Level: 2,563 square feet

● In the grand room of this home, family and friends will enjoy the ambience created by arches and access to a veranda. Two guest rooms flank a full bath—one of the guest rooms also sports a private deck. The kitchen services a circular breakfast nook. Upstairs, a balcony overlook furthers the drama of the great room. The master suite, with a deck and a private bath opening through a pocket door, will be a pleasure to occupy. Another bedroom—or use this room for a study— sits at the other side of this floor. It extends a curved bay window, an expansive deck, built-ins and a full bath. This home is designed with an island basement.

Design by
The Sater
Design Collection

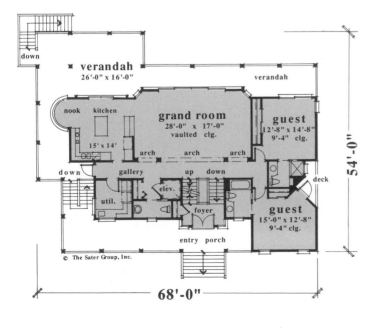

down

verandah
26'-0" x 16'-0"

verandah

nook   kitchen

grand room
28'-0" x 17'-0"
vaulted clg.

15' x 14'

guest
12'-8" x 14'-8"
9'-4" clg.

arch   arch   arch

down

gallery

up   down

elev.

deck

util.

foyer

guest
15'-0" x 12'-8"
9'-4" clg.

entry porch

© The Sater Group, Inc.

54'-0"

68'-0"

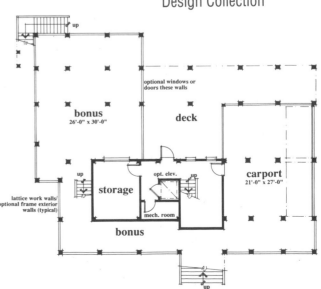

up

optional windows or doors these walls

bonus
26'-0" x 30'-0"

deck

up

storage

opt. elev.

up

carport
21'-0" x 27'-0"

lattice work walls/ optional frame exterior walls (typical)

mech. room

bonus

up

© The Sater Group, Inc.

Design 6616

First Floor: 1,136 square feet; Second Floor: 636 square feet
Total: 1,772 square feet; Lower Level: 1,928 square feet

● This two-story, coastal design is built on a pier foundation, giving it the flexibility to fit a number of different sites. The covered entry—with its dramatic transom window—leads to a spacious great room highlighted by a warming fireplace. To the right, the dining room and kitchen combine to provide a delightful place for mealtimes inside or out, with access to a side deck through

double doors. A study, a bedroom and a full bath complete the first floor. The luxurious master suite is located on the second floor for privacy and features an oversized walk-in closet. The pampering master bath enjoys a relaxing whirlpool tub, a double-bowl vanity and a compartmented toilet.

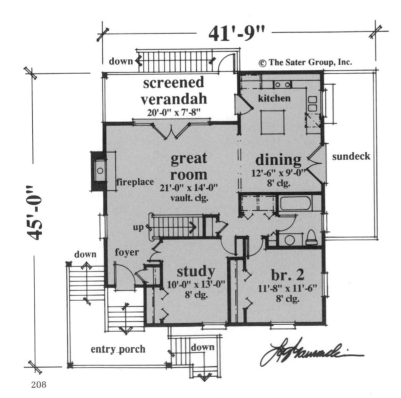

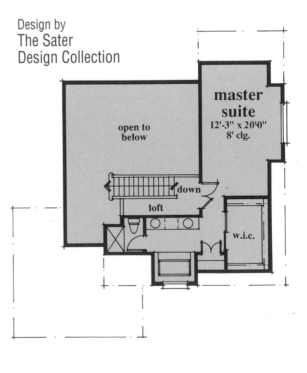

Design by
The Sater
Design Collection

© The Sater Group, Inc.

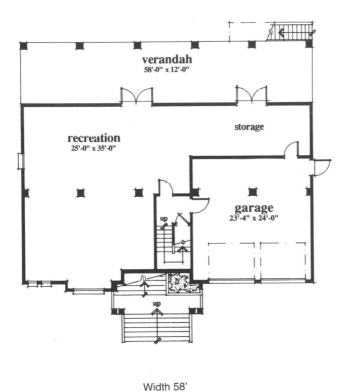

verandah
58'-0" x 12'-0"

recreation
25'-0" x 35'-0"

storage

up

garage
23'-4" x 24'-0"

up

Width 58'
Depth 54'

Design by
The Sater
Design Collection

Design 6622 Square Footage: 2,190
Lower Level: 1,966 square feet

● A dramatic set of stairs leads to the entry of this home. The foyer leads to an expansive living room with a fireplace and built-in bookshelves. A lanai opens off this area and will assure outdoor enjoyments. For formal meals, a front-facing dining room offers a bumped-out bay. The kitchen serves this area easily as well as the breakfast room. A study and three bedrooms make up the rest of the floor plan. Two secondary bedrooms share a full hall bath. A utility area is also nearby. In the master suite, two walk-in closets and a full bath are appreciated features. In the bedroom, a set of French doors offers passage to the lanai.

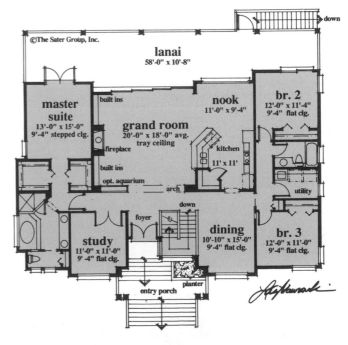

© The Sater Group, Inc.

lanai
58'-0" x 10'-8"

down

master suite
13'-0" x 15'-0"
9'-4" stepped clg.

built ins

nook
11'-0" x 9'-4"

br. 2
12'-0" x 11'-4"
9'-4" flat clg.

grand room
20'-0" x 18'-0" avg.
tray ceiling

fireplace

kitchen
11' x 11'

built ins

opt. aquarium

arch

utility

foyer

down

study
11'-0" x 11'-0"
9'-4" flat clg.

dining
10'-10" x 15'-0"
9'-4" flat clg.

br. 3
12'-0" x 11'-0"
9'-4" flat clg.

entry porch

planter

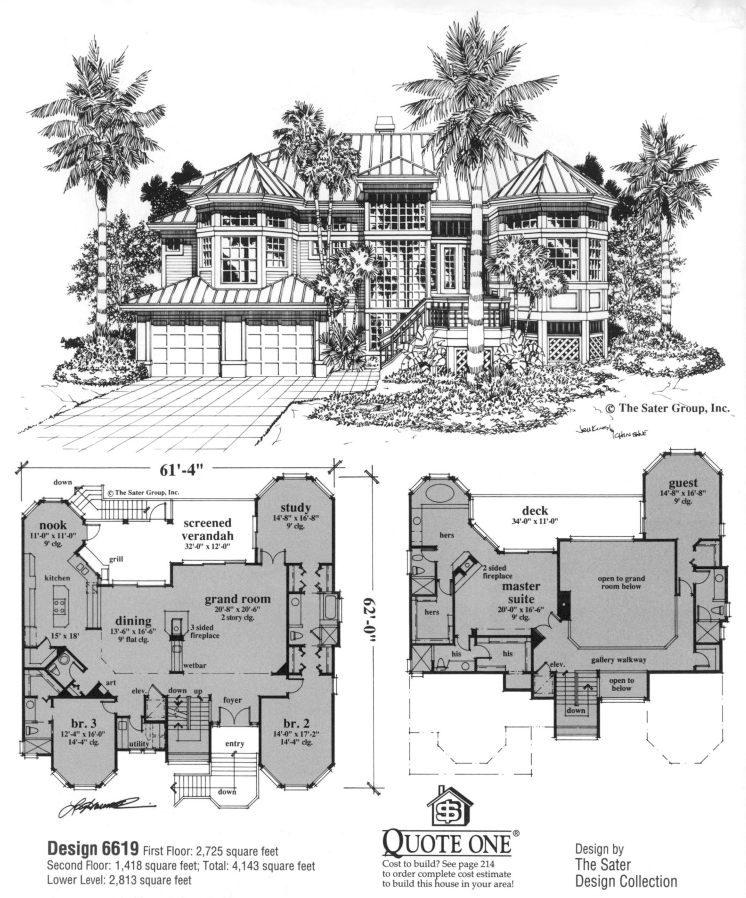

© The Sater Group, Inc.

© The Sater Group, Inc.

61'-4"

62'-0"

First Floor

- down
- nook 11'-0" x 11'-0" 9' clg.
- kitchen
- 15' x 18'
- grill
- screened verandah 32'-0" x 12'-0"
- study 14'-8" x 16'-8" 9' clg.
- grand room 20'-8" x 20'-6" 2 story clg.
- dining 13'-6" x 16'-6" 9' flat clg.
- 3 sided fireplace
- wetbar
- art
- elev.
- down up
- foyer
- br. 3 12'-4" x 16'-0" 14'-4" clg.
- utility
- entry
- down
- br. 2 14'-0" x 17'-2" 14'-4" clg.

Second Floor

- hers
- hers
- 2 sided fireplace
- master suite 20'-0" x 16'-6" 9' clg.
- his
- his
- deck 34'-0" x 11'-0"
- guest 14'-8" x 16'-8" 9' clg.
- open to grand room below
- gallery walkway
- elev.
- open to below
- down

Design 6619 First Floor: 2,725 square feet
Second Floor: 1,418 square feet; Total: 4,143 square feet
Lower Level: 2,813 square feet

Quote One®

Cost to build? See page 214 to order complete cost estimate to build this house in your area!

Design by
The Sater Design Collection

● Florida living takes off in this grand design. A grand room gains attention as a superb entertaining area. A see-through fireplace here connects this room to the dining room. Sets of sliding glass doors offer passage to an expansive rear deck. In the study, quiet time is assured—or slip out the doors and onto the deck for a breather. A full bath connects the study and Bedroom 2. Bedroom 3 sits on the opposite side of the house and enjoys its own bath. The kitchen is fully functional with a large work island and a connecting breakfast nook. Upstairs, the master bedroom suite is something to behold. His and Hers baths, a see-through fireplace and access to an upper deck all characterize this room. A guest bedroom suite is located on the other side of the upper floor and will make visits a real pleasure.

© The Sater Group, Inc.

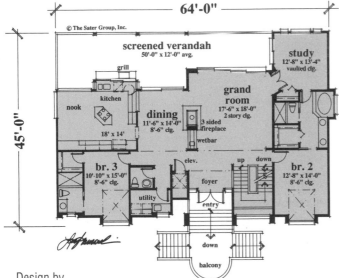

Design by
The Sater Design Collection

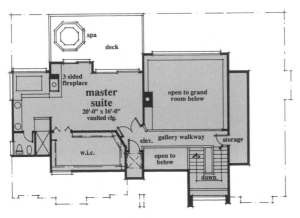

Design 6620

Main Level: 2,066 square feet
Upper Level: 810 square feet
Total: 2,876 square feet
Lower Level: 1,260 square feet

● If entertaining's your passion, then this is the design for you. With a large, open floor plan and an array of amenities, every gathering will be a success. The foyer embraces living areas accented by a glass fireplace and a wet bar. The living and dining rooms each access a screened entertainment center for outside enjoyments. The gourmet kitchen delights with its openness to the rest of the house. A morning room here also adds a nice touch. Two bedrooms and a den radiate from the first-floor living areas. Upstairs—or use the elevator—is a masterful master suite. It contains a huge walk-in closet, a whirlpool tub and a private sun deck. The garage is tucked in the lower level.

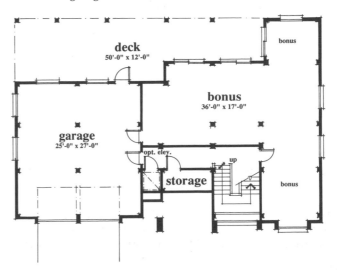

When You're Ready To Order . . .

Let Us Show You Our Home Blueprint Package.

Building a home? Planning a home? Our Blueprint Package has nearly everything you need to get the job done right, whether you're working on your own or with help from an architect, designer, builder or subcontractors. Each Blueprint Package is the result of many hours of work by licensed architects or professional designers.

QUALITY

Hundreds of hours of painstaking effort have gone into the development of your blueprint set. Each home has been quality-checked by professionals to insure accuracy and buildability.

VALUE

Because we sell in volume, you can buy professional-quality blueprints at a fraction of their development cost. With our plans, your dream home design costs only a few hundred dollars, not the thousands of dollars that custom architects charge.

SERVICE

Once you've chosen your favorite home plan, you'll receive fast, efficient service whether you choose to mail or fax your order to us or call us toll free at 1-800-521-6797.

SATISFACTION

Over 50 years of service to satisfied home plan buyers provide us unparalleled experience and knowledge in producing quality blueprints. What this means to you is satisfaction with our product and performance.

ORDER TOLL FREE 1-800-521-6797

After you've looked over our Blueprint Package and Important Extras on the following pages, simply mail the order form on page 221 or call toll free on our Blueprint Hotline: 1-800-521-6797. We're ready and eager to serve you.

Each set of blueprints is an interrelated collection of detail sheets which includes components such as floor plans, interior and exterior elevations, dimensions, cross-sections, diagrams and notations. These sheets show exactly how your house is to be built.

Among the sheets included may be:

Frontal Sheet
This artist's sketch of the exterior of the house gives you an idea of how the house will look when built and landscaped. Large ink-line floor plans show all levels of the house and provide an overview of your new home's livability, as well as a handy reference for deciding on furniture placement.

Foundation Plan
This sheet shows the foundation layout includ-

SAMPLE PACKAGE

ing support walls, excavated and unexcavated areas, if any, and foundation notes. If slab construction rather than basement, the plan shows footings and details for a monolithic slab. This page, or another in the set, may include a sample plot plan for locating your house on a building site.

Detailed Floor Plans

These plans show the layout of each floor of the house. Rooms and interior spaces are carefully dimensioned and keys are given for cross-section details provided later in the plans. The positions of electrical outlets and switches are shown.

House Cross-Sections

Large-scale views show sections or cut-aways of the foundation, interior walls, exterior walls, floors, stairways and roof details. Additional cross-sections may show important changes in floor, ceiling or roof heights or the relationship of one level to another. Extremely valuable for construction, these sections show exactly how the various parts of the house fit together.

Interior Elevations

Many of our drawings show the design and placement of kitchen and bathroom cabinets, laundry areas, fireplaces, bookcases and other built-ins. Little "extras," such as mantelpiece and wainscoting drawings, plus moulding sections, provide details that give your home that custom touch.

Exterior Elevations

These drawings show the front, rear and sides of your house and give necessary notes on exterior materials and finishes. Particular attention is given to cornice detail, brick and stone accents or other finish items that make your home unique.

Frontal Sheet

Foundation Plans

Detailed Floor Plans

Exterior Elevations

Interior Elevations

House Cross-Sections

*I*ntroducing nine important planning and construction aids

NEW

CUSTOM ENGINEERING

Our Custom Engineering Service Package provides an engineering seal for the structural elements of any Home Planners plan. This new Package provides complete calculations (except foundation engineering) from a registered professional, and offers many options invaluable to anyone planning to build. The Package includes: Structural framing plans for each horizontal framing area; Individual, certified truss designs; Specifications for all framing members; Calculation sheets detailing engineering problems and solutions concerning shear, bending, and deflections for all key framing members; Structural details for all key situations; Hanger and special connections specifications; Load and geometry information that may be used by a foundation design engineer and a Registered Professional Engineer's Seal for all of the above services. Home Planners also offers 3 Optional Engineering Services: Lateral load calculations and specifications for both wind and seismic considerations; Secondary Framing information for roofs, floors and walls; Light-gauge steel framing, providing details and cost comparisons for steel and wood.

MATERIALS LIST & DETAILED COST ESTIMATE

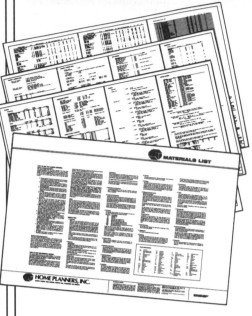

Make informed decisions about your home-building project with a customized materials take-off and a Quote One® Detailed Cost Estimate. These tools are invaluable in planning and estimating the cost of your new home.

The **Materials List** outlines the quantity, type and size of materials needed to build your house. Included are framing lumber, windows and doors, kitchen and bath cabinetry, rough and finish hardware, and much more. This handy list helps you or your builder cost out materials and serves as a reference sheet when you're compiling bids.

The **Quote One® Detailed Cost Estimate** matches line for line over 1,000 items in the Materials List (which is included when you purchase this estimating tool). It allows you to determine building costs for your specific area and for your specific home design. Space is allowed for additional estimates from contractors and subcontractors. (See **Quote One®** below for further information.)

The Materials List/Detailed Cost Estimate package can be ordered up to 6 months after a blueprint order. Because of the diversity of local building codes, the Materials List does not include mechanical materials. Detailed Cost Estimates are available for select Home Planners plans only. Consult a customer service representative for currently available designs.

SPECIFICATION OUTLINE

This valuable 16-page document is critical to building your house correctly. Designed to be filled in by you or your builder, this book lists 166 stages or items crucial to the building process. It provides a comprehensive review of the construction process and helps in making choices of materials. When combined with the blueprints, a signed contract, and a schedule, it becomes a legal document and record for the building of your home.

QUOTE ONE®

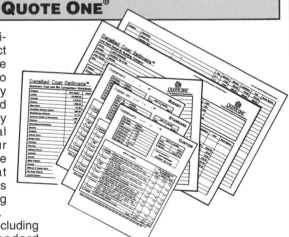

This new service helps you estimate the cost of building select Home Planners designs. Quote One® system is available in two separate stages: The Summary Cost Report and the Detailed Cost Estimate. The Summary Cost Report shows the total cost per square foot for your chosen home in your zip-code area and then breaks that cost down into ten categories showing the costs for building materials, labor and installation.
The total cost for the report (including three grades: Budget, Standard and Custom) is just $19.95 for one home; and additionals are only $14.95. These reports allow you to evaluate your building budget and compare the costs of building a variety of homes in your area.

The Detailed Cost Estimate furnishes an even more detailed report. The material and installation (labor + equipment) cost is shown for each of over 1,000 line items provided in the Standard grade. Space is allowed for additional estimates from contractors and subcontractors. This invaluable tool is available for a price of $110 ($120 for a Schedule E plan) which includes the price of a materials list which must be purchased at the same time.

To order these invaluable reports, use the order form on page 221 or call **1-800-521-6797.**

CONSTRUCTION INFORMATION

If you want to know more about techniques—and deal more confidently with subcontractors we offer these useful sheets. Each set is an excellent tool that will add to your understanding of these technical subjects.

Plan-A-Home®

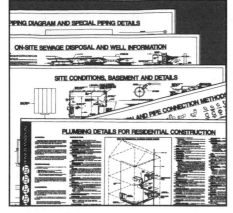

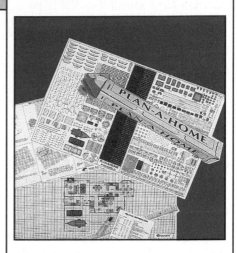

PLUMBING

The Blueprint Package includes locations for all the plumbing fixtures in your new house, including sinks, lavatories, tubs, showers, toilets, laundry trays and water heaters. However, if you want to know more about the complete plumbing system, these 24x36-inch detail sheets will prove very useful. Prepared to meet requirements of the National Plumbing Code, these six fact-filled sheets give general information on pipe schedules, fittings, sump-pump details, water-softener hookups, septic system details and much more. Color-coded sheets include a glossary of terms.

ELECTRICAL

The locations for every electrical switch, plug and outlet are shown in your Blueprint Package. However, these Electrical Details go further to take the mystery out of household electrical systems. Prepared to meet requirements of the National Electrical Code, these comprehensive 24x36-inch drawings come packed with helpful information, including wire sizing, switch-installation schematics, cable-routing details, appliance wattage, door-bell hookups, typical service panel circuitry and much more. Six sheets are bound together and color-coded for easy reference. A glossary of terms is also included.

Plan-A-Home® is an easy-to-use tool that helps you design a new home, arrange furniture in a new or existing home, or plan a remodeling project. Each package contains:

- **More than 700 reusable peel-off planning symbols** on a self-stick vinyl sheet, including walls, windows, doors, all types of furniture, kitchen components, bath fixtures and many more.

- **A reusable, transparent, 1/4-inch scale planning grid** that matches the scale of actual working drawings (1/4-inch equals 1 foot). This grid provides the basis for house layouts of up to 140x92 feet.

- **Tracing paper** and a protective sheet for copying or transferring your completed plan.

- **A felt-tip pen,** with water-soluble ink that wipes away quickly.

Plan-A-Home® lets you lay out areas as large as a 7,500 square foot, six-bedroom, seven-bath house.

CONSTRUCTION

The Blueprint Package contains everything an experienced builder needs to construct a particular house. However, it doesn't show all the ways that houses can be built, nor does it explain alternate construction methods. To help you understand how your house will be built—and offer additional techniques—this set of drawings depicts the materials and methods used to build foundations, fireplaces, walls, floors and roofs. Where appropriate, the drawings show acceptable alternatives. These six sheets will answer questions for the advanced do-it-yourselfer or home planner.

MECHANICAL

This package contains fundamental principles and useful data that will help you make informed decisions and communicate with subcontractors about heating and cooling systems. The 24x36-inch drawings contain instructions and samples that allow you to make simple load calculations and preliminary sizing and costing analysis. Covered are today's most commonly used systems from heat pumps to solar fuel systems. The package is packed full of illustrations and diagrams to help you visualize components and how they relate to one another.

To Order, Call Toll Free 1-800-521-6797

To add these important extras to your Blueprint Package, simply indicate your choices on the order form on page 221 or call us Toll Free 1-800-521-6797 and we'll tell you more about these exciting products.

⬛ *The Deck Blueprint Package*

Many of the homes in this book can be enhanced with a professionally designed Home Planners' Deck Plan. Those home plans highlighted with a ⬛ have a matching or corresponding deck plan available which includes a Deck Plan Frontal Sheet, Deck Framing and Floor Plans, Deck Elevations and a Deck Materials List. A Standard Deck Details Package, also available, provides all the how-to information necessary for building *any* deck. Our Complete Deck Building Package contains 1 set of Custom Deck Plans of your choice, plus 1 set of Standard Deck Building Details all for one low price. Our plans and details are carefully prepared in an easy-to-understand format that will guide you through every stage of your deck-building project. This page contains a sampling of 12 of the 25 different Deck layouts to match your favorite house. See page 218 for prices and ordering information.

SPLIT–LEVEL SUN DECK
Deck Plan D100

BI–LEVEL DECK WITH COVERED DINING
Deck Plan D101

WRAP–AROUND FAMILY DECK
Deck Plan D104

DECK FOR DINING AND VIEWS
Deck Plan D107

TREND–SETTER DECK
Deck Plan D110

TURN–OF–THE–CENTURY DECK
Deck Plan D111

WEEKEND ENTERTAINER DECK
Deck Plan D112

CENTER–VIEW DECK
Deck Plan D114

KITCHEN–EXTENDER DECK
Deck Plan D115

SPLIT–LEVEL ACTIVITY DECK
Deck Plan D117

TRI–LEVEL DECK WITH GRILL
Deck Plan D119

CONTEMPORARY LEISURE DECK
Deck Plan D120

L The Landscape Blueprint Package

For the homes marked with an **L** in this book, Home Planners has created a front-yard landscape plan that matches or is complementary in design to the house plan. These comprehensive blueprint packages include a Frontal Sheet, Plan View, Regionalized Plant & Materials List, a sheet on Planting and Maintaining Your Landscape, Zone Maps and Plant Size and Description Guide. These plans will help you achieve professional results, adding value and enjoyment to your property for years to come. Each set of blueprints is a full 18" x 24" in size with clear, complete instructions and easy-to-read type. Six of the forty front-yard Landscape Plans to match your favorite house are shown below.

Regional Order Map

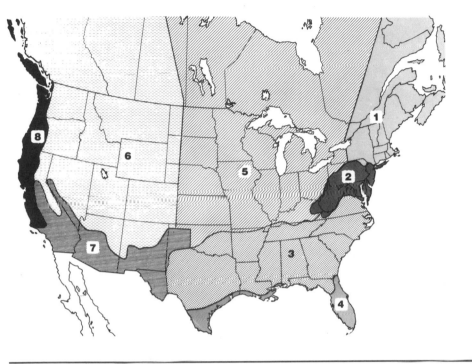

Most of the Landscape Plans shown on these pages are available with a Plant & Materials List adapted by horticultural experts to 8 different regions of the country. Please specify Geographic Region when ordering your plan. See page 218 for prices, ordering information and regional availability.

Region	**1**	Northeast
Region	**2**	Mid-Atlantic
Region	**3**	Deep South
Region	**4**	Florida & Gulf Coast
Region	**5**	Midwest
Region	**6**	Rocky Mountains
Region	**7**	Southern California & Desert Southwest
Region	**8**	Northern California & Pacific Northwest

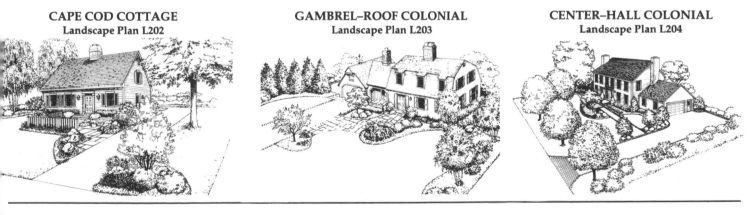

CAPE COD COTTAGE
Landscape Plan L202

GAMBREL–ROOF COLONIAL
Landscape Plan L203

CENTER–HALL COLONIAL
Landscape Plan L204

CLASSIC NEW ENGLAND COLONIAL
Landscape Plan L205

COUNTRY–STYLE FARMHOUSE
Landscape Plan L207

TRADITIONAL SPLIT–LEVEL
Landscape Plan L228

Price Schedule & Plans Index

House Blueprint Price Schedule
(Prices guaranteed through December 31, 1997)

	1-set Study Package	4-set Building Package	8-set Building Package	1-set Reproducible Sepias	Home Customizer® Package
Schedule A	$300	$345	$405	$505	$555
Schedule B	$340	$385	$445	$565	$615
Schedule C	$380	$425	$485	$625	$675
Schedule D	$420	$465	$525	$685	$735
Schedule E	$540	$585	$645	$745	$795

Prices for 4- or 8- set Building Packages honored only at time of original order.

Additional Identical Blueprints in same order................$50 per set
Reverse Blueprints (mirror image)....................................$50 per set
Specification Outlines ....$10 each
Materials Lists (not available for California Service):
    ▲Home Planners Designs.....................................$50
    † Design Basics Designs $75
    ✵ Alan Mascord Designs......................................$50
    ◆Design Traditions Designs.................................$50
If ordering a Materials List for a Schedule E plan, add $10 to above prices.
Exchanges ....$50 exchange fee for the first set; $10 for each
              additional set
              $70 total exchange fee for 4 sets
              $100 total exchange fee for 8 sets

Deck Plans Price Schedule

CUSTOM DECK PLANS
Price Group	Q	R	S
1 Set Custom Plans	$25	$30	$35

Additional identical sets:..$10 each
Reverse sets (mirror image):..$10 each

STANDARD DECK DETAILS
1 Set Generic Construction Details..................................$14.95 each

COMPLETE DECK BUILDING PACKAGE
Price Group	Q	R	S
1 Set Custom Plans 1 Set Standard Deck Details	$35	$40	$45

Landscape Plans Price Schedule

Price Group	X	Y	Z
1 set	$35	$45	$55
3 sets	$50	$60	$70
6 sets	$65	$75	$85

Additional Identical Sets ....$10 each
Reverse Sets (mirror image) ....$10 each

These pages contain all the information you need to price your blueprints. In general the larger and more complicated the house, the more it costs to design and thus the higher the price we must charge for the blueprints. Remember, however, that these prices are far less than you would normally pay for the services of a licensed architect or professional designer.

Custom home designs and related architectural services often cost thousands of dollars, ranging from 5% to 15% of the cost of construction. By ordering our blueprints you are potentially saving enough money to afford a larger house, or to add those "extra" amenities such as a patio, deck, swimming pool or even an upgraded kitchen or luxurious master suite.

Index

To use the Index below, refer to the design number listed in numerical order (a helpful page reference is also given). Note the price index letter and refer to the House Blueprint Price Schedule above for the cost of one, four or eight sets of blueprints or the cost of a reproducible sepia. Additional prices are shown for identical and reverse blueprint sets, as well as a very useful Materials List for some of the plans. Also note in the Index below those plans that have matching or complementary Deck Plans or Landscape Plans. Refer to the

schedules above for prices of these plans. Select designs can be customized with our exclusive Home Customizer® Package. See page 221 for more information. Some plans are also part of our Quote One™ estimating service, indicated by this symbol: 🏠 . See page 214 for more information.

To Order: Fill in and send the order form on page 221—or call toll free 1-800-521-6797 or 520-297-8200. If you prefer, send it on our FAX line: 1-800-224-6699 or 1-520-544-3086.

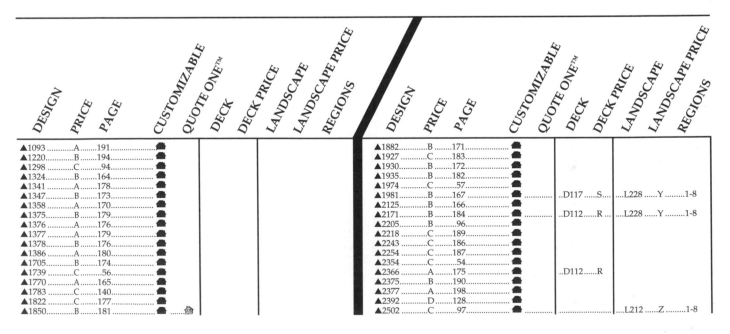

DESIGN	PRICE	PAGE	CUSTOMIZABLE	QUOTE ONE™	DECK	DECK PRICE	LANDSCAPE	LANDSCAPE PRICE	REGIONS
▲1093	A	191	🏠						
▲1220	B	194	🏠						
▲1298	C	94	🏠						
▲1324	B	164	🏠						
▲1341	A	178	🏠						
▲1347	B	173	🏠						
▲1358	A	170	🏠						
▲1375	B	179	🏠						
▲1376	A	176	🏠						
▲1377	A	179	🏠						
▲1378	B	176	🏠						
▲1386	A	180	🏠						
▲1705	B	174	🏠						
▲1739	C	56	🏠						
▲1770	A	165	🏠						
▲1783	C	140	🏠						
▲1822	C	177	🏠						
▲1850	B	181	🏠	🏠					

DESIGN	PRICE	PAGE	CUSTOMIZABLE	QUOTE ONE™	DECK	DECK PRICE	LANDSCAPE	LANDSCAPE PRICE	REGIONS
▲1882	B	171	🏠						
▲1927	C	183	🏠						
▲1930	B	172	🏠						
▲1935	B	182	🏠						
▲1974	C	57	🏠						
▲1981	B	167	🏠		D117	S	L228	Y	1-8
▲2125	B	166	🏠						
▲2171	B	184	🏠		D112	R	L228	Y	1-8
▲2205	B	96	🏠						
▲2218	C	189	🏠						
▲2243	C	186	🏠						
▲2254	C	187	🏠						
▲2354	C	54	🏠						
▲2366	A	175	🏠		D112	R			
▲2375	C	190	🏠						
▲2377	A	198	🏠						
▲2392	D	128	🏠						
▲2502	C	97	🏠				L212	Z	1-8

DESIGN	PRICE	PAGE	CUSTOMIZABLE	QUOTE ONE™	DECK	DECK PRICE	LANDSCAPE	LANDSCAPE PRICE	REGIONS
▲2504	C	95	✓						
▲2511	B	126	✓	⌂	D108	R	L229	Y	1-8
▲2536	C	192	✓						
▲2547	C	25	✓						
▲2548	C	127	✓						
▲2549	C	58	✓						
▲2560	C	59	✓						
▲2579	D	130	✓						
▲2580	C	195	✓						
▲2583	C	101	✓						
▲2588	C	193	✓						
▲2608	A	169	✓	⌂	D112	R	L228	Y	1-8
▲2624	B	185	✓		D112	R	L228	Y	1-8
▲2628	A	168	✓		D105	R	L234	Y	1-8
▲2679	C	109	✓						
▲2716	C	124	✓				L229	Y	1-8
▲2734	C	32	✓						
▲2759	C	199	✓						
▲2761	B	100	✓				L229	Y	1-8
▲2769	C	58	✓						
▲2770	B	33	✓						
▲2773	C	188	✓						
▲2786	B	162	✓						
▲2787	B	163	✓		D105	R	L228	Y	1-8
▲2788	B	24	✓				L229	Y	1-8
▲2827	C	135	✓						
▲2828	B	133	✓						
▲2837	C	198	✓						
▲2841	B	78	✓				L208	Z	1,2,5,6,8
▲2842	B	81	✓						
▲2843	C	203	✓				L228	Y	1-8
▲2845	B	200	✓						
▲2846	C	50	✓						
▲2847	C	52	✓				L220	Y	1-3,5,6,8
▲2848	C	110	✓						
▲2850	C	202	✓	⌂	D122	S	L236	Z	3,4,7
▲2856	C	108	✓						
▲2879	D	141	✓	⌂					
▲2894	C	125	✓				L229	Y	1-8
▲2901	C	196	✓				L229	Y	1-8
▲2902	B	147	✓	⌂			L234	Y	1-8
▲2913	B	137	✓		D124	S			
▲2916	B	143	✓	⌂			L221	X	1-3,5,6,8
▲2918	B	138	✓		D124	S			
▲2920	D	139	✓		D104	S	L212	Z	1-8
▲2926	D	136	✓						
▲2928	C	152	✓						
▲2931	B	142	✓						
▲2932	C	197	✓						
▲2934	D	92	✓		D109	S			
▲2936	C	93	✓				L228	Y	1-8
▲2937	C	122	✓	⌂			L229	Y	1-8
▲2940	E	148	✓	⌂	D114	R	L230	Z	1-8
▲2941	B	144	✓		D112	R			
▲2942	B	144	✓		D112	R			
▲2943	B	144	✓	⌂	D112	R			
▲2944	C	134	✓						
▲2952	E	149	✓				L235	Z	1-3,5,6,8
▲2956	E	150	✓						
▲2962	B	145	✓	⌂					
▲2966	D	151	✓						
▲3311	D	90	✓	⌂	D109	S	L220	Y	1-3,5,6,8
▲3360	D	55	✓	⌂			L207	Z	1-8
▲3361	D	91	✓	⌂			L230	Z	1-8
▲3362	D	123	✓	⌂					
▲3366	D	79	✓	⌂			L220	Y	1-3,5,6,8
▲3493	C	153	✓	⌂			L220	Y	1-3,5,6,8
▲3565	C	146	✓	⌂	D110	R	L233	Y	3,4,7
▲3645	C	40	✓						
▲3713	A	201	✓						
▲4052	B	53	✓						
▲4090	B	89	✓						
▲4101	B	88	✓						
▲4115	B	121	✓						
▲4122	B	103	✓		D106	S			
▲4133	A	119	✓				L229	Y	1-8
▲4139	A	204	✓		D120	R			
▲4141	C	116	✓						
▲4155	A	102	✓		D115	Q	L229	Y	1-8
▲4160	B	113	✓						
▲4162	B	112	✓						
▲4197	B	107	✓						
▲4209	A	26	✓				L229	Y	1-8
▲4241	C	117	✓				L230	Z	1-8
▲4254	B	118	✓						
4278	B	83	✓		D105	R			
▲4287	B	38	✓		D111	S	L230	Z	1-8
4300	B	54	✓						
▲4308	C	114	✓				L231	Z	1-8
▲4331	C	120	✓				L231	Z	1-8

DESIGN	PRICE	PAGE	CUSTOMIZABLE	QUOTE ONE™	DECK	DECK PRICE	LANDSCAPE	LANDSCAPE PRICE	REGIONS
▲4334	B	115	✓				L231!	Z	1-8
4365	C	99	✓		D112	R			
▲4376	C	99	✓		D112	R			
▲4396	B	82	✓				L211	Y	1-8
▲4408	C	106	✓						
4506	D	86			D110	R	L215	Z	1-6,8
4537	C	104							
6600	B	22							
6615	D	206							
6616	D	208							
6617	D	206							
6618	E	207							
6619	E	210							
6620	E	211							
6621	D	205							
6622	C	209							
† 7222	E	45							
† 7277	C	132							
† 7278	B	10							
† 7279	B	11							
† 7280	B	12							
† 7281	C	42							
† 7282	C	159							
† 7283	C	161							
† 7284	C	160							
† 7285	C	158							
8084	E	23							
8116	E	61							
8145	E	84							
8147	E	85							
8153	E	48							
8160	D	52							
8648	C	60							
† 9291	B	13							
† 9345	C	15							
† 9393	E	41							
9405	D	39							
✳9406	D	21							
✳9407	D	7							
✳9409	D	27							
✳9410	D	20							
✳9417	E	49							
✳9448	D	17							
✳9484	D	46							
✳9488	D	29							
✳9491	B	8							
✳9492	C	9							
✳9509	B	31							
✳9510	B	129							
✳9537	D	51							
✳9538	D	28							
✳9539	D	87							
✳9543	D	47							
✳9554	E	34							
✳9561	E	35							
✳9567	D	43							
✳9568	D	131							
✳9569	C	30							
✳9570	D	16							
✳9571	D	6							
✳9572	C	14							
✳9573	C	19							
✳9574	D	37							
✳9575	E	80							
✳9576	E	36							
✳9577	E	18							
◆9812	C	71							
9821	C	44							
9822	D	70							
◆9823	C	69							
9839	B	62							
◆9850	D	65							
9852	C	66							
◆9869	D	73							
9897	B	155							
9910	E	67							
9914	B	154							
9917	B	157							
9949	B	156							
9967	E	72							
9979	D	77							
9981	D	76							
9982	D	68							
9984	D	64							
9991	D	76							
9992	D	75							
9993	D	74							
9994	D	63							

Before You Order . . .

Before filling out the coupon at right or calling us on our Toll-Free Blueprint Hotline, you may want to learn more about our services and products. Here's some information you will find helpful.

Quick Turnaround
We process and ship every blueprint order from our office within 48 hours. Because of this quick turnaround, we won't send a formal notice acknowledging receipt of your order.

Our Exchange Policy
Since blueprints are printed in response to your order, we cannot honor requests for refunds. However, we will exchange your entire first order for an equal number of blueprints at a price of $50 for the first set and $10 for each additional set; $70 total exchange fee for 4 sets: $100 total exchange fee for 8 sets. . . *plus* the difference in cost if exchanging for a design in a higher price bracket or *less* the difference in cost if exchanging for a design in a lower price bracket. One exchange is allowed within a year of purchase date. **(Sepias are not exchangeable.)** All sets from the first order must be returned before the exchange can take place. Please add $10 for postage and handling via ground service; $20 via 2nd Day Air; $30 via Next Day Air.

About Reverse Blueprints
If you want to build in reverse of the plan as shown, we will include an extra set of reverse blueprints (mirror image) for an additional fee of $50. Lettering and dimensions will appear backward.

Modifying or Customizing Our Plans
With such a great selection of homes, you are bound to find the one that suits you. However, if you need to make alterations to a design that is customizable, you need only order our Customizer® Package. See additional information on page 221.

Architectural and Engineering Seals
Some cities and states are now requiring that a licensed architect or engineer review and "seal" your blueprints prior to building due to local or regional concerns over energy consumption, safety codes, seismic ratings or other factors. For this reason, it may be necessary to talk to a local professional to have your plans reviewed.

Compliance with Local Codes and Regulations
At the time of creation, our plans are drawn to specifications published by the Building Officials and Code Administrators (BOCA) International, Inc.; the Southern Building Code Congress (SBCCI) International, Inc.; the International Conference of Building Officials; or the Council of American Building Officials (CABO). Our plans are designed to meet or exceed national building standards. Some states, counties and municipalities have their own codes, zoning requirements and building regulations. Before building, contact your local building authorities to make sure you comply with local ordinances and codes, including obtaining any necessary permits or inspections as building progresses. In some cases, minor modifications to your plans by your builder, architect or designer may be required to meet local conditions and requirements.

Foundation and Exterior Wall Changes
Most of our plans are drawn with either a full or partial basement foundation. Depending on your specific climate or regional building practices, you may wish to change this basement to a slab or crawlspace. Most professional contractors and builders can easily adapt your plans to alternate foundation types. Likewise, most can easily change 2x4 wall construction to 2x6, or vice versa.

How Many Blueprints Do You Need?
A single set of blueprints is sufficient to study a home in greater detail. However, if you are planning to obtain cost estimates from a contractor or subcontractors—or if you are planning to build immediately—you will need more sets. Because additional sets are cheaper when ordered in quantity with the original order, make sure you order enough blueprints to satisfy all requirements. The following checklist will help you determine how many you need:

_____Owner

_____Builder (generally requires at least three sets; one as a legal document, one to use during inspections, and at least one to give to subcontractors)

_____Local Building Department (often requires two sets)

_____Mortgage Lender (usually one set for a conventional loan; three sets for FHA or VA loans)

_____TOTAL NUMBER OF SETS

Have You Seen Our Newest Designs?

Home Planners is one of the country's most active home design firms, creating nearly 100 new plans each year. At least 50 of our latest creations are featured in each edition of our New Design Portfolio. You may have received a copy with your latest purchase by mail. If not, or if you purchased this book from a local retailer, just return the coupon below for your FREE copy. Make sure you consider the very latest of what Home Planners has to offer.

Yes! Please send my FREE copy of your latest New Design Portfolio.

Name _____

Address _____

City_____State_____Zip _____

HOME PLANNERS, INC.
3275 West Ina Road, Suite 110,
Tucson, Arizona 85741

Order Form Key
| VSNDP |

The Home Customizer®

"This house is perfect...if only the family room were two feet wider." Sound familiar? In response to the numerous requests for this type of modification, Home Planners has developed **The Home Customizer® Package**. This exclusive package offers our top-of-the-line materials to make it easy for anyone, anywhere to customize any Home Planners design to fit their needs. Check the index beginning on page 218 for these plans.

Some of the changes you can make to Home Planners plans include:

- exterior elevation changes
- kitchen and bath modifications
- roof, wall and foundation changes
- room additions and more!

The Home Customizer® Package includes everything you need to make the necessary changes to your favorite design. The package includes:

- instruction book with examples
- architectural scale and clear work film
- erasable red marker and removable correction tape
- ¼"-scale furniture cutouts
- 1 set reproducible, erasable Sepias
- 1 set study blueprints for communicating changes to your design professional
- a copyright release letter so you can make copies as you need them
- referral list of drafting, architectural and engineering professionals in your region who are trained in modifying Home Planners designs efficiently and inexpensively

The price of the **Home Customizer® Package** ranges from $535 to $775, depending on the price schedule of the design you have chosen. **The Home Customizer® Package** will not only save you 25% to 75% of the cost of drawing the plans from scratch with a custom architect or engineer, it will also give you the flexibility to have your changes and modifications made by our referral network or by the professional of your choice.

Now it's even easier and more affordable to have the custom home you've always wanted.

CALL TOLL-FREE 1-800-521-6797

BLUEPRINTS ARE NOT RETURNABLE

ORDER FORM

**HOME PLANNERS, INC., 3275 WEST INA ROAD
SUITE 110, TUCSON, ARIZONA 85741**

THE BASIC BLUEPRINT PACKAGE
Rush me the following (please refer to the Plans Index and Price Schedule in this section):

_____ Set(s) of blueprints for plan number(s) _____.	$_____
_____ Set(s) of sepias for plan number(s) _____.	$_____
_____ Home Customizer® Package for plan number(s) _____.	$_____
_____ Additional identical blueprints in same order @ $50 per set.	$_____
_____ Reverse blueprints @ $50 per set.	$_____

IMPORTANT EXTRAS
Rush me the following:

_____ Materials List: $50 Home Planners Designs; $75 Design Basics Designs; $50 Alan Mascord Designs; $50 Design Traditions Designs. Add $10 for a Schedule E Plan Materials List.	$_____
_____ Specification Outlines @ $10 each.	$_____
_____ **Quote One**™ Summary Cost Report @ $19.95 for 1, $14.95 for each additional, for plans _____.	$_____
Building location: City _____ Zip Code _____	
_____ **Quote One**™ Detailed Cost Estimate @ $110 Schedule A-D; $120 Schedule E for plan _____. (Must be purchased with Blueprints set; Materials List included)	$_____
Building location: City _____ Zip Code _____	
_____ Detail Sets @ $14.95 each; any two for $22.95; any three for $29.95; all four for $39.95 (save $19.85). ❑ Plumbing ❑ Electrical ❑ Construction ❑ Mechanical (These helpful details provide general construction advice and are not specific to any single plan.)	$_____
_____ Plan-A-Home® @ $29.95 each.	$_____

DECK BLUEPRINTS

_____ Set(s) of Deck Plan _____.	$_____
_____ Additional identical blueprints in same order @ $10 per set.	$_____
_____ Reverse blueprints @ $10 per set.	$_____
_____ Set of Standard Deck Details @ $14.95 per set.	$_____
_____ Set of Complete Building Package (Best Buy!) Includes Custom Deck Plan _____. (See Index and Price Schedule) Plus Standard Deck Details	$_____

LANDSCAPE BLUEPRINTS

_____ Set(s) of Landscape Plan _____.	$_____
_____ Additional identical blueprints in same order @ $10 per set.	$_____
_____ Reverse blueprints @ $10 per set.	$_____

Please indicate the appropriate region of the country for Plant & Material List. (See Map on page 217): Region _____

POSTAGE AND HANDLING		1-3 sets	4+ sets
DELIVERY (Requires street address - No P.O. Boxes)			
• Regular Service (Allow 4-6 days delivery)		❑ $8.00	❑ $10.00
• 2nd Day Air (Allow 2-3 days delivery)		❑ $12.00	❑ $20.00
• Next Day Air (Allow 1 day delivery)		❑ $22.00	❑ $30.00
CERTIFIED MAIL (Requires signature) If no street address available. (Allow 4-6 days delivery)		❑ $10.00	❑ $14.00
OVERSEAS DELIVERY		fax, phone or mail for quote.	

NOTE: ALL DELIVERY TIMES ARE FROM DATE BLUEPRINT PACKAGE IS SHIPPED.

POSTAGE (from box above) $_____

SUBTOTAL $_____

SALES TAX (Arizona residents add 5% sales tax; Michigan residents add 6% sales tax.) $_____

TOTAL (Sub-total and tax) $_____

YOUR ADDRESS (please print)

Name _____

Street _____

City _____ State _____ Zip _____

Daytime telephone number (_____) _____

FOR CREDIT CARD ORDERS ONLY

Please fill in the information below:

Credit card number _____

Exp. Date: Month/Year _____

Check one ❑ Visa ❑ MasterCard ❑ Discover Card

Signature _____

Please check appropriate box:
❑ Licensed Builder-Contractor
❑ Homeowner

**ORDER TOLL FREE
1-800-521-6797 or
520-297-8200**

Order Form Key

VSBP

Helpful Books & Software

Home Planners wants your building experience to be as pleasant and trouble-free as possible. That's why we've expanded our library of Do-It-Yourself titles to help you along. In addition to our beautiful plans books, we've added books to guide you through specific projects as well as the construction process. In fact, these are titles that will be as useful after your dream home is built as they are right now.

COUNTRY

1 200 country designs from classic to contemporary by 7 winning designers. 224 pages $8.95

BUDGET-SMART

2 200 efficient plans from 7 top designers, that you can really afford to build! 224 pages $8.95

FAMILY HOMES

3 200 stylish designs for today's growing families from 7 hot designers. 224 pages $8.95

NARROW-LOT

4 200 unique homes less than 60' wide from 7 designers. Up to 3,000 square feet. 224 pages $8.95

REGIONAL BEST

5 200 beautiful homes from across America by 7 regional designers. 224 pages $8.95 NEW!

EXPANDABLES

6 200 flexible plans that expand with your needs from 7 top designers. 240 pages $8.95 NEW!

BEST SELLERS

7 NEW! Our 50th Anniversary book with 200 of our very best designs in full color! 224 page $12.95

NEW ENGLAND

8 260 of the best in Colonial home design. Special interior design sections, too. 384 pages $14.95

AFFORDABLE

9 430 cost-saving plans specially selected for modest to medium building budgets. 320 pages $9.95

LUXURY

10 154 fine luxury plans-loaded with luscious amenities! 192 pages $14.95

ONE-STORY

11 470 designs for all lifestyles. 860 to 5,400 square feet. 384 pages $9.95

TWO-STORY

12 478 designs for one-and-a-half and two stories. 1,200 to 7,200 square feet. 416 pages $9.95

VACATION

13 345 designs for recreation, retirement and leisure. 312 pages $8.95 NEW!

MULTI-LEVEL

14 312 designs for split-levels, bi-levels, multi-levels and walkouts. 320 pages $6.95

OUTDOOR

15 42 unique outdoor projects. Gazebos, strombel-las, bridges, sheds, playsets and more! 96 pages $7.95 NEW!

DECKS

16 25 outstanding single-, double- and multi-level decks you can build. 112 pages $7.95

ENCYCLOPEDIA

17 500 exceptional plans for all styles and budgets—the best book of its kind! 352 pages $9.95

MODERN & CLASSIC

18 341 impressive homes featuring the latest in contemporary design. 304 pages $9.95

TRADITIONAL

19 403 designs of classic beauty and elegance. 304 pages $9.95

VICTORIAN

20 160 striking Victorian and Farmhouse designs from three leading designers. 192 pages $12.95

SOUTHERN

21 207 homes rich in Southern styling and comfort. 240 pages $8.95 NEW!

WESTERN

22 215 designs that capture the spirit and diversity of the Western lifestyle. 208 pages $9.95

EMPTY-NESTER

23 200 exciting plans for empty-nesters, retirees and childless couples. 224 pages $8.95

STARTER

24 200 easy-to-build plans for starter and low-budget houses. 224 pages $8.95

Landscape Designs

FRONT & BACK

25 The first book of do-it-yourself landscapes. 40 front, 15 backyards. 208 pages $12.95

BACKYARDS

26 40 designs focused solely on creating your own specially themed backyard oasis. 160 pages $12.95

EASY CARE

27 NEW! 41 special landscapes designed for beauty and low maintenance. 160 pages $12.95

Design Software

BOOK & CD ROM

28 NEW! Both the Home Planners Gold book and matching Windows™ CD ROM with 3D floor-plans. $24.95

HOME ARCHITECT

29 The only complete home design kit for Windows™. Draw floor plans and landscape designs easily. Includes CD of 500 floor plans. $42.95

Interior Design

HOME DECORATING

30 Special effects and creative ideas for all surfaces. Includes simple step-by-step diagrams. 96 pages $8.95

BATHROOMS

31 An innovative guide to organizing, remodeling and decorating your bathroom. 96 pages $8.95

KITCHENS

32 An imaginative guide to designing the perfect kitchen. Chock full of bright ideas to make your job easier. 176 pages $12.95

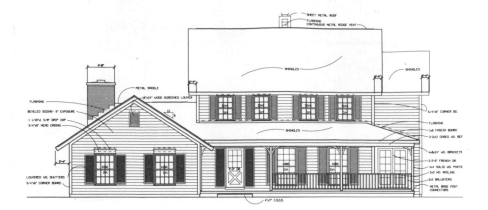

OVER 3 MILLION BLUEPRINTS SOLD

"We instructed our builder to follow the plans including all of the many details which make this house so elegant... Our home is a fine example of the results one can achieve by purchasing and following the plans which you offer... Everyone who has seen it has assured us that it belongs in 'a picture book.' I truly mean it when I say that my home 'is a DREAM HOUSE.'"

S.P.
Anderson, SC

"We have had a steady stream of visitors, many of whom tell us this is the most beautiful home they've seen. Everyone is amazed at the layout and remark on how unique it is. Our real estate attorney, who is a Chicago dweller and who deals with highly valued properties, told me this is the only suburban home he has seen that he would want to live in."

W. & P.S.
Flossmoor, IL

"Home Planners' blueprints saved us a great deal of money. I acted as the general contractor and we did a lot of the work ourselves. We probably built it for half the cost! We are thinking about more plans for another home. I purchased a competitor's book but my husband only wants your plans!"

K.M.
Grovetown, GA

"We are very happy with the product of our efforts. The neighbors and passersby appreciate what we have created. We have had many people stop by to discuss our house and kindly praise it as being the nicest house in our area of new construction. We have even had one person stop and make us an unsolicited offer to buy the house for much more than we have invested in it."

K. & L.S.
Bolingbrook, IL

"The traffic going past our house is unbelievable. On several occasions, we have heard that it is the 'prettiest house in Batavia.' Also, when meeting someone new and mentioning what street we live on, quite often we're told, 'Oh, you're the one in the yellow house with the wrap-around porch! I love it!'"

A.W.
Batavia, NY

"I have been involved in the building trades my entire life... Since building our home we have built two other homes for other families. Their plans from local professional architects were not nearly as good as yours. For that reason we are ordering additional plan books from you."

T.F.
Kingston, WA

"The blueprints we received from Home Planners were of excellent quality and provided us with exactly what we needed to get our successful home-building project underway. We appreciate Home Planners invaluable role in our home-building effort."

T.A.
Concord, TN